W9-BNI-769

# *Consumer Reports*
# *Guide to*
# *Personal Computers*

# Consumer Reports Guide to Personal Computers

Olen R. Pearson
and the Editors of
Consumer Reports Books

Consumer Reports Books
A Division of Consumers Union
Yonkers, New York

To my mother,
who always believes in me,
even when I don't deserve it,
which is probably much too often!

Copyright © 1996 by Consumers Union of United States, Inc., Yonkers, New York 10703.

The phrase "From America's #1 Consumer Test Center™" is a trademark belonging to Consumers Union.

Published by Consumers Union of United States, Inc., Yonkers, New York 10703.

All rights reserved, including the right of reproduction in whole or in part in any form.

Library of Congress Cataloging-in-Publication Data
    Pearson, Olen R.
    Consumer Reports guide to personal computers/Olen R. Pearson and the editors of Consumer Reports Books
    p. cm.
    ISBN 0-89043-832-3
    1. Microcomputers—Purchasing. I. Consumer Reports Books.
    II. Title.
    QA76.5.P368 1996
    004.16'029'7—dc20                                     95-37501
                                                          CIP

Design by Joseph DePinho

Page composition by Jennifer Dixon

First printing, February 1996

This book is printed on recycled paper.

Manufactured in the United States of America

*Consumer Reports Guide to Personal Computers* is a Consumer Reports Book published by Consumers Union, the nonprofit organization that publishes *Consumer Reports*, the monthly magazine of test reports, product Ratings, and buying guidance. Established in 1936, Consumers Union is chartered under the Not-for-Profit Corporation Law of the State of New York.

The purposes of Consumers Union, as stated in its charter, are to provide consumers with information and counsel on consumer goods and services, to give information on all matters relating to the expenditure of the family income, and to initiate and to cooperate with individual and group efforts seeking to create and maintain decent living standards.

Consumers Union derives its income solely from the sale of *Consumer Reports* and other publications. In addition, expenses of occasional public service efforts may be met, in part, by nonrestrictive, noncommercial contributions, grants, and fees. Consumers Union accepts no advertising or product samples and is not beholden in any way to any commercial interest. Its Ratings and reports are solely for the use of the readers of its publications. Neither the Ratings, nor the reports, nor any Consumers Union publications, including this book, may be used in advertising or for any commercial purpose. Consumers Union will take all steps open to it to prevent such uses of its material, its name, or the name of *Consumer Reports*.

# Contents

## Acknowledgments

While the idea for this book was my own, it might well have never been written without the encouragement, support, and many helpful comments and suggestions from my family, friends, and colleagues. To those who unselfishly contributed their time and energy to the improvement of this book and the preservation of my sanity, I am indebted.

I also wish to express my special appreciation to the editors and staff of Consumer Reports Books for their confidence in this project as well as their most capable guidance and assistance in converting my technical jargon into a readable presentation. Special thanks to Dean Gallea for all his help and advice.

# *Introduction*

It is very important to establish your needs and ascertain what equipment is available to fit those needs before you can decide what type of computer and accessories are best for you. Few people would buy a car without first having driven it, yet many people purchase a personal computer without first giving it a "test run" to see if it's comfortable for them or if it's right for their needs. The entire system as a whole as well as each of its components should be **user-friendly** to you, which means no more than the term implies—it is easy for you to understand and use.

Even more amazing, some people buy a computer without ever having used *any* computer. This is why it's crucial to become **computer literate**, knowledgeable about computers and your needs.

The first microcomputer designed for personal use was introduced more than two decades ago. In 1974, the Altair 8800 was announced but was available only in kit form and interested mainly the electronics hobbyists and computer enthusiasts. Nonetheless, about 10,000 kits were sold at $400 each. There soon followed models by such now-familiar names as Apple, Atari, Commodore, and Tandy (Radio Shack), which were suitable for anyone, whether or not they'd had any prior experience with computers.

The early 1980s saw an explosion in the number of companies offering personal computers, but many firms had to withdraw from the field because of either an inferior product or the inability to market their wares successfully against intense competition. IBM was somewhat late entering the microcomputer race, not introducing its first PC until September 1981. However, its leadership in the personal computer market was soon firmly established. After IBM's successful entry into this rapidly growing market, a number of IBM clones (copies) or compatibles were introduced that now permeate the market.

The early microcomputers, although inferior by today's standards, were marvels for their era. For the first time you could bring the power of a computer into your home, office, or business without connecting into a large mainframe system—and at a reasonable cost.

Consumer choice from among the earlier systems was limited. There were only a few places to buy your computer, and the availability of models and accessories was limited. Today, not only do computer and most electronics stores carry microcomputers, but there are numerous other places to shop, including many department, discount, toy, and office-supply stores. Entire, ready-to-use systems can be purchased via mail order. There is also a mind-boggling array of models, options, accessories, add-ons, and other hardware from which to choose to build a computer system.

This book is intended to help lead you through this potentially confusing landscape. It will help you make informed and appropriate decisions before purchasing your personal system, decisions that suit your wants and needs as closely as possible.

The microcomputer world is changing so rapidly that models discussed today may be outdated or even out of production in a short time. This book discusses the basic capabilities and general features of microcomputers, as well as their major accessories, in straightforward, nontechnical terms.

This guide starts off with a review of how to buy a computer, followed by an outline of the seven basic steps that will take you through the process of preparing for and making your purchase. The chapters that follow cover learning how to gather information, assessing your individual needs, comparing and selecting equipment, and setting up and caring for your system. Plus, brand name tests of notebook computers, printers, and a first look at Windows 95 are also included. Finally, we've provided a comprehensive Glossary to assist you in understanding the required terminology. Rather than constantly defining all of the technical and nontechnical language throughout the book, words or expressions in boldface indicate a term covered in the Glossary.

In addition, two appendixes are included. The Manufacturers Resource Guide (Appendix A) provides names and telephone numbers for many computer product manufacturers. Most of these companies will provide literature or answer specific questions on their products upon request. Appendix B gives a selected list of online services and bulletin board systems (the Internet and World Wide Web) for those interested in linking their computer to outside resources.

# How to Buy a Computer

## ▸ A Road Map to the Right Gear

Because computer makers incessantly trumpet the marvels of their newest products, anyone setting out to buy a computer may suffer from purchase paralysis, the inability to choose for fear that their equipment will soon be obsolete and quickly supplanted by cheaper and faster gear.

## ▸ The Types: IBM and Mac

There are two main types of personal computers—various brands of IBM-compatibles and Apple's Macintosh. Once an IBM-compatible was much cheaper, a Macintosh far easier to use. But now those differences aren't as pronounced. For most typical home-computing tasks, the choice between the two hinges largely on your preference.

Most new IBM-compatibles are easier to use than their ancestors because of the ubiquitous Microsoft Windows user interface. (An interface connects you with the program you're running; you use the interface to start and run a program, store and retrieve data, and so on.) And IBM-compatibles still run a wider selection of software. To compete, Apple has accelerated the Macintosh processing speed and dropped its price. It's still a bit easier to learn how to use a Mac than an IBM-compatible and to add components such as a modem or CD-ROM drive.

Apple's Power Macintosh can also run Windows and other IBM-compatible software. That would seem to make the choice of computer somewhat academic. But the Power Mac isn't quite the bridge to IBM-land it might seem. The Power Mac's processor, called the PowerPC, uses a technology that makes the machine a lot faster than an ordinary Macintosh. But that's true only with specially written programs. To run Windows and other IBM-compatible software on a Power Macintosh, you need SoftWindows, a $300 extra. Even then, Windows runs very slowly.

# ▸ Where to Buy It

The days are over when "prestige" names like IBM, Compaq, and Apple could be found only at selected stores. Mail-order upstarts like Dell and Gateway have become major brands by selling the latest technology at the lowest prices. Now companies such as IBM and Compaq also sell computers directly.

Computer outlets now include:

## ◆ Computer Stores

There are two types, traditional local shops and superstores like CompUSA. Both will likely have knowledgeable salespeople. A local shop specializes in personal service, so you're more apt to be remembered should you call with a problem after you buy. A superstore has the widest range of computers, as well as printers and software, so you can do all your related shopping at once. With either type of store, you can easily have a computer repaired or customized.

## ◆ Consumer Electronics Stores

Don't expect the selection of brands and models to be as wide as that in a computer store, and don't expect the salespeople to be as knowledgeable. But if the store has an on-site repair shop, you can easily have equipment customized and won't have to send faulty hardware elsewhere.

## ◆ Office Supply and Department Stores

These offer only a few brands. Salespeople can be fairly knowledgeable, or, at worst, quite ill-informed. Don't count on having your computer customized on-site.

## ◆ Warehouse Clubs

Don't expect much in the way of selection or service at places such as Sam's Club or the Price Club. Warehouse clubs also don't necessarily sell the most up-to-date models.

## ◆ Mail Order

You can buy through a dealer or directly from the manufacturers that advertise in computer magazines. Some ads list individual models in order of power and price; *Zeos* presents its dozens of combinations in a table from which you pick the processor and other components. Options are listed sep-arately. You should be able to get exactly the system you want; direct-mail companies specialize in customizing computers. The main catch, of course: You can't see what you're getting. Mail-order buying often costs less.

## ▸ What's in the Box

Personal computers start at around $1,200 and range as high as your bank account allows. All but the lowest-priced IBM-compatibles have a processor that's fast enough and powerful enough for most needs; video capabilities to do justice to most computer games; and enough software, already installed, for serious work or play. Many models also include a fax/modem and intro-ductory membership to an online service like America Online, CompuServe, or Prodigy. (Information from *Consumer Reports* is part of the basic content of all three online services.)

Some systems are designed to spring into action right out of the box—pro-vided you connect the cables and wires to the right places. If you can't get the machine running, or if you have trouble later on, you can contact the manufacturer for help. Most companies have a toll-free number. Several also offer software that lets their technician operate your computer over the phone to diagnose and remedy problems.

Unfortunately, telephone help isn't always immediate. *Consumer Reports* tried calling a couple of manufacturers at hourly intervals for a week, and, depending on the day, time, and manufacturer, got through immediately or waited—sometimes up to an hour. Occasionally, it took so long to get through that it wasn't worth it to continue to stay on the line.

Some manufacturers also include handy software, known as a front-end, that acclimates you to the computer, answers basic questions, and helps you get around.

## ▸ To Avoid Getting Taken

To minimize the chance that you'll be talked into expensive, unnecessary upgrades or steered away from the computer that best meets your needs, watch out for the following selling ploys:

——◆ *Prices too good to be true.* In the fiercely competitive computer market, there are only two ways a retailer can advertise at impossibly low prices: the computers are priced below cost or the merchandise isn't what it appears to be in the ad.

——◆ *Bait and switch.* Be suspicious if the salesperson tries to steer you away from an advertised model or talk you into paying hundreds of dollars for a better monitor, CD-ROM drive, speakers, or more video RAM. If the machine really needs better components, the original price was probably contrived to lure you in.

——◆ *Stingy store policies.* A store that won't give refunds is suspect. If you buy there, pay with a credit card so you can dispute the purchase if something goes awry.

——◆ *Lowballing the monitor.* The most common ploy found: A retailer advertises a low price by including a very low-quality monitor. Be sure to view the monitor you're buying. One quality check you can do in the store: See how well the monitor displays black letters on a white background.

——◆ *Altered packaging.* Make sure all packaging has the manufacturer's name and part number on it and hasn't been altered. A buyer for a major retailer showed us a factory-sealed printer package labeled "refurbished." Minus that word, the package could be sold as new.

——◆ *Switched parts.* Ask whether the hard drive, CD-ROM drive, and such are the ones that are supposed to come with the computer. Otherwise, they won't be covered by the computer's warranty and must be serviced by their manufacturer.

——◆ *Future compatibility.* When choosing an IBM-compatible, ask if the computer carries the "Designed for Windows 95" logo (an assurance that it will work well with the newest version of Windows).

## ▸ What to Look for: Major Parts

All computers are made from the same basic components—keyboard, monitor, circuit boards. Often manufactured by a company other than the computer maker, each part influences a different aspect of performance, from how fast the computer processes information to how much space it takes up. Manufacturers consider dozens of alternatives before selecting components that strike the best balance between cost and performance.

Computer ads contain a considerable amount of detail about the components, since many customers consider it essential to choose the right parts. Some companies will custom-assemble a computer from a menu of components priced à la carte. Whether you buy a custom-assembled machine or an off-the-shelf model, expect a jungle of buzzwords, acronyms, and technical terms. Take heart. Even if you don't speak technobabble, you can get the components right by sticking to the essentials described here and in the Glossary of this book.

### ◆ Processor

*What it is:* The computer's brain, which performs calculations and controls the software. More than any other part, the processor determines how fast the computer runs and what it will cost. Machines with the latest, fastest processor command the highest prices.

*Buzzwords:* Intel, whose chips dominate the processor market, produces families of processors identified by a five-digit number like 80386 and 80486. Each family represents a different level of technology. Terms such as SX, DX, DX/2, and DX/4 represent a chip's place in its family. The speed of the processor's internal clock is expressed in megahertz (MHz), usually between 25 and 100 MHz. Combine those elements and you get the designations shown in ads: "486SX-33," say, denotes an 80486SX, 33-MHz chip. New generations of processors arrive every couple of years. The 80286 and 80386 families, popular a few years ago, have been supplanted by 80486 processors. Intel's premium chip, the Pentium, has a direct competitor in the PowerPC, which directs Apple's Power Macintosh and is available in a few IBM-compatibles.

*What you need if you're a first-time buyer:* An IBM-compatible computer should have at least a 66-MHz 486DX/2 processor. To maximize the computer's useful life, look for an upgradable machine that Intel has certified can accept a Pentium replacement processor (you can call Intel at 800 321-4044 for a list of such machines). A Macintosh with a 68040 processor will probably have the most attractive price. A Power Mac, although more expensive, will be better for the future.

If you have a computer at the office and also need one for work at home, buy one that's neither significantly faster nor slower than the office machine, to ease the transition. Otherwise, choose either an IBM-compatible with a 66-MHz 486DX/2, preferably upgradable to a Pentium processor, or an actual Pentium machine. Likewise, if you use a Macintosh at work, choose one for the home with comparable capabilities.

*What you need if you're upgrading:* Consider only processors that have at least twice the performance of the one you own.

## ◆ Video

*What it is:* The components that determine how sharp an image you'll see and how quickly images can change. The video component you actually see is the monitor. Inside the computer are other elements that govern the resolution of the images on the monitor and the pace of changes on the screen.

*Buzzwords:* Monitors come in various sizes, the most popular being 14, 15, and 17 inches (as measured diagonally across the face of the tube). A monitor's resolution, a measure of the fineness of detail it can display, is represented by the number of rows and columns of pixels (dots) on the screen. The coarsest resolution commonly available for IBM-compatibles is VGA (640 by 480 pixels, rendering 16 colors), whereas SuperVGA can display more detail. Monitors also come in two types, interlaced and noninterlaced. A noninterlaced monitor will be easier on your eyes.

Many ads highlight a measurement called dot pitch, the spacing between the monitor screen's color phosphors. Dot pitch typically ranges from 0.21 to 0.39 inch. The smaller the pitch, the sharper the image and the less eyestrain. A noninterlaced monitor with the largest screen size, highest resolution, and smallest dot pitch is the most expensive.

Inside the computer, the video card (or controller) limits the display's maximum resolution and, to a lesser extent, its sharpness. The video card requires its own memory, known as VRAM (Video Random Access Memory).

The bus, though not strictly a video component, nevertheless affects the display. The bus connects the processor to the video card and other elements. The newest designs are VESA Local Bus (VLB), found on many systems using an 80486 processor, and Peripheral Component Interconnect (PCI), found on most Pentium systems.

*What you need if you're a first-time buyer:* For an IBM-compatible machine:

You should choose a noninterlaced 14-inch monitor, capable of at least SuperVGA resolution, with a dot pitch of 0.28 inch or less. Don't spend more for a 15-inch monitor; the size difference is mostly a marketing ploy. If you can test a computer in the store, try to see how well it displays high-resolution photos or black letters on a white background. For an 80486 system, choose a model with a VLB local bus and at least 512 KB of VRAM video memory.

*What you need if you're upgrading:* Your choices will be limited by the computer's expansion slots. If they can accept a VLB or PCI video card, get one with at least 1 MB of VRAM. Before buying a video card, make sure your monitor can handle the capabilities you are trading up to. Text resolutions greater than 800 by 600 pixels, for example, practically demand a 17-inch noninterlaced monitor.

## ▸ What to Look for: Memory and Such

### ◆ Hard Drive

*What it is:* The electronic storage compartment, where software and data reside from day to day.

*Buzzwords:* Storage space is measured in megabytes (MB); common sizes range from 300 MB to about 1,000 MB. The largest drives are measured in gigabytes (GB), equal to 1,000 MB. The larger the drive, the better, but also the more expensive. Prices run about 50 cents per MB and are constantly dropping. The two most popular types are Integrated Drive Electronics (IDE) and Small Computer System Interface (SCSI). They are roughly equal in speed for most purposes; SCSI, which tends to be more expensive, is the only type available for most Macintoshes.

*What you need if you're a first-time buyer:* An IBM-compatible running Windows ought to have a minimum of 300 MB of hard-drive space if you'll be sticking with the "Works" integrated software package that comes with the machine. Otherwise, get at least 400 MB. Make sure the computer has at least one empty bay for a second hard drive. You should allow plenty of additional megabytes for the data files you create, as well as "breathing" space. For a Macintosh, *Consumer Reports* recommends at least 250 MB of disk space.

*What you need if you're upgrading:* You may be able to forestall a purchase by removing little-used software and data to diskettes. Or you may uncover a few large, long-forgotten files that can be deleted. One cost-effective way to get more disk space is to use file-compression software. Such products are supposed to double the available disk space, but the improvement is more like 70 to 80 percent, with a slight reduction in disk speed.
Before installing a new hard drive, copy critical files onto diskettes. Since it's easy to get in over your head installing a hard drive, consider having the dealer do it.

## ◆ Fax Modem

*What it is:* A device that combines fax capability with a modem, which computers use to communicate over the telephone. A fax card, although cheaper than a separate fax machine, isn't as useful. You can only transmit information already inside the computer; and, to receive faxes at any time, you must leave the computer on. Some fax cards can send but not receive. A modem is far more useful, essential if you want to use an online service.

*Buzzwords:* A plug-in—or internal—modem resides inside the computer, whereas an external modem sits outside, connected to a communications socket in the back. Modem speeds are measured in baud, the number of symbol elements transmitted each second. Speeds range from 2,400 to 28,800 baud. Higher-speed modems can also operate at the lower speeds. Price directly reflects speed.

*What you need if you're a first-time buyer:* Consider it a plus if the computer comes with a fax modem. But if the modem is the common 2,400 baud, you'll probably want to buy a faster modem for any serious communications. Get at least 14,400 baud, which shouldn't run you much more than $100.

*What you'll need if you're upgrading:* The best choice is usually a 14,400-baud modem. Slower models don't save you much and are on the way out; faster ones cost a lot more and aren't any better unless you can connect with one that's just as fast.

## ◆ Memory

*What it is:* Random access memory, or RAM, determines how much data the computer can access efficiently. RAM affects a computer's performance. A program will run slowly (and may not run at all) if the computer has insufficient memory.

*Buzzwords:* Memory size is measured in megabytes (MB). Most IBM-compatibles come with at least 8 MB.

*What you need:* An IBM-compatible computer running Windows should have at least 8 MB of RAM. Consider more only if you expect to run several applications simultaneously. Macintosh computers come with 5 MB as standard, which is a bit skimpy. You should upgrade the computer to 8 MB; upgrade to 12 MB for desktop publishing or other memory-intensive applications. For best performance, a computer with a 486DX/2 or faster processor should also have 128 KB (or more) of additional memory, known as cache.

## ◆ Diskette Drive

*What it is:* The slot on the front of the computer into which you insert disks containing a program you want to run or a file you want to access.

*Buzzwords:* Most computers have a 3½-inch drive that accommodates a 1.44 MB diskette. Some IBM-compatibles add the older, 5¼-inch drive for a 1.2 MB floppy disk.

*What you need:* Virtually all software comes on 3½-inch diskettes. Unless you have a particular need for a 5¼-inch drive—to exchange diskettes with an older computer, for example—spend money on other components. If the 5¼-inch drive takes up space that could be used for a CD-ROM or hard drive, your computer may even be better off without it.

### ◆ Multimedia

*What it is:* Accessories to run interactive encyclopedias, talking children's books, and games with hi-fi sound.

*Buzzwords:* A CD-ROM drive, the central multimedia component, plays compact discs that can contain up to 680 MB of information. The most popular drive type is double-speed, meaning it conforms to MPC-2, the current standard for multimedia hardware and software (CD-ROM drives up to 6X speed are now available). A sound board (a plug-in circuit board for IBM-compatibles) translates the sound track on a CD-ROM disc into a sound signal for loudspeakers. A 16-bit card is best suited for processing the sound data on the newest CD-ROM discs.

## WHAT UPGRADES COST

Hard Drive
| | |
|---|---|
| 200 MB | $150 |
| 420 MB | $200 |
| 540 MB | $300 |

Monitor
14-in., 0.28-in. dot pitch, noninterlaced $250
15-in., 0.28-in. dot pitch, noninterlaced $300
17-in., 0.26-0.28-in. dot pitch, noninterlaced $500

Memory
| | |
|---|---|
| 4 MB | $150 |
| 8 MB | $300 |
| 16 MB | $600 |

Multimedia
Double speed CD-ROM drive, 16-bit sound card, rudimentary speakers $250

Fax/modem
14,400 baud modem $100

*What you need if you're a first-time buyer:* Buy a computer with multimedia components already installed. Look for a double-speed (or quad-speed) CD-ROM drive, a 16-bit sound board, and self-powered, magnetically shielded speakers. Choose a 66 MHz 486DX/2 (or Pentium) processor to keep pace with future demands.

*What you need if you're upgrading:* First check the software you intend to run to be sure the kit is compatible. Have the dealer install it.

## ◆ Computer Case

*What it is:* The box holding the electronics, with places to connect the monitor, printer, and other equipment.

*Buzzwords:* The all-in-one (case combined with monitor) takes up less space than the traditional desktop case and is a bit easier to move around but typically has less expansion room inside. A minitower can free up even more desk space by sitting on the floor and offers the most extra plug-in slots and bays for upgrades. An additional bay makes it easier to add a hard drive or CD-ROM drive later. Serial and parallel ports, standard on most computers, are the outlets for the external modem, printer, and the like.

*What you need:* Pick the type that best suits the space in your home. Make sure the machine will have ample plug-in slots and a free drive bay.

# Seven Basic Steps

**W**hat *is* the best computer to buy? Of course, there is no single *best* computer, no specific manufacturer's model that suits everyone's needs. The computer you should buy is the one that fits your individual needs. If you purchase an inexpensive system that does not have the capabilities to run your favorite software packages, then you will almost certainly be dissatisfied with it. In this case, most either stop using their system or end up spending additional money to create a more powerful system that could have been purchased in the first place. On the other hand, buying a system that has many times the computing power and features you need or want can be just as financially imprudent.

Here are the basic steps that you should follow when planning for your system:

1. Become computer literate.
2. Learn what is available.
3. Thoroughly assess your needs.
4. Select your software.
5. Select your hardware.
6. Buy intelligently.
7. Set up, use, maintain, and care for your computer.

Each step is related to and dependent on the others. For example, you can't adequately assess your needs until you become informed about computers and what is available. But what and how much you need to learn depends on what you intend to do with your computer—for example, whether you'll be running a word processor, graphics applications, or multimedia games.

## ▸ Step 1. *Become Computer Literate*

Becoming computer literate basically involves three things: (1) learning the terminology or language (**computerese**) surrounding computers;

(2) learning what is available in basic equipment and accessories; and (3) gaining some hands-on experience. You should not underestimate the importance of the last item. It is not uncommon for someone to become knowledgeable about computers yet remain so intimidated by or afraid of them (**computerphobic**) that the new system remains virtually untouched.

There are many sources available to help you learn about computers. The Glossary at the end of this book will help you learn basic terminology. Your local library and bookstore can provide other books and magazines, both on general as well as more specialized topics. Also, if there are computers available at your place of work, school, library, or friends' homes, you may be able to gain some of the all-important hands-on experience.

## ▶ Step 2. *Learn What Is Available*

As you become computer literate, you will learn much about which computers and accessories are available and what they are capable of doing, enough to know at least what you will need and where to look for further information. The wealth of sources available provides more information than you will need, so it is essential to narrow your focus.

Make a list of your "wants" or "would likes." When you find something that interests you, add it to your list. You can then look for further information on those particular items. You should be able to gain a rough idea of the cost of each item that you want and estimate what the total system will cost.

## ▶ Step 3. *Thoroughly Assess Your Needs*

Your "want list"—which may change several times—should summarize your requirements and lead you to final judgments as to your true needs.

Rigorously edit your "want list" in light of the projected cost. For example, if your only use for a CD-ROM drive or sound board (**multimedia**) is to play a few games, the extra cost will make the CD-ROM drive a luxury item rather than a necessary component.

Be aware that, over time, your computer needs will likely change. As you become more familiar with your system, you may want your computer to embrace new technology and features. Keep in mind that you may want to add more items in the future. Factor in the capability for expansion. For example, if you are not sure about computer games now but would like to leave that option open as a future possibility, be sure any system you consider will permit you to add the CD-ROM drive and sound board later (see Chapter 4 for more details). Bottom line: Consider only those systems that offer adequate expansion potential.

## ▶ Step 4. *Select Your Software*

*Software should be selected first.* Many people make the mistake of purchasing the hardware first, under the assumption that the software they want will be available. Unfortunately, this is not always the case, and some of these buyers become disappointed and discouraged when their system does not meet their needs.

There are two basic reasons for selecting your software first. For one thing, it is primarily the software that determines the applications that will run on your system, and this is the best way to ensure that your system will do what you want. Don't settle for general types of programs. If you ask a salesperson whether a computer will run a software package such as a word processor, he or she will say yes because virtually all computers will run some type of a word processor. But will it have the features you want? The best way to be sure is to decide which word-processing software fits your needs and then find a computer that runs it. If you can't find the exact package you want, at least have a list of the features you like and ask the salesperson if the software is available. You should do this for *all* the software that you know you want, even if you do not intend to purchase some of it until later.

Second, if you know what software you will be using, you can select the specific computer components that you need. For example, if you plan to run desktop publishing or engineering applications, you may want a larger screen monitor with high-resolution graphics. If you will need to produce professional-looking printed reports, then the additional cost of a laser printer may be justified. If you plan to link your computer to other systems, then a higher-speed modem will likely save money in connect or long-distance charges. Without prior knowledge of the programs and applications you are going to run on your system, you could make a serious mistake in your choice of these items by purchasing components with inadequate, unnecessary, or wrong features.

"Software first" is intended more as a rule of thumb than an inflexible edict. The software generally acts as a guideline to the selection of the hardware; however, there are exceptions. For example, you might require a specific brand or model of computer or certain types of components for a particular reason, such as gaining compatibility with a system at work or at school. In such cases the available selections will be more limited but not substantially restricted.

## ▶ Step 5. *Select Your Hardware*

Once you have selected your software, you can begin your search for a system to handle it. Keep in mind the additional software you may consider buying at a later time; your system should be able to run these packages as well—or at least have the expansion capability to do so. It is not necessary to purchase all hardware components together; you can delay the purchase of some optional items such as a modem or extra memory until you actually need them. Remember, however, that many such items will have to be installed inside the computer. If you are not comfortable doing this, it may mean a service charge.

## ▶ Step 6. *Buy Intelligently*

One of the best ways to buy a system is to consult with a friend or colleague who has a fair amount of computer knowledge. However, a resource like that is not available to everyone, which is why we wrote this book.

If you do not have anyone advising you, resist buying the first computer you see, even if you think it's perfect for your needs. To get the right computer at a fair price, you must take the time to do some comparison shopping. Prices do vary from store to store, depending to a great extent on the type of store and the services provided. There is also a significant price difference on some items, depending on your location (such as urban or rural) or the area of the country in which you live.

## Smart Computer-Buying Questions

No matter which computer system and accessories you think are best for you, some basic considerations should be kept in mind when shopping and making your decision. When looking at a system or individual product, ask yourself the following questions:

- ◆ Have you thoroughly examined similar products?
- ◆ Does the product meet your needs?
- ◆ Is there adequate expansion capability?
- ◆ Is the product well-known and tested?
- ◆ Is sufficient documentation provided?
- ◆ Have you actually used the product?
- ◆ Have you talked with other users?
- ◆ Are you comfortable with the product?
- ◆ Is the cost within your budget?

If your answer to any of these questions is no, then you may not yet be ready to make your purchase.

The choice of where to buy your system is as important as which system you buy. When shopping, ask yourself the following questions about the retail computer dealers you are considering:

- ◆ Has the store been in business very long?
- ◆ Does the store have a good reputation?
- ◆ Are the salespeople knowledgeable, cooperative, and helpful?
- ◆ Are post-purchase support and services provided?
- ◆ Is special training available?
- ◆ Are prices competitive?
- ◆ Are prices clearly and freely stated?
- ◆ Are the products you want in stock?
- ◆ Are past-customer references available?
- ◆ Are there many brand names you've never heard of?

When you have selected all the components of your system as well as what you consider the best place to make the purchase, stop and take one last look. Ask yourself the following questions:

——◆ Do you have firm assurances of the delivery of any out-of-stock items?
——◆ Do you know exactly what you're getting and whether it meets your original needs?
——◆ Do you understand all costs?
——◆ Will local help be available should you need it?
——◆ Will additional products be available if needed?

If you cannot answer yes to all these questions, go back and reexamine the areas in which you are uncertain and see what you need to do to correct the problems.

## ▸ Step 7. *Set up, Use, Maintain, and Care for Your Computer*

Most system hardware requires very little special care other than what common sense would dictate. Your software and the files you create need more care, but you will find this small investment in time well worth it in the long run. Unfortunately, once a problem with a computer makes itself known, it is often too late to do anything to prevent its recurrence. For this reason it is essential that you do the few small things for your system that under normal circumstances prolong its useful life, such as keeping it free of dust and any other harmful contaminants.

Take your time, do your homework and be well prepared before actually making your purchase. If in doubt, *wait.* Something new that better suits your needs may become available, and if the current trends persist, prices are likely to go down rather than up (multimedia and upper-end Pentium systems, for example); the cost of some systems has dropped by more than 50 percent over the last five years, while the overall capabilities have increased significantly. It is also possible that a particular item you want could drop out of the market, but a better, more powerful version is likely to replace it. If you take care in making your choices, you should be able to purchase a system that will provide many years of service and enjoyment.

# Learn What Is Available

Computer information and educational resources vary from region to region, but you should have access to most of them, since many of the potential sources of information, such as magazines, books, and retail catalogs, are nationally distributed.

Information resources have been organized into three categories: (1) *What to Look For* explains the general features to keep in mind when shopping for a personal computer. (2) *General Product Information* lists places you might consult for basic ideas of what is available as well as to search for more details on particular items. (3) *Advanced, Special, and Hard-to-Find Information* gives you some idea of where you might turn if the usual references fail to provide you with the data you need or if you have a special requirement.

This list begins with a general source of information and then moves to the more specific references to determine which individual system components you want before you search for firm prices. Most potential buyers have little or no need for the resources listed in the third group until after the sale, when they may want to join a computer club or user's group.

The diversity of available information can seem overwhelming. If you haven't already decided where to start, first talk with someone you know who has a computer. Then consider a magazine or two and visit a few local computer stores. If you don't yet know what to ask, tell the salesperson that you are gathering information and ask for some literature. You will soon develop an understanding of what type of system you want and what you want it to do. Carefully organize your research. Retain copies of articles, advertisements, and other literature that are helpful, and remember to make notes of specific features you find attractive about various products.

# ▸ What to Look For

Always keep in mind that your primary objective is to design a whole system. It is not uncommon for someone to become so concerned about obtaining a particular component or feature that far more important features or capabilities don't receive the required attention.

You must be concerned about the *specifics* of each component, but only after you have satisfied yourself that it will work well with your potential system in a *general* way. Does it have the general features you want? If not, the specifics are irrelevant. For example, if you need to produce huge amounts of printed materials you'll require a printer with a moderately fast print speed of at least 8 to 12 pages per minute (ppm). You may desire some other features such as different fonts, pitches, and enhancements but still consider the speed to be your principal need. You should collect data only on printers with print speeds of about 300 cps or higher and select a printer for your system that offers these features and compatibility.

## ◆ *Compatibility*

Perhaps the most important factor to consider when selecting and designing a successful computer system is *compatibility*. This does not mean that everything you have must be compatible but that everything that will operate at the same time must be.

Suppose you decide that you want to have a word processor, spreadsheet, data base manager, and graphics program on your system, but you will be running only one of these at a time. Your computer, its operating system, and your printer must work well with all of these software packages if you are to take full advantage of their features. However, since you do not plan to run more than one program at a time, it might be that these would not have to be compatible with one another. (Even though most microcomputers are single-task systems, some programs such as Windows or OS/2 permit multitasking or running more than one program simultaneously.)

As you consider various components, check their features and specifications very carefully and verify that they satisfy the requirements of the other components you have previously selected. Be flexible. If you find something you really like but it does not seem to fit with an earlier product you had tentatively settled on, you may want to reconsider the first item (for more on compatibility, see Chapter 5).

## ◆ *Capacity*

Capacity refers very generally to your computer system's ability to perform its functions adequately and is usually determined by the values of certain parameters or basic parts of the system. At some point you will be forced to make decisions about the capacity of your system. For example, you will have to decide on the amount of memory and disk-storage space you need. You will have to choose from a number of different computers with various types of microprocessors and a wide range of performance capabilities. Similar decisions will have to be made about many of the other components of the system.

Sometimes these decisions will be made for you. You may have little choice concerning the amount of memory needed for your software. Or the program will not run unless you have a certain processor or type of graphics. However, in many cases you will have to make most of these choices on your own by carefully balancing your present needs, your anticipated future requirements, and your financial capabilities.

### ◆ Options

Options generally refer to capabilities above those minimally required for basic performance. There is not always a clear distinction between what is a basic capacity requirement and what is an option. In fact, these can change as you change your mind about what you want in a system.

Look carefully at the various options provided by your software and hardware. Often, a relatively simple addition can save you much in time or provide much in enjoyment. For example, it can easily require hundreds of diskettes and many hours to back up a medium-size hard disk. The process can be completed easily and in much less time with a cartridge tape system. (For more explanations on backups, see Chapter 5.) If you plan to use games or educational applications, the addition of a CD-ROM drive and sound board would provide such enhanced capabilities and enjoyment that you would likely find the extra investment well worth it.

Think carefully before simply rejecting anything outright. Consider your possible future needs when looking at options. Be certain that you will have the capability to add them.

### ◆ Level of Power

When you have collected a substantial amount of data, you are likely to find that you have found several computers (or components) that would satisfy your needs but at various levels. Buying a more expensive model could provide for some future expansion or options that will make the system more usable and enjoyable for you. However, a simpler and more affordable system might be easier to learn—and save you money.

You may be faced with similar decisions for many of your system components. Decisions have to be made concerning such items as the amount of memory, the size of the hard disk, the resolution of the graphics, the speed of the printer and the quality of the print it provides, the transmission rate of the modem, and features of various software packages.

### ◆ Special Requirements

You may know from the very beginning of your search for a computer that you have some special or unusual requirements, but you may not discover until later that some of your needs are unique. For example, you may need to accommodate someone with a physical disability, handle a business or unusual hobby, or operate in a particularly difficult physical location. In any case, as soon as you know about your exceptional needs you should begin to take these into consideration when selecting components and designing your system.

### ◆ *Relative Costs*

Keep track of the relative costs of each component of your system. Sometimes adding a single feature (even an inexpensive one) requires changing other components to accommodate this new capability, resulting in a considerable price increase. For example, adding desktop publishing may affect the type of printer, graphics resolution, and monitor you require. If the total cost begins to get out of hand, don't panic. Before you eliminate something that you really want or need, check to see if you can cut back in other areas.

## ▸ General Product Information

These resources will provide you with a general overview of the computer world, what is available, and what the various components will do. Check your local newsstands for the many periodic product reviews and industry summaries that are published by *Consumer Reports* and many of the major computer magazines. After consulting some of these sources, you should have a reasonably good idea of the features and capabilities that you might want in a computer.

### ◆ *Computer Stores*

Many computer salespeople are more than willing to answer your questions and show you their systems, as well as demonstrate hardware and software packages. Nearly all dealers with demonstration systems permit you to try them out for yourself with a variety of programs. "Trying it out for yourself" means just that—not simply watching the salesperson demonstrate what he or she wants you to see, but asking to use the system yourself. If this isn't possible, perhaps you would do better elsewhere. (You might get more hands-on time when the store is less crowded, such as immediately after it opens.)

There are several things to keep in mind when reviewing a product at a retail store. The salespeople want to make a sale and are going to push their products. They are not likely to tell you about problems or weaknesses unless you specifically inquire about them—and maybe not even then. Also, you will see only a small selection of the available computers at most places, and a salesperson cannot be expected to tell you about the systems not for sale at that store. Unfortunately, some salespeople are not very informed about their products and can give you poor information or advice. (After a time, you may actually find that you are more computer literate than many of those selling computer equipment.) It is often a good idea to verify details with specification sheets from the manufacturer or some other source.

### ◆ *Magazines*

There are many magazines that describe personal computer systems and include reviews of new computers, accessories, and programs. They also carry retailers' and manufacturers' advertisements. Most include articles on various parts of systems, such as memory, monitors, disk drives, printers, and software, as well as what is new on the market. Many also provide excellent reviews of the most current software. But remember: Much of what you read is intended to *sell* you something in addition to providing information.

### ◆ *Product Catalogs*

Many special product catalogs are published each year that list nothing but computer products of a particular type. Some list computers, whereas others provide a current roster for accessories such as printers, modems, or monitors. Sometimes you may find several different components listed in the same source, but these lists are not usually as complete.

These catalogs are of two basic types. One type lists only what is currently new on the market, such as hardware lists, which are part of a periodical or provided by consumer groups. The other type is a software catalog, which provides a more comprehensive list of what is available on the market and is distributed by private or independent organizations. You are more likely to find the hardware summaries on the newsstand or library near the end of the year. Check the major publications for special issues, reports, equipment summaries, or compendiums. Whereas some descriptive material may be provided, most of these hardware lists have a brief summary of the technical specifications for each product along with the suggested retail price. Although brief, this is usually sufficient to provide a basis for further comparisons.

Software catalogs provide a brief description of the currently available programs for a specific type of computer or on a particular subject. Some of these catalogs are very extensive, with listings of many thousands of products. Software catalogs are available for most popular computers. Check with your local computer dealer or library for the availability of a catalog for any system that you might be considering. Software catalogs can be expensive, so you may want to review one before deciding whether or not to actually purchase it.

Catalogs are also published that list software by subject, such as educational programs and games. Also, some are dedicated to products that run under a particular type of operating system. If you have trouble finding a catalog of a specific type, check your library for catalogs that list catalogs. You should keep in mind that any of these catalogs will reflect a certain delay between the time it was written and when you read it, even the current issue.

### ◆ *Reader's Service Cards*

Many magazines contain special reader's service cards that permit its readers to obtain additional information on products described or advertised in that issue. Descriptive literature will be sent directly from the manufacturers.

### ◆ Manufacturers' Literature

Aside from the reader's service cards, literature from manufacturers can be found in most computer stores as well as in many retail stores with a large computer sales department. If you want more information on a product and cannot obtain it locally or through a reader's service card, you can always write directly to the manufacturer. (The telephone numbers for many computer product companies are given in Appendix A.) If you cannot locate a specific manufacturer there, the information can usually be obtained from any store that carries their product line. You can also check an advertisement in a magazine for an address or telephone number.

When contacting a manufacturer, specify the exact models on which you want data and at what level you want the information—general and descriptive or specific and technical. Remember that information obtained directly from a manufacturer is designed as much for sales purposes as any advertisement in a magazine and should be treated as such; however, the brochures can provide information that may be hard to find locally and is often more detailed than what is available elsewhere. They can also provide you with a good way to verify questionable information obtained from other sources.

### ◆ Performance Reports

Performance reports are useful because they can give you valuable information on the technical performance of a particular product, and they usually provide data on how the product performs compared to other similar products or to industry or lab standards. Performance reports are available in many computer magazines and from many consumer groups. If you cannot find a report on a particular item in a recent issue of any publication, check annual or other indexes for a list of articles that have been published recently. If this also fails to provide the desired report, look for articles on a similar product, which you may find listed as comparable.

Be cautious, however, when reading such reports. Be aware of the source, and satisfy yourself as to the objectivity of the report. Be certain that the authors and publishers have no ax to grind or product to push. You may encounter a publication that is not entirely objective, whose self-interests may have prejudiced the story. If you are uncertain about whether to trust the results of a report, look elsewhere.

### ◆ Computer Shows

The number of computer shows all over the country is increasing. These range from huge national shows like COMDEX to tiny open houses sponsored by individual dealers. If you attend one of these shows, you will not only see many of the latest products, some of which have not been released for retail sale yet, but you will also have the opportunity to talk directly to the manufacturers' representatives and gather information and literature.

Check with some of your local computer stores about upcoming computer shows in your area. Ask about how to obtain tickets. If they can't provide them, they should be able to tell you where to write or call to request them. There is usually an admission fee to the larger shows.

### ◆ Books

When you have a better idea of the type of system you want, you may wish to review one or more books written specifically for that computer or particular software. For the most popular models, there are books that explain in detail how the system operates and what types of tasks it handles best.

### ◆ Advertisements

Read advertisements in your local newspapers and magazines, on radio and television, in store windows, and even in direct-market mail. You will find your best deal by knowing the market and doing a careful job of comparison shopping. But remember: If it sounds too good to be true, it probably is.

### ◆ Retail Catalogs

As a source of information do not ignore product catalogs, such as those from discount, department, electronics, computer, and specialty stores. These can provide you with realistic price quotations for your area, as well as help you locate specific items.

### ◆ Retail Stores

There are a number of different types of stores where you might look for a computer or some part of your system. These vary from full-service, dedicated computer dealers that offer a full range of computers and services to discount or mail-order stores that provide little more than a price, a box, and a bill. The choice of your retailer may be as significant as the choice of your computer. Check with people you know who have bought items from the store, and consult the Better Business Bureau or the state attorney general's office for any record of consumer complaints.

In consulting sources for prices, you must be careful to distinguish between the *suggested retail price* and the *actual selling price*. It is not always easy to tell which price is being quoted. It may be that these two are the same, but in most cases the latter may be substantially lower than the former. Resources such as performance reports, buying guides, manufacturers' advertisements or literature, and product catalogs are more likely to list the manufacturer's suggested retail price. On the other hand, a dealer's advertisements, retail catalogs, and in-store prices generally reflect the actual selling price. Sometimes you will get lucky and both prices will be given for comparison.

If you cannot tell from the information given which price is being quoted, check before taking any action. Ask, if possible, and compare with other sources. It would be wise to avoid any dealers who quote prices that are very much out of line with the rest of the market, but be certain you are comparing the same exact models at similar kinds of retailers.

# ⧩ Advanced, Special, and Hard-to-Find Information

The following resources deal with special needs or unusual applications. They may not be as readily available or, in some cases, may not be free to you.

## ◆ *Computer Clubs and Users' Groups*

There are many microcomputer clubs throughout the United States. Some clubs are dedicated to a specific type or model of computer, whereas others are made up of members with a variety of systems. Most members of such clubs would be more than happy to answer your questions and discuss your needs with you. You might be able to attend a meeting and talk to several members to get more than one opinion. This may be especially helpful if the club represents many different computer systems. Check with your local schools (students are frequently members of such clubs) and computer dealers for possible clubs in your area.

Users' groups are similar to computer clubs except that they frequently draw their membership from a wider geographical area; are dedicated to a single brand, model, or operating system; and offer their members (and sometimes others) special opportunities for acquiring software or other items. They can help you find additional information about the system they support, as well as inform you about the availability of software. Some users' groups sponsor a buying club or other method through which its members can acquire current computer products at a discount price. Once you have decided on the computer you want, you might check with your local dealer for any local users' groups for that particular model. Computer clubs and users' groups sometimes advertise in the classified sections of computer magazines.

The membership of both computer clubs and users' groups is normally composed of people with a wide variety of backgrounds and capabilities. You will likely find some novice users as well as seasoned professionals. The computer club is more likely to provide you with a direct and personal learning experience with someone on a one-to-one basis, but you may find a wider data base of information to draw on from a users' group. Consider and investigate both possibilities, and take advantage of one or both if you feel that doing so can be helpful to you.

## ◆ *Computer Professionals and Other Resources*

Most communities of any size have a number of computer professionals—ranging from programmers to systems analysts to college instructors—who are skilled at their work. If you don't abuse the privilege, most professionals will be happy to take a few minutes to answer your questions and give you some advice. Your friends or the computer or data processing department at your place of work can provide leads.

Excellent but rarely used sources of information are students of computer studies. These students are usually very knowledgeable about microcomputers and the newest developments in personal computer systems, and most are eager to be of help. If there is a college in your area that offers computer studies, you might ask an instructor if one of the advanced students could be of help to you. Most instructors would be happy for their students to get the experience and would put you in touch with a capable student if one is available. Such students would help you gain a general knowledge and understanding of concepts, especially if you already know something about what you want and just need some technical details, and they could also be a real asset in helping you research the solution to any special need or application you have.

Other valuable resources are instructors at high schools, technical or vocational schools, and colleges; computer programmers; service technicians; sales representatives; computer buffs; and anyone else with a good working knowledge of computers. These people are often experts with one or more facets of microcomputers and can provide you with straight facts and also helpful hints you will not find in any published reference. You might even get a demonstration or some hands-on experience on a system.

If all your sources fail to give you the information you need, you might consider a professional consultant. For a fee, these knowledgeable people will assist you with your individual needs. If you decide to use a consultant, research your choice thoroughly before making any commitment. Also, since you will likely be charged an hourly or daily rate, be very specific with your requests so you will get what you want the first time.

# ▶ Spotting Trends

It is difficult to determine which products will be the new industry pacesetters and which will lose out. Even the largest computer companies have had their failures. No matter how advanced or revolutionary a design, the only proven methods for evaluating a product are through direct marketing, consumer testing, and user reactions. There are, however, several ways that you, as a future buyer, can spot a potentially successful product.

### ◆ *Product Reviews*

Product reviews in national computer magazines are usually thorough. These reviews rarely say anything negative about a product, but the absence of reviews for a major entry into the market may indicate a weak product or the presence of a problem that the reviewers do not wish to tackle. The objectivity of the reviews in these magazines is difficult to judge. The manufacturers whose products are reviewed also pay for advertisements in these same publications.

### ◆ *Consumer Reports*

Included in this guide are actual product reviews done by the engineers at *Consumer Reports*. Chapter 8 contains a review of Windows 95 and complete brand name tests and Ratings of notebook computers and printers.

### ◆ *Response to Established Needs*

Look for products that are being offered in response to an established need. For example, 24-pin dot-matrix printers caught on very quickly, despite their somewhat higher price, because they offered letter-quality print on a dot-matrix printer, fulfilling a long-standing need.

### ◆ *Multiple Market Entries*

Experimental, one-of-a-kind products are risky no matter how terrific they appear to be. It would be unwise to buy a computer with a new operating system or hardware design until you know that it will be supported by other hardware and software companies. Otherwise, you might find yourself with a computer and no software to run on it. Once several companies invest in the production of a specific technology, it is more likely to become successful.

# Select Your Software

Software is a collective term for the **programs**, or sets of instructions, that make a computer function. Even the most expensive computer is no better than the programs that direct its actions. If the program contains errors, or **bugs**, then the computer will not properly process the data that is fed into it. Likewise, if the data that is entered into the system is incorrect, then the results cannot be correct either. (This is referred to by computer users as GIGO—garbage in, garbage out.)

Most major software programs are now too large to run on floppy disks alone and require a hard disk. Many take advantage of the advances in graphics displays, high-quality printers, and sound output now available with all computers.

## ▶ The Operating System

The computer's operating system is a set of programs that activates the computer when you first turn it on and permits you to perform certain basic and routine functions necessary for the operation of the system. It is normally (but not always) supplied with the computer when you purchase it, and you may need to know no more about it than what system and version you have. This is necessary because not all programs run on every version of a given operating system. Also, some computers support more than one operating system, and you may wish to acquire a second one either to give you more versatility or to provide a more user-friendly environment.

The operating system resides on and is loaded from a disk; therefore, it is normally referred to as the **disk operating system (DOS)** or sometimes the **basic disk operating system (BDOS)**. Though any operating system is technically a DOS, the term "DOS" has now come to refer to the **PC-DOS** or **MS-DOS** operating system used on IBM and IBM-compatible computers, respectively.

The **microprocessor** serves as your computer's brain. However, this brain "thinks" very differently than a human brain. The operating system provides an **interface**, or method, for you to communicate with the computer, which includes all the necessary instructions you and the programs need to tell the microprocessor what operations you wish to perform. It provides the link that permits software applications to communicate with the hardware components of the system. This is illustrated schematically at the left:

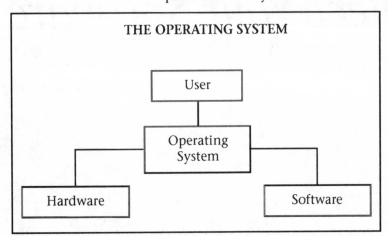

**THE OPERATING SYSTEM**

User

Operating System

Hardware

Software

Without the operating system, it would be extremely difficult to communicate with the computer.

An operating system is always written for a specific computer or group of computers, usually being linked to the kind of processor being used. For example, **MS-DOS** works only on IBM-compatible computers. It is important to select an operating system that is comfortable for you. Several types of operating systems offer various capabilities and features, and different ways for the user to interact with the computer. There are programs called **shells** and **emulators** that can simulate the operating system of a different system, let programs written for one system run on another, or make a relatively awkward operating system more user-friendly.

*Figure 4.1*
*Operating systems have the capacity to run many functions.*

### ◆ MS-DOS Versus Macintosh

The two most popular computers in the home and small-business markets today are the IBM-compatible and the Apple Macintosh systems. Coincidentally, these two computers represent the opposite ends of the spectrum in the general design of operating systems.

IBM-compatible computers, which use the **MS-DOS** (**PC-DOS** on IBM-made computers), rely primarily on direct keyboard entry and a command-oriented structure; that is, if you have a file named OLDFILE that you want to delete from your disk, you would simply enter DEL OLDFILE from the keyboard. Many commands are more complex than this, but the idea is basically the same.

Macintosh computers rely primarily on screen **icons** and a **mouse** to enter commands. Icons are simply graphic images representing a particular item or idea. To delete OLDFILE on a Macintosh computer, you would use the mouse to locate the file on the screen and capture it with the button on the mouse. To delete the file you have just grabbed, you would move (or "drag") it to the icon for delete (a trash can) and drop (delete) the file with the button. **System 7**, the current version of the Macintosh operating system, supports many advanced features such as **multitasking** (running more than one program simultaneously), **multimedia**, and **TrueType** fonts (described later) that are available on MS-DOS systems only through individual application software or a **graphical user interface (GUI)** such as Windows (see below).

Unless you have a reason for needing a particular type of system, you should try both in person before making a decision. Each has advantages and disadvantages. For example, the Macintosh is generally considered to be easier for the first-time user to learn and begin to use. Also, if you plan to use graphics extensively, you may find the Macintosh preferable. However, these benefits are offset by the limited selection of **peripherals** such as printers, and you will find the market for additional programs more limited than that for MS-DOS–compatible systems.

The distinction between the text-based IBM-type commands and the graphics-oriented Macintosh environment, while still clear, is rapidly narrowing. This is due primarily to the widespread use of programs like Windows (see below), although other factors such as hardware and software advances also contribute. Since the Apple-IBM alliance was established in 1991 to bring the systems closer together, models of the Macintosh (**Power Macintosh**) that can run software written for IBM-compatible computers have become available. Because of the increasing joint ventures within the industry, expect more of these mergers.

## ◆ *Other Choices*

Whereas the operating systems for the IBM-compatible and Macintosh computers are the leaders in the market, you may wish to consider other options.

***OS/2 Warp.*** This is a graphics-oriented operating system similar to that of the Macintosh for IBM-compatible machines that provides many additional features. It can run DOS and Windows applications and can boot (or, bring the system into operation) as either DOS or OS/2. It is reported to be a robust operating system that avoids lockups from unruly applications.

OS/2 (Operating System/2) Warp, introduced in 1994, includes improved memory management, enhanced multimedia support, a group of Internet (discussed later in this chapter) utilities with access through IBM's Global Network, and a large set of application software. It is, however, large and considered slow and awkward by some users, which may be one reason it has never caught on as expected.

***Windows NT.*** This network-oriented operating system was released in 1993 and is derived from OS/2. Windows NT (Windows New Technology) is a self-contained operating system, but it can run DOS applications. Available in both client and server versions, it is becoming increasingly popular with network users.

***UNIX.*** For many years, one of the most popular and powerful operating systems on mainframe computers has been UNIX. It has not been commonly used on personal computers because of its complexity and difficulty of use. However, in recent years several versions have been developed for the personal computer including AIX and XENIX as well as Motif, a user-friendly graphical interface for UNIX-based systems. UNIX would not be for all users, but for those who may use this system at work, it may be an option.

***Future Options.*** With the developments that will come about as a result of the Apple-IBM alliance, a number of new operating systems or standards for compliance are sure to appear. Those for PowerPC-based systems are already becoming available.

### ◆ *System Utilities*

Most operating systems are accompanied by a set of utility programs that permit you to do certain housekeeping and disk maintenance chores such as copying, renaming, and deleting files; formatting, copying, and organizing disks; and checking on the contents, available space, and status of a disk. If you run only purchased programs on your system and do not do any development of your own, you may have only a limited need for many of these facilities. With time and experience, however, you will likely find them very useful. There are tutorials for most computers to help you learn how to use the system's utility programs.

## ▶ Software Interface Programs

If you like the user-friendliness of a Macintosh but must have an IBM-compatible, you might want to consider one of the many programs that can assist you with managing your DOS operations. These vary in type and capabilities and range from simple shells to full-system managers with many exotic features. However, most are menu-driven, and many include icons and permit using a mouse.

Such programs are collectively referred to as a **software interface.** In general, an interface provides a communications link between the user and some part of the computer. A keyboard is a **hardware interface** that permits the user to easily communicate with the computer's microprocessor. The monitor provides another kind of interface by which the computer communicates with the user.

In the case of a software interface, the interface is a program that provides some link between the user and the computer, usually the operating system. A software interface does not alter the capabilities of the system but will provide an alternate and hopefully easier means to interact with and take advantage of the many functions of the system. In some cases, the interface may actually add functions not provided by the basic operating system.

Additionally, many interface programs come with their own set of special application or utility programs. Typical of these are clocks (maybe with alarms), calendars (some with daily reminder features), appointment books, address/phone books (may work as phone dialers), calculators, notepads, clipboards, word processor, telecommunications, games, and possibly much more. While these are rarely equivalent to the best programs independently available, the convenience of having such a collection all in one place and quickly accessible at all times is often worth the sacrifice.

### ◆ *Microsoft's Windows*

The most popular operating system is Microsoft's Windows, which offers mouse control, pull-down menus, and an icon-based graphics environment similar to the Macintosh. The name of the program is derived from the way it displays applications in movable, sizable windows. Windows is now reported to be running on over 85 percent of all IBM-compatible personal computers.

Windows provides a more user-friendly interface to a DOS-based system and enhances many of the computer's capabilities. For example, Windows provides **multitasking** capability, which means that you may work with more than one application simultaneously; you can leave one program and switch to another without having to close and exit from the first one. It also permits communication between applications, such as moving text or graphics using the clipboard. Windows also supports **multimedia**, common printer management, and **TrueType** fonts.

Although Windows will run nearly any application, an increasing number of programs are now being written specifically for the Windows environment; only these programs can take full advantage of the features of Windows. However, a **graphical user interface** such as Windows reduces the available memory, may be sluggish at times, takes some effort to set up and maintain, and may introduce certain compatibility problems with other software. Yet, most Windows users consider these drawbacks to be well worth the enhancements provided by the interface.

**Windows 95** is the latest upgrade of Windows that replaces all previous versions except Windows NT; however, like Windows NT, it is a self-contained operating system that can run either Windows or DOS applications. Windows 95 has many enhancements, but one of the most promising is "**Plug and Play**" capability, which gives a computer the added ability to automatically configure new components (especially **expansion boards**) without the need for guesswork and manual settings. For more on Windows 95, see Chapter 8.

### ◆ *Other Interface Programs*

Though Windows is sufficiently popular to warrant special mention, there are other options for those users whose needs may not be well-suited to the Windows environment. There are both text-based and graphics-oriented interfaces available whose features vary from "bare-bones" to extensive, including system management and **multitasking**. These programs may offer the advantages that they are easier to set up and manage than Windows, do not require the system resources that Windows does, and may run more easily with DOS based applications. On the negative side, few, if any, will enjoy the wide support or provide the comprehensive features that are available for Windows.

A simple, limited interface program can be found for as low as $10, but such a program may prove inadequate for most users' needs. Full-featured, graphical interface programs such as Windows may cost in excess of $100; however, Windows is often included as part of a built-in software package on many systems.

## ▸ Other System Software

A number of programs are available to help you enhance the performance of your computer. A few of the most popular and commonly available ones are listed below.

### ◆ *System Managers*

Whereas most system utilities are quite easy to learn to use, a few are not. For these systems you can get a system management package that will perform the most commonly used functions in a user-friendly manner. Most of these are menu-driven interfaces. Some of these packages are very simple and do only a few of the basic functions; others are complex and do almost everything for you, including controlling your entire system. The better programs may even provide capabilities not available through the basic operating system commands. These are priced from about $10 and up, with their capabilities roughly proportional to the price.

### ◆ *Shells*

Shells are menu-driven programs that are most often used as interfaces between the user and the operating system. They generally serve to make the present operating system more user-friendly and/or to simulate the environment of another operating system (that is, act as an emulator; see the section on emulators that follows). Many shells will also provide extended system management capabilities.

### ◆ *Backup Programs*

One of the most important precautions to safeguard the data placed on a computer is to keep a current backup copy for use in case the original is damaged or lost. Both operating system utilities and many system managers provide means for maintaining a backup copy of the data on disk. However, because of the importance of this operation, there are a number of stand-alone programs designed for this purpose. These usually provide a number of options, including a simple, complete backup of an entire disk; a backup of user-selected files; a backup of only those files that have been changed or added since the last backup was made; and automatic, unattended backups. Not all provide tape backup handling capability.

### ◆ **Speed Utilities**

Some operations can take a relatively long time to execute. A variety of programs are available to accelerate systems in such circumstances. Some examples of these programs are speed loaders (to reduce the amount of time it takes a program to load into memory), disk cache and optimization programs (to increase the speed and efficiency of disk operations), and memory managers (to optimize the main memory). Such programs are often found as part of a system manager and may best be purchased that way.

### ◆ *Print Spoolers*

A print spooler is used to permit the computer to continue with a printing operation while freeing the system for you to do something else. Spoolers are often found as part of the utilities that accompany many shells or other application programs such as word processors.

### ◆ *Emulators*

Some operating systems are more user-friendly than others. A few systems may offer emulators, which make one operating system look to the user as if it were another. For example, a microcomputer running under MS-DOS might be made to appear as if it were running the UNIX operating system. Terminal emulators are also available to make one computer or terminal respond like another.

### ◆ *Virus Protection Software*

The spread of computer virus programs (see Chapter 7) has created a demand for programs to counter that threat. These programs normally scan for and then remove known viruses from a computer system. Some may provide a type of sentry to monitor computer activities for possible infection. However, since new virus programs are constantly being introduced, an older virus-protection program may not be effective against the newest types of virus hazards. For this reason, it is especially important that such programs be easily and inexpensively updated, something that should be done at least yearly. (See Chapter 7 for more details.)

### ◆ *Diagnostic Programs*

Computers are complex pieces of machinery that can often present unusual symptoms that may or may not mean signal trouble. Diagnostic programs can help to determine whether or not the various hardware components of the system are functioning properly.

Such programs perform fairly standard tests on the various components, either one at a time or as a group. Using a diagnostic program *can* help to prevent needless repairs when the problem is only a transient **glitch** that may never recur. However, no diagnostic routine is foolproof, so false results are possible. Also, many tests involve very basic system components and can cause problems (to a ROM chip or the data on a disk, for example) if not operated properly. These programs may not be for the novice. Carefully read any warnings on the package regarding the use of the program before purchase, and be alert to any warning messages during the operation of the product.

Diagnostic programs are available in a variety of formats ranging from those that test only one or two components to those that look at the entire system. A good program will cost from $50 up. (Note: More powerful diagnostics are available as hardware components, but these are rarely employed by the home user.)

### ◆ *Screen Savers*

Monitors on computers that are left on but unattended for long periods can develop permanent ghost afterimages of the patterns that linger, or "burn," on the screen. Of course, this is preventable by simply turning the monitor (or the brightness) off, but a simpler and more convenient method is to use a **screen saver** program.

Screen Savers are programs that produce a moving image on the screen that will not damage the display. The image may be anything from geometric patterns to cartoon animations. These may be either terminate and stay reside (TSR) programs that automatically pop up after a certain period of inactivity or they may be manually activated. Some will even provide a low level of system security by requiring a password to restore the regular display. A **screen blanker** is a screen saver that simply causes the screen to go blank.

Although the problem of images burning into screens has been significantly reduced with modern color monitors, screen savers continue to be very popular for their entertainment value and visual impact—from "flying toasters" to images of lush landscapes.

# ▶ General-Purpose Utilities

One problem with the operating system utilities is that they are often very difficult or awkward to use. Some are limited in their available options. Programs designed to replace the utilities singly or in part are fine but clearly limited in their use.

In recent years, a number of multipurpose programs on the market perform most of the operating system utility functions as well as several other special and often very useful functions. These additional operations may include procedures that range from restoring or retrieving an accidentally erased file to rearranging the data on a disk to make the system operate faster.

Aside from the obvious advantage of performing many very useful operations, most general-purpose utilities are very user-friendly and make routine operations and proper maintenance of a system's data much easier to perform. However, some can be complex and may take some time to learn. Also, because they are often very powerful and comprehensive, some of the processes can involve an element of risk to data if not used properly.

# ▶ CD-ROM and Multimedia Formats

There are two kinds of software that are beginning to permeate the market that do not represent a new kind of application but rather a new way of *presenting* an application. These are supplied in the CD-ROM format and/or take advantage of the multimedia capability of many new computer systems.

### ◆ *CD-ROM Based Software*

CD-ROMs hold huge amounts of data, equivalent to about 500 diskettes. Although this has not opened the door to many new types of applications, it has made it possible to offer far more extensive data or powerful programs than were previously available. For example, 5-digit zip code directories are small and easily managed by most computers; however, 9-digit directories are huge and too extensive for all but the largest systems. Now, with the capacity of the CD-ROM format, these larger directories are easily available to anyone with a CD-ROM drive.

Many software companies are beginning to offer their products on CD-ROM. Other than capacity, they offer a number of advantages over diskettes, including being more durable, more difficult to illegally duplicate, and immune to infection by a computer virus. Also, it is easier and cheaper to manufacture, package, and ship a single CD-ROM than the dozen or more diskettes that often accompany the larger applications.

### ◆ *Multimedia Applications*

Multimedia refers to using more than one medium for the presentation of an application. Traditionally, with the exception of a few games, software has consisted almost totally of still images, with a few beeps from the computer speaker. This is now changing. An increasing number of programs make use not only of sound (via a sound board) but also of high-resolution, motion graphics, often in the form of videos. These are frequently integrated together into a harmonious presentation.

The first thought for such a concept may be games, but this is only the beginning. Multimedia encyclopedias now offer not just the text but accompanying photos, drawings, maps, and frequently audio or video clips. For example, an article about Beethoven might have a picture of the composer along with a short sample of his work. One home medical program offers not only written medical information but also audio pronunciations of terms, photos of various conditions, and videos of treatment procedures.

Although not for every application, multimedia is truly the direction in which much computer software is moving. Not all multimedia products are supplied on the CD-ROM format, but because of the large amount of storage space required for the graphics and audio files, it is becoming increasingly difficult to fit the huge programs on diskettes.

The cost of CD-ROM and multimedia software has dropped dramatically so that it is now competitive with software on diskettes. In fact, considering what you get on a CD-ROM as compared to diskettes, most CD-ROM applications might even be called a bargain! But, as with any software, the quality of what is available ranges from very poor to truly outstanding. Use the same precautions you would with any software purchase—for example, try it in the store before purchasing.

# ▶ Word Processors

The most common use for personal computers is word processing. Word processing is much like typing with a regular typewriter except that what you type appears on the screen and is printed only after you issue a command. Errors are corrected and changes made directly on the screen. Words, sentences, and entire paragraphs can be deleted, moved, and inserted as needed. Control over such things as margins, page length, breaks, tabs, **headers** and **footers**, and general layout are commonplace. An assortment of highlights and special effects such as boldface, underline, italics, superscripts, and subscripts, as well as different type styles and sizes, are usually available.

Some very inexpensive word processors ($5) may feature only a **line editor,** which means you may work on only one line at a time. If you need to work on a second line, you must move the text to align it with the edit line. Nearly all packages offer a **full-screen editor,** which permits you to work at any position on the screen simply by moving the **cursor,** or position marker, to the location on the screen and then entering the appropriate commands or text. Although virtually all word processors now feature **word wrap,** in which the text automatically continues on the next line without having to hit the Return key, a few very simple, inexpensive ones may not. Avoid these, because the small saving isn't worth the inconvenience. Another valuable feature is automatic page breaks and page numbering.

Many word processors contain a spelling checker that finds and informs you of most spelling errors. Many also have a thesaurus and a hyphenation dictionary, with a few programs now including a grammar checker. Although not foolproof, these tools can not only improve the quality of your work but also save incalculable time in proofreading. (Such tools should be thought of as aides and not replacements for the human eye. For example, although any spelling checker will find a misspelling such as typing "thnik," none would be alerted by typing "bear" for "bare" or "mouse" for "house" because these are all correctly spelled words, even if they are not the ones you intended.)

The more expensive word processors offer such features as automerging, which permits you to insert names and addresses in separate form letters and then print them without having to edit and print each one manually. Others offer indexing, which locates key terms and then generates an index. Others assist in the creation of spreadsheets, outlines, tables, and figures, even permitting drawings, diagrams (graphics), and mathematical equations to be incorporated directly into the text. A few now even provide direct document transfer via modem or FAX. These capabilities may come as part of the original package or may be available as an option.

### ◆ *Keyboard*

If one of your primary uses for a computer is word processing, you need to give careful consideration to the type of keyboard your system has. No computer keyboard is arranged or functions exactly like a typewriter, but some are closer than others. You will want to consider whether the keyboard is comfortable for you. Unless there is some very unusual feature, do not be too concerned with the arrangement of the keys; you will learn to adjust to this. More important is the presence of full-size and **full-stroke keys.**

### ◆ *Monitor*

Most serious word processing makes use of an 80-column-wide screen, which means that you may enter up to 80 characters on one line across the screen. Each character is fairly small and requires a sharp, steady image on the monitor screen. Many lower-priced models give a very poor quality picture. The letters may be fuzzy or even wiggle. Look at the monitor and use it with a word processor before purchasing it to be sure it is suitable for you. If the word processor has the ability to work with graphics images, be sure the monitor can adequately display these as well.

### ◆ *Printer*

The ability of word processors to produce a variety of outputs, both text and graphics, ranges widely. The upper end packages can generate an amazing variety of print combinations with capabilities rivaling a professional print shop. You should take care to see that any printer you are considering supports the printing features of your word processor and provides a suitable quality print to meet your needs.

Also, check to verify that any printer you like is supported by the word processor. It is rare that all popular printer models are not supported by the better word processors, but it can happen. If you encounter this situation and cannot find a good alternate, check with the maker of the word processor. A new driver for the printer may have been developed since the word processor was released and will usually be sent to you at no extra cost.

Word-processor packages range in price from about $10 to several hundred dollars. Many of the professional programs offer special and advanced features that are valuable mainly to those who write complicated reports or prepare long manuscripts.

## ▸ Desktop Publishers

**Figure 4.2**
**An example of the**
**many capabilities**
**of desktop**
**publishing.**

If you are involved with the publication of a newsletter, newspaper, or any other printed material, desktop publishing may be for you. These programs provide the capability to produce camera-ready copy—including large headlines, special type styles, pictorials, and other graphics—directly from your computer. A top-of-the-line desktop publishing program, together with the appropriate hardware, can rival a small printing press in its capabilities and product. The sample at left could have been prepared with most any desktop publishing program and many word processors.

A few desktop publishers incorporate many of the basic features of word processors, such as text entry, editing, and perhaps even spell checking, but these products are generally aimed at a somewhat different end product. Most packages assume that the text has been prepared with an outside word processor and provide the capabilities for incorporating text or graphics files into a document and moving these files around as needed. They also normally include features that provide for special formatting of the output. This most often includes extended printer support for graphics, additional print typefaces and fonts (see pages 40–41) to produce headlines and other special text printing requirements, extended character sets, columns, borders, and other special features needed to provide customized printouts. There may also be a collection of special graphics files called clip art (see page 40) that can be placed directly in a document and printed.

Although desktop publishers and word processors have traditionally been quite different and aimed at a different usage and user, this is slowly changing. Within the past few years, word processors have been gradually incorporating many of the special printing capabilities of desktop publishers, especially in the areas of clip art images and extended printer-font support. Even though the desktop publishers have been somewhat more reluctant to increase their text-processing capabilities, and the word processors are still lagging behind the capabilities of desktop publishers, the trend is toward merging both categories of programs. Good desktop publishers are priced with the upper-end word processors.

## ▶ Clip Art

**Figure 4.3
Many images
and characters
are available in
clip art.**

This and the next section are devoted to two types of software that are not actually programs but rather support for those programs that make use of them. **Clip art** refers to the image files that are most commonly employed by word processors and desktop publishers but may be compatible with other packages that make use of graphics.

Clip art images may, quite literally, be of anything and of any quality. Two examples are shown at left. If you need a certain image or group of images, be patient; you are likely to find what you are looking for in a software package. Images can also be custom drawn or scanned from photographs.

**Figure 4.4
Clip art quality
varies from image
to image.**

The two images shown above are of average quality. Low-quality clip art will be very "grainy" and disappointing. The image of the dog at left is an example of a low-quality clip art image. Notice how the individual dots that make up the image are clearly visible. High-quality images will resemble a photograph. Clip art may be in either black and white or color; however, only the best images can do justice to color reproductions.

No matter how fine the clip art, it is no better than the equipment used to display or reproduce it. For example, if the monitor or printer is not capable of reproducing the beauty of a high-quality image, then the desired effect will be lost.

Clip art includes individual images or sets of images, sometimes numbering many thousands of files in a set. It is usually far more economical to purchase sets than to try to find the separate image files.

## ▶ Typefaces and Fonts

| | | |
|---|---|---|
| Arial | Camberic | *Brush Script* |
| Bodoni | **COLLEGIATE** | Black Forest |
| Bauhaus | Durango | Black Chancery |
| Caligula | Charlie Chan | CHILI PEPPER |

**Figure 4.5
Typefaces.**

The second class of support software is collectively referred to as **fonts**. The term "font" is often used generically to designate any kind of type style or size, but more precisely it refers to any variation *within* a specific **typeface**. The typeface is the actual design of the type. There are literally thousands of typefaces to choose from, ranging from standard-looking to exotic. At left are just a few examples of typefaces.

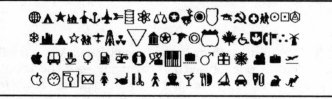

**Figure 4.6**
**Special characters.**

| | |
|---|---|
| Helvetica Regular | *Helvetica Italic* |
| Helvetica Light | ***Helvetica Bold Italic*** |
| **Helvetica Bold** | Helvetica Smaller Size |
| **Helvetica Black** | Helvetica Larger Size |

**Figure 4.7**
**Fonts.**

Clearly, a choice of typefaces can go a long way in improving any output that involves printed text.

If you want to print in a foreign language or to incorporate special symbols into your work, there are typefaces for nearly any need. Font sets are available for alphabets ranging from Greek to Hebrew to Cyrillic. In addition, special character sets are abundant. On this page are samples of a few of the many thousands of symbols that can be found in these sets. Sets of special symbols are often referred to as **dingbats**.

Fonts refer to variations in the presentation of a specific typeface. For example, see Figure 4.7 for several common fonts for the Helvetica typeface. These represent only a few of the many possible combinations.

Font enhancements such as boldface or italics are relatively common in even entry-level printers; however, font size is a little more complex. Some fonts are measured by **pitch**, which refers to the number of characters per inch that will be printed. (This will be discussed in some detail along with printers in the next chapter.)

Most fonts are scaled to the desired size. Some are prepared beforehand and set to specific sizes; these are referred to as **bitmapped fonts**. Others are scaled (sized) as needed and are called **scalable fonts**. The latter variety take longer to process because they must be generated every time they are used, but they take much less disk space to store. One of the most popular scalable fonts is **TrueType**, which is compatible with both the Windows and Macintosh platforms.

The size of scaled fonts is measured in **points** where a 72-point font is one inch high. The following comparison in Figure 4.8 should give you a good idea of point sizes.

Common computer type is normally about 12 points.

With the increased use of fonts by many programs, especially word processors, they have become both common and economical. Like clip art, fonts are best acquired in groups. It is not uncommon to find collections numbering in the hundreds. Special utility programs are also available to permit viewing, printing, editing, and even creating your own fonts.

It should be apparent that using clip art and fonts extends the abilities of desktop publishers and many word processors to produce a significantly wider range of outputs. However, the weak link in the system is often the printer. A laser printer is usually required to take full advantage of the features offered by programs that fully employ fonts.

This is 8 point type
This is 12 point type
## This is 18 point type
# This is 24 point type
# This is 36 point type

**Figure 4.8**
**Point sizes.**

# ▸ Financial Software

Software is available to do almost anything in the financial area. Many small programs are designed to do only one job, such as balancing your checkbook or planning a budget, whereas others are comprehensive, providing complete financial management. Most programs do not require graphics but may provide charts if adequate graphics is available. (Common price range: $10 to $75.)

### ◆ Checking Account Programs

These are programs that keep track of your checking account transactions (checks, deposits, service charges, interest, and so forth) and automatically keep them up-to-date. The dreaded monthly chore of balancing is done automatically for you simply by checking off those items that have cleared your account. Most programs permit working with multiple accounts. These programs are usually inexpensive and easy to use. (Common price range: $10 to $20.)

### ◆ Budget Planners

These programs permit you to plan and examine many possible budgets. Some packages may suggest choices based on the financial information you enter. As your finances change from month to month, the program automatically alters your budget for future months. This means that if you wish to make a purchase and pay it off in installments, you can enter the amount of the payments into the program, and it will indicate your new budget. (Common price range: $15 to $25.)

### ◆ Financial Planners

These types of programs are similar to budget planners except that they are more comprehensive and usually permit you to develop a more detailed financial plan that may include long-term or anticipated items. (Common price range: $15 to $30.)

### ◆ Assets Managers

Many packages have been written to assist you in keeping track of your personal assets. Some simply maintain an inventory list, whereas others also allow you to include such things as bank accounts, investments, debts, assets, and income. Many also automatically factor in interest, dividends, depreciation, and other adjustments to your overall financial worth. (Common price range: $25 to $50.)

### ◆ Financial Analyzers

Analyzers permit you to make projections of possible financial situations and then factor these into your present and future budgets. For example, you might ask the program to determine the payments on a new car and then see how this would fit your budget. You could enter the prices of several models and more than one loan rate and time, if that is available to you. You would see which car, if any, you could best afford—or possibly even which would be the best deal in the long run.

### ◆ Financial Managers

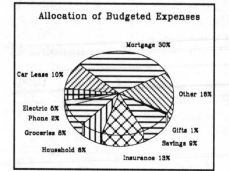

This package may offer a combination of most of the features of the other financial software plus such additional options as personal inventory, automatic depreciation, net worth, projected income, insurance analysis, and catastrophe control. These packages are often complex and more difficult to set up initially but are well worth the extra effort, especially if your financial situation is complicated. Some of the better programs even allow you to produce charts and graphs such as the one shown at left. You will also find that managers tend to be somewhat more expensive, but the cost is less than buying the included programs individually. (Common price range: $10 to $75.)

*Figure 4.9
Many financial
software packages
have the capacity
to produce charts
and graphs.*

### ◆ Tax Preparers

Up-to-date programs are available every year to assist you with your federal income tax preparation. They can be very comprehensive, with step-by-step guidance in completing the various forms. These packages may even print the forms for you. However, do not look at the program as a solution to your tax problems; it will only give as good a result as your tax situation and your skills in completing the process permit. The purchase price may exceed $50, and you will need an updated version every year, but most tax preparers charge you that much or more. Take care, however, when choosing a program; recently, many programs have had major glitches and have caused users serious headaches. (Common price range: $15 to $50.)

## ▶ Spreadsheets

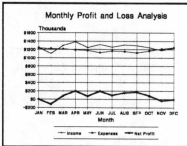

Spreadsheets are generalized financial management systems designed to be customized to your individual needs. You can use a good spreadsheet to do nearly any financial planning, analysis, or report required. They have a simple screen of rows and columns that you can set up to do the calculations and present the figures you need. The better packages can even construct graphs and charts based on the information you enter. A simple example of a line graph is shown at left; bar, pie and other types of graphs may also be available.

One significant advantage of spreadsheets is their power to project changes in a financial situation based on a set of numbers. Once you have defined your spreadsheet (which can be done directly on-screen with simple mathematical expressions), you can change some of your input data to see how it affects the end result. For example, in the sample shown at

*Figure 4.10
Spreadsheets are
common in most
financial software.*

| UNITS SOLD IN 1995 | | | | | | |
|---|---|---|---|---|---|---|
| Month | Smith | Jones | Davis | Logan | Owens | Totals |
| January | 3,125 | 1,825 | 2,329 | 2,231 | 2,930 | 12,440 |
| February | 2,921 | 2,231 | 921 | 1,822 | 3,202 | 11,097 |
| March | 3,004 | 2,202 | 2,802 | 2,121 | 2,884 | 13,013 |
| April | 3,421 | 2,476 | 2,723 | 2,042 | 3,200 | 13,862 |
| May | 2,862 | 2,102 | 2,526 | 1,996 | 3,016 | 12,502 |
| June | 3,072 | 1,983 | 3,181 | 2,120 | 2,891 | 13,247 |
| July | 3,327 | 2,087 | 2,275 | 2,213 | 2,736 | 12,638 |
| August | 2,525 | 2,718 | 2,523 | 2,529 | 2,813 | 13,108 |
| September | 3,036 | 2,103 | 2,631 | 2,013 | 3,175 | 12,958 |
| October | 3,530 | 1,481 | 2,710 | 1,820 | 2,987 | 12,528 |
| November | 3,316 | 946 | 2,379 | 2,046 | 3,137 | 11,824 |
| December | 3,003 | 2,063 | 2,284 | 2,235 | 2,837 | 12,422 |
| TOTALS | 37,142 | 24,217 | 29,284 | 25,188 | 35,808 | 151,639 |

*Figure 4.11 Spreadsheets are designed to adjust automatically to changes in data.*

left, if one of the sales figures had to be adjusted, the totals would automatically be updated to reflect the change. Or, in a more personal application, if you have set up a screen to see how your retirement account might grow over the next 20 years, you can see instantly how it will change for different values of monthly contributions, inflation adjustments, and interest rates just by changing these values.

These programs range in price from about $10 to several hundred dollars. There are some relatively good and inexpensive packages, but you may find them disappointing and lacking desired features. If you are interested in doing a number of financial applications on your system, you would likely find that the greater initial investment for a good spreadsheet will more than pay for itself in time. Like a word processor, an 80-column screen is normally used, so either a moderate- or a high-resolution color monitor gives the best results.

# ▶ Household Applications

You will find a variety of software designed to help you with many aspects of daily life. The following is a list of just a few of the packages you might find of value. Graphics is usually not required. The cost may be as low as under $10.

### ◆ Address Books

These are very simple programs that maintain a list of names, addresses, and telephone numbers. With these programs, information usually must be retrieved by name. However, a few of the better ones might permit you to retrieve by city, state, zip code, or even area code, giving you a list of only those people who live in a certain area. This could be of particular value if you have a very long list of names to handle, for business as well as personal use. (Common price range: $10 to $25.)

### ◆ Phone Books/Dialers

These very simple programs maintain lists of names and phone numbers. Most such programs will provide some kind of automatic dialing capability. (Common price range: $10 to $20.)

### ◆ Reminders

These are relatively simple programs that permit you to enter future events or appointments. Later, you can ask to see a schedule for the day, week, month, or even year. Reminders are often found as part of a larger program and may require or make use of a system clock, which automatically keeps track of the correct date and time. (Common price range: $10 to $20.)

### ◆ *Calendars*

These are sophisticated reminders. They function not only as a reminder to inform you of your upcoming plans but also usually include holiday notices. Calendars may also show you actual calendarlike screens with your schedule superimposed. These screens are very helpful in planning events such as shopping, parties, vacations, household repairs, and so forth. Whereas you can usually see any scheduling problem directly on the screen, some programs may alert you to possible or definite conflicts. Some of these programs employ graphics and will likely require a system clock. (Common price range: $10 to $50.)

### ◆ *Personal Information Managers (PIM)*

The basic idea behind PIM software is to provide an information-handling facility that permits data to be entered, managed, and retrieved in a manner that is matched as closely as possible to normal daily activity. A PIM will offer a combination of the features listed above. This most often will include address/phone book with dialer, calendar with reminder, notepad for entering and later reviewing notes, alarm clock, calculator, and other useful utilities. (Common price range: $20 to $100.)

### ◆ *Contact Managers*

A contact manager is somewhat similar to PIM in that personal or business contacts can be maintained with name and full contact information. In addition, a contact manager provides facilities for keeping track of the contacts made with each entry in the list and the results obtained. Although these programs have been used most frequently by sales representatives for listing prospective clients, they are also useful to those involved in other endeavors such as fund raising, recruitment, membership maintenance, and follow-up studies. (Common price range: $25 to 300.)

### ◆ **Organizers**

These programs will permit you to enter, organize, and retrieve information for recipes, records, tapes, tools, books, toys, collectibles, clothes, or even your computer software. Retrieving information in an organizer is usually accomplished by using one or more identifying words or phrases.

One example of an organizer is a recipe file. With such an organizer, you enter all your recipes into the system, then retrieve them by one or more key words or phrases. For example, you might request to see all your seafood recipes or maybe only those that use scallops. Some programs might even permit you to see all the recipes that make use of both chicken and onions and that can be prepared in less than 30 minutes. (Common price range: $15 to $50.)

### ◆ Catalogs

Catalogs are a more sophisticated form of organizer. These programs are intended for professional rather than casual applications. They generally offer more flexible retrieval capabilities, with detailed cross-referencing of entries. Such packages are very useful for large collections of items such as coins, music, stamps, books, and cards. (Common price range: $25 to $200.)

### ◆ Project Managers

If you have many tasks to schedule in a short time, one complex job with many parts, or a high demand on a particular item, such as a car or a room, then you may need a project manager. These programs not only assist you in assigning times to events but also allow you to see how changes in one or more events will affect the overall project or other related projects. Some may also analyze how long individual events (and entire projects) may take, and possibly even what materials or facilities will be required. (Common price range: $20 to $100.)

### ◆ Video Production

These packages, which are relatively new to the market, permit you to convert your home videos into professional-looking productions with titles, subtitles, graphics, and even animations. Special hardware to interface with your VCR is required to run these packages. (Common price range: $50 to $500; hardware can be several hundred dollars extra.)

### ◆ Hobbyists' Interests

Special programs have been prepared for a wide variety of hobbies, including coin collecting, health and fitness, genealogy, amateur astronomy, music, lotteries, trivia, ham radio, handwriting analysis, palm reading, and nearly any sport or game. Some of these programs can offer a challenge. For example, there are a number of packages that permit you to manage your own sports team with a high degree of realism. (Common price range: $10 to $100.)

### ◆ Timers/Controllers

Programs are available to permit your system to control certain external devices, such as turning lights or air conditioners on and off. These require a system clock and special hardware and wiring. Such packages can be fun, but the expense of the additional hardware is often not worth it unless you make extensive use of this application. Your money may be better spent on individual timers. (Common price range: $25 to $100; hardware can be several hundred dollars extra.)

### ◆ Security Software

Microcomputers can be set up to control your home security system. You should carefully study the economic practicality of this feature, since the same cautions mentioned above about extra items required for timers apply here as well. (Common price range: $10 to $50.)

# ▸ Health and Diet

A number of programs are available to assist with daily health and diet needs. These range from simple recipe files to detailed medical reference programs.

### ◆ Recipe Programs

The array of recipes currently available in these programs is mind-boggling to even the most avid cook. It is not unusual for these programs to contain tens of thousands of entries that can be searched in seconds. Searches are usually permitted by such areas as category, title, ingredients, or any combination of these. Most also permit the recipes to be edited or deleted, or new recipes to be added. Some also will automatically adjust the amounts of the ingredients as you change the number of servings you need. (Common price range: $10 to $50.)

### ◆ Diet and Calorie Programs

These programs contain a list of common foods and the number of calories for each. The calories are often broken down by carbohydrates, proteins, and fats. Other elements such as sodium and cholesterol are also frequently given. Suggestions for better dietary substitutes are offered by some programs. (Common price range: $10 to $25.)

### ◆ Menu Planners

Menu planners do precisely that—plan menus according to the information you feed into them. These programs often have options for special menus for diabetics, as well as sugar-free, sodium-free, or lactose-restricted diets. (This feature is often found as an option on more comprehensive recipe programs.) (Common price range: $10 to $25.)

### ◆ Fitness Assistants

These packages will assist in planning a fitness program of measured exercise and caloric intake to help in weight reduction. They are often very heavily dependent on the accuracy of the information fed into them, which often limits their effectiveness. However, some have fairly nice graphical displays of your progress as the weight-loss plan is followed. (Common price range: $15 to $25.)

### ◆ Medical History Programs

A medical history program helps you organize and continuously update medical histories for each member of your family. These programs are relatively simple but are very useful for those with chronic or multiple medical problems. This kind of program is often included as a feature in more comprehensive medical programs. (Common price range: $15 to $30.)

### ◆ Home Pharmacist

These programs contain a list of drugs along with a description of each. Commonly, such items as indication, side effects, contraindications, potential conflicts with other drugs, and dosages are given. (Common price range: $15 to $50.)

### ◆ Home Doctors

There are several programs that combine the features of many of the smaller medical programs and provide information on symptoms, diseases, drugs, medical terms, diagnostic tests, health care costs, and other aspects of your medical needs. Some even supply an interactive diagnosis capability based on answers you provide to a series of questions.

A common feature of most such programs is a personal medical history file for the entire family that may include tracking of family medical expenses. Nearly all provide detailed information on first aid. Some may include information on personal health interests such as diet and exercise. A few have good graphical displays to accompany the text explanations. (Common price range: $20 to $50.)

# ▶ Maps and Travel

With the increasing use of high-resolution graphics, the number of good-quality map programs has increased dramatically. These vary in purpose and presentation, but they all require a good-quality graphics display to function optimally. Because of the need to make use of huge amounts of data, a number of the more comprehensive map programs now come in CD-ROM format.

***Figure 4.12
Map details and
clarity vary from
program to program.***

### ◆ Geographical Map Programs

These maps provide information on the various geographical features, both man-made and natural, of the surface of the earth. They primarily show land masses, national boundaries, major cities, rivers and other bodies of water, and other significant features. Sometimes various topological features such as altitude scales and mountain ranges can also be displayed.

These programs may offer a variety of displays ranging from the entire globe to a single country or state. Often, more than one view will be available for a given region. The information provided

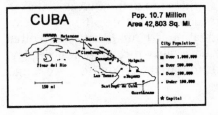

is normally restricted to the map display without an associated data base of political or demographic data. The figure on page 48 depicts how Cuba might be displayed by such a program. (Common price range: $20 to $50.)

### ◆ *Informational Map Programs*

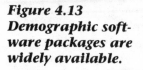

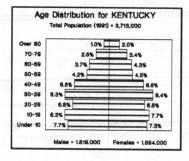

These programs provide some map detail, but they concentrate more on political and demographic information than on detailed displays. The maps are usually fairly static with little ability to adjust or switch to an alternate view.

The data available is often very comprehensive. It can cover such topics as population, crime, weather, the economy, business opportunities, politics, taxes, health care, the environment, education, cultural opportunities, and much, much more. Two typical graphical displays from this type of program are shown on this page. One shows the ten states having the highest number of total hospital beds; the other gives a breakdown of the population of Kentucky by age and sex. (Common price range: $20 to $50.)

**Figure 4.13 Demographic software packages are widely available.**

### ◆ *Road Atlas Programs*

It is now possible to obtain a complete road atlas for your computer. In fact, some of the software atlas programs are more detailed than a printed atlas. Unlike their paper forerunners, you can usually adjust the amount of detail you want to see. For example, if you want to see only major highways, you can delete all topographical features and other points of interest from the display.

Atlases begin with those that show roads and features much as a standard paper atlas does. This would include most cities and towns and the connecting roads, political borders, bodies of water, forest, mountains, and various points of interest. However, some computer atlas programs offer much more. They can provide detail maps down to the street (block) level for every place in the United States (or other countries), often providing the ability to select by an address range. You can then zoom in or out to see as much or as little detail as you need. A section of downtown Atlanta as displayed by one such program (not yet at its maximum detail) is at left.

**Figure 4.14 Road atlas programs can be customized to fit your needs.**

There is one special precaution that should be observed when selecting an atlas program. With most packages, you get the full atlas just as you would expect. However, a few companies supply only the display mechanism and a few sample maps. Whereas the remainder of the map data base is contained in the material you have purchased, you must pay extra for special codes, passwords, or keys to access these maps, either individually or as a group. If you need only a few maps, this kind of package may be fine, however, this can often become very costly if your need is for a comprehensive map program. In general, programs requiring these additional fees should be avoided. (Common price range: $30 to $200.)

### ◆ *Trip Planners*

Nearly all trip planners offer an accompanying map display; however, a few cheaper ones do not. This program will draw on a data base of hotels/motels, restaurants, and other features to assist you in planning an itinerary. Most programs will also provide you with trip information, including the estimated travel time and distance as well as suggested routes. Trip planners are sometimes incorporated within atlas programs. (Common price range: $15 to $50.)

## ▶ Data Base Managers

A data base manager (sometimes called an **electronic file cabinet**) may be the most powerful single software package you will encounter. A good **data base management system (DBMS)** can be a very effective and efficient organizer, catalog, calendar, and financial manager, and can facilitate the orderly storage and handling of data. A DBMS is designed to be customized to your individual needs. Many are very powerful, amazingly versatile, and creative in the ways they set up and manage specific applications.

The power of a good data base is its ability to retrieve information in a variety of ways. The output can be listed in a special order or to fit certain conditions. For example, suppose you are going to Cincinnati on a business trip and wish to know whom to contact for possible sales while in that area. You can ask for an alphabetical list of all clients who live in Cincinnati and have expressed an interest in your product division within the past six months. Or, you might ask for an alphabetical list of all the names of United States presidents. However, the ability to get data out of a data base depends on how the data base was set up. Some data bases are much more flexible and easier to manage than others, and this should be a primary consideration when comparing these packages.

Data base managers vary greatly in price, ranging from about $10 to several hundred dollars. As with a word processor or spreadsheet, you would be well advised to invest carefully in a data base manager that will suit your needs. This means not only considering the data you will need to handle and how you will need to retrieve it, but also any compatibility requirements with other software. Very cheap versions are not powerful or versatile and may prove to be a disappointment. A package should be chosen wisely. Many data base management systems use graphics. Most require an 80-column display.

## ▶ Informational Data Bases

Specialized data base systems are available for a rapidly increasing number of topics. These include general references (such as dictionaries, almanacs, atlases, encyclopedias, and books of quotations), lists (such as colleges, companies, libraries, government agencies, newspapers, and broadcast media), recipes and electronic bartenders, magazines, literature (from selected passages to complete works), geographic and demographic data, census results, travel distances and times, movie guides, star catalogs, scientific data, catalogs of electronic and other components, home and business phone books for the entire United States, zip codes (including complete 9-digit codes), and consumer information (such as price and feature comparisons). The costs of such a reference source will depend on its size and media, and will range from under $10 to over $500.

Whereas some informational data bases are available on floppy disks, because of the huge amounts of data involved, most now make use of the expanded capacity of the CD-ROM format and may be found exclusively on that media. Occasionally, data bases (especially those still on diskettes) may be supplied in simple text files, and you will need to use a data base manager, word processor, or other program to make use of these. Other diskette-based data bases will come with their own simple data base manager, but the features of such systems are often limited and highly specialized. A data base on CD-ROM, while more expensive, is generally much more extensive and visual in its presentation. Some CD-ROM data bases use sound (often stereo), which may require a **sound board** (see Chapter 5).

# ▶ Integrated Software

Integrated software packages combine the features of several types of software into a single package that offers you the capabilities of each individually. Although many different types of programs are found in an integrated package, the five most commonly incorporated in such software are word processors, spreadsheets, data base managers, presentation graphics, and telecommunications.

One major advantage of this type of program is that information created by one section of the package can be referred to and used by another. For example, suppose you need to include part of the information from the data base in a report you are preparing using the word processor. With an integrated package, the information can be easily transferred. This type of cross-referencing compatibility is often lacking with software packages that are purchased separately.

Another advantage is price. You can get an integrated package for much less than what the individual parts cost when purchased separately—and usually without significantly sacrificing features or overall capabilities. However, integrated software packages range widely in price and features. They are available for as low as about $20 and cost as much as several hundred dollars for the top-of-the-line professional packages. As with any software of wide-ranging capability, the extra initial investment is usually well worth it.

If there is a disadvantage to integrated software, it is that you must take all three packages as a unit and therefore will not have as much flexibility in selecting their individual features. To get a word processor that does all that you want it to do, for example, you may have to settle for a spreadsheet or data base manager that is not quite up to your preferred standards.

A special type of integrated package known as an **application suite** is a group of programs designed to work together and be run under the Windows environment. Applications suites are similar to conventional integrated packages in that data and features are shared among the components of the package. The biggest difference is that each part of the application suite is normally a stand-alone program, which is not the case with standard integrated software.

# ▸ Telecommunications Software

The software that links your system to others is called a telecommunications (also **data communications**) package. These programs permit your computer to send and receive information from other computers over **data communications channels**, such as telephone lines, microwaves, and communications satellites. You will need access to a telephone line (or maybe just a jack) and a **modem** (which requires a **serial port** on your computer). A modem links a computer to a data communications channel, which for home systems is nearly always the telephone line. The telephone can be your regular home phone or an extension located at your computer. The expense of establishing telecommunications, including both the software and the modem, will likely cost between $100 and $500.

If you have a friend with a personal computer similar to yours that also has a telecommunications program, the two of you can exchange messages, programs, data files, and other information over the telephone lines. You might transfer files directly from your computer at work to your home system, or students might send their homework directly to the computer at school. Your computer could be set to answer the phone automatically and receive data from other computers when you are not available.

## ◆ *Bulletin Board Systems (BBS)*

One of the most popular uses of telecommunications is accessing electronic bulletin boards. These are computer systems that are accessible over the phone lines and provide some service or information. One common type is dedicated to a particular computer system and provides information to the users of that system. This may include information on new software or hardware products, comments from users on software or hardware currently in use, or even free software that you can **download** (copy) onto your system. Other bulletin boards provide more general information. Most provide an **electronic mail** (e-mail) service that allows its users to leave messages for one another. Some even provide interactive games in which you play other users. Many bulletin boards are free to access, whereas others charge various fees depending on your usage. If the bulletin board is not local, there probably will be a long-distance telephone-type charge.

## ◆ *Online Information Services*

There is an increasing number of electronic information services, both local and nationwide, including Prodigy, CompuServe, GEnie, Delphi, and America Online (AOL). A list of several nationally available online services and bulletin board systems is provided in Appendix B.

Online services offer data bases that include information in such areas as daily news summaries, stock quotations, catalogs, shopping (many types), education, health and medicine, literature, science, real estate, legal data, computer games (some may be interactive with other users), software markets, government, business, book and article reviews, weather reports, sports updates, traffic reports, and airline schedules. In some cases, you may interact with other systems, such as an airline data base. You can actually make, confirm, and pay for reservations for flights, rental cars, and hotel rooms while online.

One service might give you access to several hundred subjects ranging from Dow Jones stock quotes to daily horoscopes. Many features, such as games and airline schedules, must be used while connected to the system; others, such as news summaries and reviews, can be downloaded to your system for later viewing at your convenience, saving connect-time and long-distance phone charges. All online services provide a wide range of bulletin boards (not to be confused with the electronic bulletin board systems mentioned above), also called conferences or forums, which can number in the hundreds and are each dedicated to a specific topic. For example, if you are a teacher who is interested in cooking and crafts, you might like to exchange ideas on the several boards that deal with education, food, and crafts.

These services can be valuable and a lot of fun, but they can also be expensive. There may be several different rate options, and the procedure for calculating charges is sometimes complex. There is usually a basic monthly charge (about $9 to $17) for limited time and features, but total fees could be substantially more depending on how, when, and how frequently you use the service. For example, you may be charged for time beyond your allotment for signing on during prime-time hours, accessing certain areas of the service, or performing special actions such as downloading or sending a FAX. In addition, you may or may not have to make a long-distance call to access the service. *Be very sure you understand all potential charges before signing up for any online service because these costs can add up quickly.*

Many services employ simple, text-based displays and are accessed using regular telecommunications software. Others make use of extensive graphics-based screens and require special access software that is normally supplied free of charge with membership. Nearly all have versions of their software for both IBM-compatible and Macintosh computers as well as for those using Windows.

If you are in doubt about whether such a service is for you, watch for free trial offers. Most services periodically provide some kind of promotional offer to try to attract new subscribers. These offers usually give you a limited period during which you can use the system (or some restricted part of it) for free or with a money-back guarantee. This is a good way to assess your needs and find out what is available. If you do not wish to continue, be certain that your membership is canceled at the end of the trial period. Also, should you continue to use the service, it is common practice to include the trial period in your first billing cycle so it would have been free *only had you canceled.*

## ◆ *The Internet*

The Internet is a global collection of tens of thousands of individual networks from government, military, university, and commercial sources. Although the original idea of the Internet was to promote communication and information exchange between those within the network and enhance and promote research, it has now been opened up to virtually anyone with a computer.

Everything is available on the Internet from high-level technical data to NASA photos of the planets to gossip on bulletin boards. The information is both archival and current. There are millions of files for review and down-loading. The system can be overwhelming to even the experienced computer user, but with a little patience it is a wonderland for anyone.

The Internet was not designed for ease of use, and it is often very intimidating to the novice user. There are programs that provide a more friendly interface into the Internet by permitting the use of more easily understood commands. Some of the bulletin board systems and online services mentioned above provide Internet access (**gateway**), whereas a few specialized services exist primarily for the sole purpose of being an Internet gateway.

### ◆ *The Information Superhighway*

The bulletin board systems, online services, and the Internet are only examples of three types of stops available along the **information superhighway**. The latter is a term used to loosely refer to the growing ease and ability to access and exchange information via electronic means. Although the term "Internet" is sometimes used synonymously with "information superhighway," in reality it is only one stop along the way—although indisputably the largest one at the moment.

The information superhighway is still in its infancy—so news about what its exact nature will eventually be like is only a guess. Some envision it as a giant super Internet that will reach into and link every home and office. Others see it as being rooted in interactive cable and other entertainment media. A collection of different access methods, by our best guess, will likely be the reality.

Whatever the eventual evolution of the information superhighway, personal computers will play an integral part in the access and exchange of information.

# ▶ Graphics Programs

One of the fastest growing areas in personal computer software is that of graphics packages. Not only are these becoming much more reliable, versatile, and sophisticated, but the better graphics of the newer computers offer sharper pictures and new applications. In the past, games came to mind when people thought of computer graphics. Although games were one of graphics' primary uses for many years, excellent graphics packages are now available for many applications in education, engineering, art, drafting, business, word processing, and manufacturing. Many even come with a variety of ready-made images of geometric figures and other familiar objects that you can incorporate into your own designs.

If you anticipate the need to run any programs on your system that will make use of graphics, you must be certain that the computer has the appropriate capabilities. Most graphics software now uses moderate- to high-resolution graphics. Some may require accessories for input or cursor (screen position) control, which may include **joysticks**, a **mouse**, a **light pen**, or even a **tablet**. Check that your computer system can adequately handle all the graphics software you will need. Acceptable graphics packages are available from about $50 and up, which does not include the cost of any special equipment that may be needed.

### ◆ *Drawing Programs*

These programs permit you to draw directly on the screen, usually with a special, manually controlled instrument such as a mouse or a light pen. Some of these may permit very detailed drawings with variable-width lines and many colors. (Common price range: $10 to 30.)

### ◆ *Painting Programs*

Painting programs are similar to drawing packages except that they tend to be more "artistic" in nature. These usually permit varied types of brush strokes and a wide variety of colors (the **palette**). Often, a touch-sensitive pad called a **tablet** can be used to paint and transfer the image to the screen. (Common price range: $10 to 50.)

*Figure 4.15 These graphics programs are limited only by your creativity.*

### ◆ *Sign and Banner Makers*

Many relatively simple but often very versatile programs are now available to print signs, banners, posters, titles, headings, greeting cards, or other items requiring large or special print. (These may even be executed in color.) Such programs normally come with a variety of fonts, borders, and graphics images from which to select in making designs. Two typical examples, a sign and a banner, are shown at left.

These programs usually work rather well, but they require a printer capable of similar graphics. There are now variations of these packages designed to work with a word processor to enhance its printing capabilities. (Common price range: $10 to $50.)

*Figure 4.16 Professional-looking graphic programs can be an asset to any business*

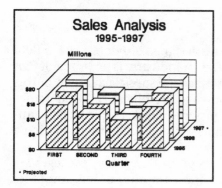

### ◆ *Presentation Graphics*

This refers to professional-level graphics programs that are designed to produce various kinds of charts and provide a variety of output formats. These programs can normally display information not only as the common text, line, bar, and pie charts, but also as area, pyramid, organizational, and other kinds of charts, including various combinations. There is usually a wide latitude in display choices, including colors and patterns.

Once a chart has been created, it can be displayed or printed, but many programs also have slide show or film recorder output abilities. In the latter case, the chart can be transferred directly to photographic film for display as a slide or transparency. A simple example of the kind of chart this program can produce is shown at left. In fact, most of the line, pie, and bar charts shown in this chapter were prepared with this type of program.

Although inexpensive programs to produce simple charts are

available, they may be disappointing. Good presentation graphics programs are not cheap, often costing $200 or more. However, because of their versatility, they usually prove to be a wise investment over the long run. If you need this kind of application, buy the best available package. (Common price range: $25 to $500.)

***Figure 4.17***
***There are software packages available to help you design almost anything, even a house.***

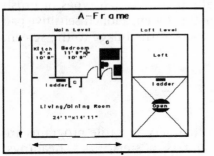

### ◆ Home Design Packages

An increasingly popular kind of graphics program is one that permits a complete architectural design to be easily drawn. These programs include special symbols for doors, windows, fireplaces, and other features. A simple floor plan for an A-frame cabin is shown at left.

Some programs of this type even have supplements or companion programs that allow you to add furniture within individual rooms and even perform landscaping. (Several collections of floor plans are also available, but these may not be in a format that is compatible with the program you like.)

Although the programs may not be a substitute for a professional architect, they can be both helpful and enjoyable to use. Good, complete packages are about $50 and up.

***Figure 4.18***
***Complex scientific programs have improved dramatically.***

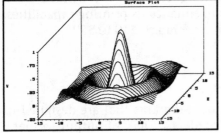

### ◆ Plotting Programs

Among the earliest attempts at graphics programs were those designed to draw plots of mathematical functions. The early programs could make use of very limited graphics. However, today's high-resolution graphics systems have given new life to this kind of application. A typical plot of a complex function is shown at left.

Typically these programs can display and print (or plot) a graph of most any valid math function supplied by the user. Some programs are more user-friendly than others and permit the function and its associated parameters to be entered directly; others may require that a separate data file be generated. In either case, these programs are invaluable to anyone who needs to draw function graphs. (Common price range: $15 to $30.)

***Figure 4.19***
***Professional design software is available in a wide price range.***

### ◆ Design Packages

This is basically professional-level software designed either to teach a field such as drafting or assist with design projects in industry. (The home design and plotting programs just described are special examples of this kind of software.) They normally require high-resolution graphics, making use of three-dimensional displays, **plotters, scanners,** or other special equipment. A typical drawing from such a program is shown at left.

Two of the most popular types of general design packages are **computer-aided design (CAD)** and **computer-aided manufac-**

turing (CAM). Not only are these packages widely used in education for instruction and simulations, but they are also useful in fields such as engineering, architecture, product testing, production, and tooling. Many CAD/CAM systems come as a unit with both the basic hardware and software, and may be very expensive. Although simple products can be found for under $50, these often prove to be disappointing; reasonably good programs can be obtained for under $300. Full-featured packages can cost as much as several thousand dollars in both software and hardware.

### ◆ Graphics Utilities

These programs are different from those discussed above because they are not graphics development or design programs. Rather, these are programs that permit you to perform some operation with a graphics file. For example, you may have a graphics design that was created by one program that you would like to use in another, but they are of a different format. A graphics utility program may permit you to convert between a number of the many different formats used by graphics programs.

Some utilities may perform only a single function; others will do a number of jobs that may include viewing images, cropping, scaling (changing the size or resolution), manipulating (flipping, rotating), dithering (adjusting the colors), and other special effects. If you plan to do a lot of work with graphics applications, a good graphics utility program will be a valuable companion. (Common price range: $20 to $50.)

## ▶ Educational Programs

Many of the educational programs make extensive use of motion graphics and sound. Some employ joysticks, a mouse, a light pen, or even a tablet. Excellent programs are available for virtually every subject area and at any level of study from preschool to college. Educational packages cost less than $10, but some comprehensive programs can cost hundreds of dollars.

*Figure 4.20 Children's software is very popular.*

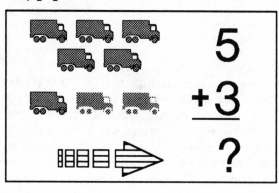

### ◆ Drill and Practice

These programs are very simple in concept but tend to be dull, so they are often included with games to stimulate interest. Drill and practice packages offer repeated examples on a given subject for the student to answer. Many provide automatic grading and review (if the student does not do well). Some offer work on more than one topic or level. The figure at left is a simplified example of a screen that might be included in such a program for young children learning basic arithmetic. (Common price range: $15 to $50.)

### ◆ *Tutorials*

Tutorials are designed to teach something, ranging from a single topic to an entire subject or course. They offer instruction on the subject followed by a test. Then, based on the results of your score, you are directed to either review or go on to the next lesson. (Common price range: $10 to $50.)

### ◆ *Computer-Assisted Instruction (CAI)*

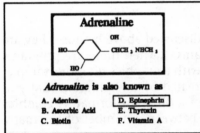

*Figure 4.21 Educational software is available for all learning levels, including this program on biochemistry.*

Whereas drill and practice and tutorial packages can be used along with other material, most are designed to stand alone and be used without any other assistance. **CAI** software is more often used as part of a course to supplement the regular material. Many good CAI programs are available for personal computers to help you study and master new skills or learn new subjects. For example, the figure at left is an example of what might be found on a CAI program on biochemistry.

CAI software is used at all levels and in virtually every field covering basic to advanced topics. It comes in a very diverse variety of presentation formats and is sometimes referred to as **computer-assisted learning (CAL)** or **computer-based training (CBT)**. (Common price range: $15 to $200.)

### ◆ *Instructional*

Whereas the three categories just described all involve software that is designed to teach you a body of knowledge, some programs are intended simply to explain or show you how to do something. For example, there are packages available that explain how the system works, what it can do, and how to begin to operate it.

### ◆ *Preparatory*

These packages are designed to assist you in preparing for some specific event. For example, there are programs that offer sample tests to help you study and prepare for certain national standardized tests. (Common price range: $10 to $40.)

*Figure 4.22 Software packages such as this help you keep accurate records.*

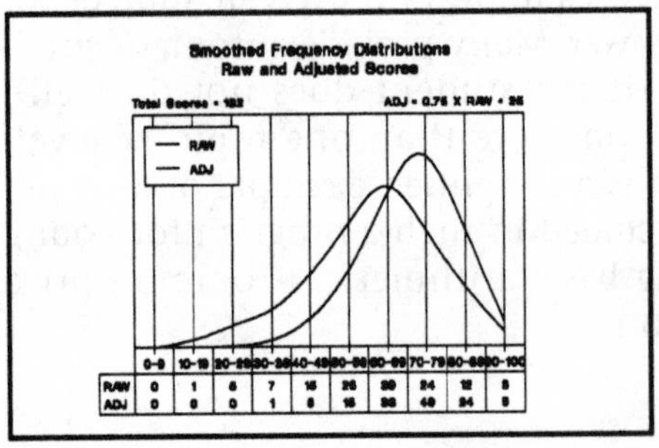

### ◆ *Professional*

Professional packages are designed primarily for teachers and administrators. They are intended to assist with professional chores such as test writing, record keeping, and grading. Many provide detailed, often advanced analysis capabilities ranging from simple score or item analysis to complete statistical data treatments. Graphical presentations of analyses are common with the better programs. A sample display of a score analysis is shown at left. (Common price range: $25 to $100.)

### ◆ *Design*

Many programs are now available for design projects ranging from art and drawing to drafting and engineering. These normally make use of graphics and special input devices, such as tablets and scanners, and can offer real versatility and creative expression for artistic or creative design. (Common price range: $50 up to several thousand dollars.)

### ◆ *Simulations*

Many real-life situations, ranging from counseling to chemical reactions, have been simulated by a computer program. The user can then react to various sets of conditions and observe the results. (Common price range: $25 to $200.)

## ▶ Games

From the beginning of computer use in educational applications, some students who resisted "normal" instruction were coaxed to learn when the lessons were presented as a game. For this reason, much of the educational software is based on some sort of game to induce the student to learn. You can find games at all levels and on most subjects. In addition, some noneducational games, such as adventure, mystery, strategy, simulations, and even some arcade varieties, may be of value in teaching and developing logical reasoning and problem-solving skills.

Games have been written that present almost any topic normally taught in grades 1 through 12, including math, biology, history, grammar, social studies, spelling, chemistry, and literature. Most of these require the student to solve a problem or answer a question in order to proceed with the game. Rewards are often given for correct results and penalties for incorrect ones. The format may be presented either as tutorials or as drill and practice.

Games constitute the third largest category of computer software, with over $700 million in sales in 1994. There is a wide selection available for most computer systems. Most games packages range in price from about $5 to $50, with some very good programs available for $15 or less. A game often costs more if it is new or trendy, and it may become available later at a much reduced price.

If you plan to run many games on your computer, you will likely need a good, high-resolution graphics system to get a sharp image for games that employ greatly detailed or motion graphics. Sound is also becoming an integral part of game design with many of the more sophisticated and expensive games now being supplied on CD-ROM format. You may also need one or two joysticks to control the action on the screen.

### ◆ *Arcade/Action*

These are the familiar graphics action games that first come to mind when most people think of computer games. Even if you have never used a computer, you may have heard of some traditional favorites such as PacMan, Space Invaders, JumpMan,

*Figure 4.23
An example of
how the game
Tetris would look
on your screen.*

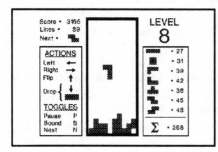

Asteroids, and Mario. Many of the more recent games build on the formats made popular by these early "standards." A game called Tetris, in which you must align the falling blocks, is illustrated in Figure 4.23.

### ◆ Adventure

These games often involve an adventurous "journey" in search of a hidden treasure, or an attempt to rescue a captive and resolve a dilemma. There are normally many perils and pitfalls to impede your progress.

An adventure game may be a mystery, strategy, or other type, but it usually requires you to enter word commands to control the action. A key to the solution to the game may be the decoding of one or more clues hidden in a word, phrase, or other part of the game. Many adventure games do not employ graphics and operate satisfactorily using a text display.

### ◆ Mystery

In this type of game you act as a detective or spy or other sleuth to try to solve a mystery. This may involve anything from a "whodunit" to recovering secret papers from "the enemy." Some of these resemble adventure games in their plot, but they normally make more use of graphics and screen action.

### ◆ Strategy

These may be based on almost any topic from sports to international intrigue. You are asked to develop a strategy for the solution to a specified problem or set of problems. Many are similar to adventure and mystery games, which are often based on trial and error, but strategy games are usually more organized and less forgiving of mistakes.

*Figure 4.24*
*A display typical of hangman programs is pictured.*

### ◆ Word

Word games come in a wide variety of types ranging from the familiar puzzles, such as crossword, word scramble, and hangman, to more exotic and unusual offerings.

Unlike many of the other kinds of games, word games often allow you to generate your own puzzles. In other words, a crossword puzzle game might not only present you with its own puzzles to solve, but also permit you to develop your own puzzles.

### ◆ Simulations

You are put into a real-life situation and asked to guide the action in a realistic manner. This might be an arcade-type presentation, such as the pilot of a jet fighter or a race car driver. Or the setting may be historically based, with you as a general in charge of an army in the American Revolution or Civil

War, with your results compared to the actual situations. Whereas many of these games involve a battle setting, others might cast you as a stockbroker, bobsled pilot, football coach, or even a doctor.

### ◆ Game Shows

Several popular TV game shows are now available as computer games. These are close simulations of the actual TV show (without the "fabulous" prizes).

### ◆ Sports

Nearly any sport that you can imagine from baseball and hockey to golf and skiing has been simulated for play on the computer. Naturally, there are sports games that permit you to play the sport, either against the computer or a human opponent, but there are also more sophisticated offerings that permit you to manage a team or act in other more general capacities.

### ◆ Card Games

Most popular card games, such as poker, bridge, and cribbage, plus a number of less well-known games, have been programmed by several companies in various forms for the computer. Although these tend to be accurate representations of the games, they frequently lack imagination in play, and it is often not very difficult to figure out how the computer "thinks" and learn to beat it most of the time.

### ◆ Casino Games

These are similar to card games, but they simulate popular casino games such as craps, keno, and roulette. These also tend not to be too imaginative, but many faithfully reproduce the actual game.

*Figure 4.25*
*A relatively simple screen for a computer Othello game is shown.*

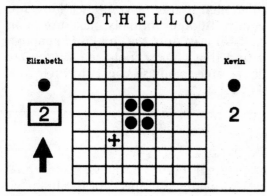

### ◆ Board Games

Nearly every popular board game has been programmed into a computer game, some more successfully than others. Many are offered by several companies, and some are only close clones. The computer tends to be "smarter" when you are playing against it in these games than in the card or casino games.

Do not be misled by the simplicity of the display in the sample game: Some can be very complex. For example, there are three-dimensional chess games in which the game pieces actually walk from square to square as moves take place and then engage in "combat," complete with sound effects, when a capture occurs!

### ◆ *Number Games*

If you like working with numbers, then these are for you. They normally require the manipulation of one or more numbers to achieve a stated result.

### ◆ *Educational Games*

See the discussion of Games under Educational Programs.

### ◆ *Virtual Reality*

This is a software design that places the user into a three-dimensional playing field. The more sophisticated systems employ special helmets and gloves for interacting with your "reality"; however, many games now use 3-D graphics with the action at the viewpoint of the player. The "world" then moves in response to the actions of the user, who directs things by using the keyboard, mouse, or joystick. Typical settings for virtual reality games include flight and driving simulators and the familiar "hero storms fortress" scenario.

These games obviously require detailed graphics. They also normally employ sound to simulate speech, gunfire, opening doors, or other actions as the game proceeds. Such games are a combination of arcade, adventure, and simulations and are usually very challenging. (Note: Virtual reality designs appear in other applications as well, but these are often very expensive and are not of much interest to the average home computer user.)

## ▶ Children's Software

If you have children who will have access to the computer, do not overlook the wealth of software that is available for young users. The bulk of the programs are either games or educational applications, but this in no way limits the diversity of the selection. Most of the programs make use of animations and sound to help maintain the child's interest and to enhance the enjoyment of the overall experience, especially for the very young user.

Do not think your child is too young. If a child is old enough to use a mouse or joystick, he or she is old enough to use the computer. Programs that are specifically written for young children normally make use of an input device other than the keyboard—at least until the child is old enough to know the alphabet. (You may find that your school-age children are already computer literate and may be able to advise you as to their own needs.) (Common price range: $10 to $50.)

## ▶ Business Packages

If you plan to use your computer system in your business, professional programs are already on the market to handle all aspects of the financial

**Figure 4.26
A typical
prescription label.**

record keeping, such as payroll, billing, sales, inventory, personnel development, contact management, and so forth. There are software programs for pharmacies, farmers, doctors, dentists, churches, truckers, barbers, retail stores, schools, politicians, and almost everyone else. A typical prescription label that might be printed as part of a complete record-keeping package for a pharmacy is depicted at left. If a suitable package is not available for your unique needs, one could be specially written. As another alternative, an appropriate set of programs can be customized from a data base manager, spreadsheet, or integrated software package, but this approach would require considerably more thought, planning, and time to set up. (Common price range: $50 to $1000.)

# ▸ Professional Software

Whatever your profession, it is likely that you can find software to assist you with your work. Several general application–type packages can be used for many on-the-job projects. We have mentioned professional-level packages for education and business applications as well as the plotting and CAD/CAM programs. There are many excellent professional-level packages for other fields as well. For example, there are statistical analysis programs, report generators, equipment controllers, data analyzers, and many more. These programs are usually complex and powerful, and may be fairly expensive; they are not designed for the average user and do not work on some computers. (Common price range: $25 to $1,000.)

# ▸ Programming Languages

All of the software discussed thus far involves preprepared programs that you purchase and execute on your computer. If you want to write programs for yourself, you need to acquire one or more programming languages. Capable and reliable versions of programming languages are expensive. You may expect to pay from around $20 to well over $1,000, depending on the specific language and its capabilities. Less expensive ones are available, but you may find them disappointing.

## ◆ *Text Editors*

If you wish to get into program development, you need a text editor to write your programs. This is a very simple word processor designed for producing basic output files without special formats or control codes. Such files are commonly referred to as **ASCII** (American Standard Code for Information Interchange) files. Text editors are frequently only line editors, and may be both simple and awkward to use. They are usually included as part of the operating system utility package. They can also be purchased separately, or a word processor can be used, provided it has a text editor mode or the ability to save files in DOS or ASCII format. (Common price range: $5 to $50.)

### ◆ Development and Run-Time Systems

Some languages come in two separate parts: the development and the run-time systems. The run-time system allows you to run only programs that have already been written. You must also have the development system in order to construct your own programs. Languages are sometimes offered this way to provide a less expensive package to those who do not plan to do any program development of their own. Whereas a full-development system for a language may cost as much as $1,000 or more, the separate run-time module, if available, may cost only a fraction of that.

### ◆ Compilers and Interpreters

You may also have a choice between a compiled and an interpreted version of a language. This is especially true for many versions of the BASIC programming language. Interpreters process a program line by line, interacting with and assisting you as you write the program. But they tend to be slow. Versions that employ a compiler are faster; however, you must construct the entire program (or an independent segment) and compile it to get any feedback. Interpreters are recommended for beginning programmers. If you desire, the programs that you write this way can always be compiled later, provided a compiler is available for your particular interpreter version.

### ◆ BASIC

This is the most commonly used language on microcomputers and is supplied with many systems. If it does not come with the initial system software, it should be available for your computer, probably in several versions. It was designed to be easy to learn and use by persons with little or no prior experience with computers. BASIC is the best language for the new programmer to learn first because it is straightforward and non-intimidating.

You should not be deceived by the ease with which you can learn BASIC; it is a very powerful language that can be used to solve many complex problems. Although it has lost some popularity to C and Pascal, newer versions—such as Microsoft's Visual Basic—that provide advanced features and user interface are restoring BASIC as a popular programming language. (Common price range: $30 to $500.)

### ◆ COBOL

This language is designed to be used specifically for programming business applications. It is a very complex and powerful language that requires a lot of memory and disk space to operate. For this reason, it has neither been available for nor popular with many microcomputers. However, with today's more powerful systems this is no longer a problem, and there are a few very good versions available for personal computers.

COBOL is not a difficult language. It is based on "English-like" statements, but it is highly structured and detailed, which may make it confusing for the beginner.

### ◆ FORTRAN

This was the first major programming language to be developed. It is a language oriented primarily for science, math, and engineering applications. FORTRAN has not been widely used on microcomputers, having lost out to newer languages such as Pascal and C. Although somewhat more complicated, the newer versions of FORTRAN resemble BASIC in many ways. (Common price range: $25 to $300.)

### ◆ Pascal

This language, which is very popular with programmers, is available for any computer. It was developed specifically to make use of structured or more ordered programming design. It is recommended by some as a first language because you are less likely to develop bad programming habits with it than you might with BASIC. However, it is more difficult to learn and can be intimidating to the novice programmer. (Common price range: $25 to $300.)

### ◆ LISP

This is an unusual, nonnumeric language that will not be for all users. It is well-suited for **artificial intelligence (AI)** applications, including those used in robots, **expert systems** (such as medical diagnostic, trip routing, and investment advisers), voice recognition, and foreign language translation. LISP can be found in many forms and is normally available in both interpreted and compiled versions. (Common price range: $100 to $500.)

### ◆ Assembly Language

If you are very interested in program development, you may want to try programming in assembly language. These programs normally execute faster on the computer; however, they are very tedious and time-consuming to write. Unlike all the other high-level languages mentioned here, assembly languages are dependent on the computer in which they are intended to run. (Common price range: $15 to $100.)

### ◆ C/C++

C is a very powerful, high-level programming language with the speed and flexibility of a low-level language. It manipulates the computer much like assembly language, but the compiled version is machine independent. C has become the language of choice for many programmers. C++ is an even more powerful version that is increasing in popularity. (Common price range: $100 to $500.)

### ◆ *Other Languages*

This list is only representative and is far from complete. Additional languages, including Ada, ALGOL, APL, Forth, Logo, PILOT, PL/1, Prolog, RPG, and SNOBOL, may also be available for some microcomputers. Many languages come in several, often equally good but functionally different, versions.

# ▸ Public Domain Software

Public domain software refers to programs that are not protected by copyright and are not restricted from being freely duplicated and distributed. Such software is normally available for roughly the cost of duplication. Collections are usually maintained by users' groups and some dealers, and can often be found advertised in the classified sections of computer magazines. For some systems this can amount to many thousands of programs. In many cases the author is unknown. Public domain libraries tend to consist primarily of operating system utilities and games.

Most of the programs in public domain libraries are functional and perform a specific job, but some are not user-friendly or well written. Many assume that the user has a basic understanding of such things as operating system commands or the very process they are designed to accomplish. Whereas they may not actually contain errors, they can lack the edit checks to catch improper entries that the better programs incorporate. Much public domain material will not meet the standards of its commercial counterparts, but if you have the patience to look, a few real gems are out there.

# ▸ Shareware

The increasing complexity of programs has made commercial publication by the individual software author more difficult. However, with the proliferation of IBM compatibles, the number of such programs has become enormous. The immediate solution to this problem by the software authors has been the distribution of shareware, or **user-supported software.** This concept was born in the idea that the users of a product will pay for and support it if they use it and find it of value.

Shareware authors protect their work by copyright but distribute their programs for little or no initial fee; they place few restrictions on the further distribution of the program by its intermediate distributors or end users. If there is an initial charge, it is nominal, usually about $1 to $5 per disk. Each program carries a message that if the user finds the program of value or continues to use it beyond a certain period, commonly thirty days, the author requests either a voluntary contribution or legal registration fee of a certain amount, normally from $5 to $50. This can go much higher with the distribution of such materials as the program source code, printed copies of manuals, hints to or solutions for games, templates, and other "special" offers.

Authors can be creative about enticing you to pay the registration fee. Sometimes, the shareware version of a program is limited, being only a demonstration version or having only a few of its features implemented, requiring that you pay a registration fee to receive a fully functional version. At other times, the author offers special additions or enhancements to the basic program, free samples of other shareware programs, or other bonuses if you register. Usually, registration will bring you some level of technical support, but normally not to the degree offered by a commercial product.

Shareware programs can be freely copied or given away as long as they are kept in their entirety and not sold or altered. These programs range in value from almost useless to as good as their commercial counterparts. They tend to be better written than public domain material and are available for almost any purpose or application. Both public domain and shareware programs are normally available from many retailers and bulletin boards.

There is no reason to avoid shareware as a whole, but you should be fully aware of the sources of the programs and rules governing their use. Since a program could pass through several hands before you acquire it, be extra careful to verify that the disks have been certified as virus free or that you have the capability to check them yourself. It might not hurt to do both. If there is a physical defect in the disk, you can complain to the source from which it was acquired. However, third-party dealers do not provide much, if any, technical support. If you have a problem with the program, you will have to contact the author for assistance.

As a final note, shareware authors have formed an organization to police their own work. It is referred to as the **Association of Shareware Professionals (ASP)**. Program authors who are members of this organization will prominently display the ASP logo (shown at left), usually in their program's initial or final screen or the documentation.

**Association of Shareware Professionals**

**MEMBER**

*Figure 4.27 Logo for the Association of Shareware Professionals (ASP).*

If you have difficulty resolving a problem with a shareware author *who is a member of ASP,* the organization will endeavor to help. Their policy statement reads in part: "ASP wants to make sure that the shareware principle works for you. If you are unable to resolve a shareware-related problem with an ASP member by contacting the member directly, ASP may be able to help. The ASP Ombudsman can help you resolve a dispute or problem with an ASP member, but does not provide technical support for members' products." This is not a guarantee of a resolution to your problem, but it is another avenue of appeal, something that is not always available with commercial software publishers.

## ▶ Access Software

A computer can be equipped so that nearly anyone can use it. There is a wide array of software designed to assist persons with disabilities to make use of a computer. For example, persons with visual impairment can benefit from screen magnifiers that make the images on the screen larger or screen readers that actually *read* the text on the screen. Many such devices, such as the screen reader, may also require special hardware.

Unfortunately, the cost of the software and hardware for equipping a computer for a user's special needs can be significant, so it would be especially wise to shop around. Ask your dealer for guidance. If this does not prove to be fruitful, contact someone at your state department of rehabilitative services for assistance.

# Select Your Hardware

Once you have a firm idea of what applications or specific software packages you want for your system, you are ready to look at the **hardware,** or physical equipment. In this chapter, hardware will be discussed in general terms; refer to Chapter 8 for complete test results of notebook computers and printers.

The variety of available products you will have to select from may vary significantly, depending on the system that interests you. For example, the market is flooded with monitors, printers, and other equipment for IBM-compatible computers, whereas the products from Apple are more proprietary in design and therefore your choices are more limited. This fact alone does not necessarily limit the performance of one computer relative to another and should not influence your final decision.

## ▶ Compatibility

**Compatibility** is a key word in selecting any computer system. There are several important considerations that apply to nearly every system.

### ◆ *Software*

The software and hardware must be compatible. Not only must the software be compatible with the computer itself (including the operating system), but it must also function properly with *all* other system components that it will use, such as the graphics display, sound board, and printer. A lack of compatibility in this area could mean anything from a minor annoyance to a total failure of the software to run.

### ◆ *System*

Many computers are designed to be compatible with and use the software designed for other brands. The most common examples are the IBM PC compatibles, which are supposed to run whatever is on the IBM-band computers. To achieve compatibility, you must be certain that you are looking at a model that works with the corresponding IBM machine, such as the XT, AT, or PS/2. Although there may be some cross-compatibility, selecting the wrong model will ensure trouble. Sometimes computers that are advertised as "compatible" are not 100 percent compatible, and a few are not even close. Some may also require expensive add-ons to achieve claimed compatibility.

### ◆ *IBM Versus Apple*

With the introduction of the **PowerPC** chip, a product of the Apple-IBM alliance to promote communications between the two giant but separate systems, the historic gap between the two is now rapidly closing. No longer are users of one locked out of the other. For example, the newest Macintosh models, the **PowerMacs**, are capable of running not only the traditional Macintosh applications but also those written for MS-DOS and Windows. Likewise, IBM offers a line of PowerPC-based machines that can run Macintosh programs. The day may eventually arrive when the artificial barriers between brands are gone forever.

### ◆ *Plug*

Many independent companies make computer components, such as disk drives, monitors, printers, and modems, that are designed to work with certain popular computers by simply "plugging" the two together. These so-called plug-compatibles are supposed to plug directly into the computer and function properly. Note that some of these may not utilize all the features of your software, even when they have the desired features. This is not necessarily the fault of either the hardware or the software but rather a communications problem between the two. Such troubles frequently are resolved by a **patch**, or modification to your software program(s). If, however, the communication problem is between two hardware components, the difficulty may be more serious and require the replacement of one or both components to resolve.

### ◆ *Other Standards*

Computers, in general, and individual system components subscribe to no universal standards, but several informally established norms may be important to you in selecting the parts of your system. These will be mentioned when applicable as each component of the computer system is described in the remainder of this chapter.

# ▸ The Computer

The computer itself consists of several specific components within a case. The **computer system** is the basic computer plus all the items attached to it (monitor, printer, etc.). There is a wide variety of possibilities for system designs, limited only by your imagination and budget.

A basic computer system can be pictured schematically as shown in the diagram here.

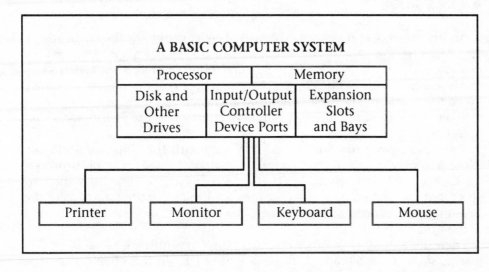

**A BASIC COMPUTER SYSTEM**

| Processor | | Memory |
|---|---|---|
| Disk and Other Drives | Input/Output Controller Device Ports | Expansion Slots and Bays |

| Printer | Monitor | Keyboard | Mouse |
|---|---|---|---|

Minimally, the computer itself will normally include a microprocessor chip, memory, a hard disk drive, at least one floppy disk drive, a display adapter, and assorted expansion ports and slots. Optionally, models may also include such items as FAX/modem, sound board, a CD-ROM drive, tape backup units, or other special equipment. These are attached to various external components such as the keyboard, mouse, monitor, printer, or other accessories. Depending on what is included with the computer, the price could be as low as under $500 for a very simple model with limited capabilities. Typical mid-range systems run from about $1,500 to $2,500, with high-performance, upper-end systems costing up to several times that amount.

Here are some of the considerations you may encounter when comparing individual computers.

## ◆ *Processors*

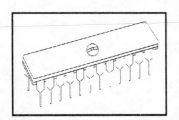

**Figure 5.1**
**This is what a computer chip looks like.**

The heart of any computer is the microprocessor, (also referred to as the CPU—Central Processing Unit or just processor). This is a chip or small but complex set of electronic circuits that controls the entire system and performs all the arithmetic and logical (comparison) operations needed to execute processing activities. A few computers even have more than one processor but use only one at a time for any given application. Although a number of companies are now getting into the business of making processors, for the past decade or so the industry has been led and the standards set by Intel and Motorola, whose chips have been used in IBM-compatible and Apple computers, respectively.

## ◆ *Word Size*

A wide variety of processors is currently used in microcomputers, with new ones constantly appearing. Most now employ **32-bit** or even occasionally

**64-bit** words, but you may encounter one of the older **16-bit** processors in a used machine. Basically, this **bit specification** refers to the size of the block of data, or **word**, that the processor can handle at a time. The larger the word, the more data the computer can process in a single operation. This means that fewer operations are required with larger words to get a job done, and as a result it will be completed faster.

### ◆ Clock Speed

Another feature of processors you will likely encounter is the **clock speed**. This refers to how rapidly the processor can complete an operation or how many operations can be completed in a given unit of time. Most systems currently available run at rates from 25 to 12 megahertz (**MHz**), but you may find a few top-of-the-line machines that are faster.

Some of the most popular microprocessors presently used with microcomputers are listed in Table 5.1.

The values given for clock speed may vary with the chip manufacturer. (Note: You may occasionally encounter a computer based on an older processor such as a 386 or even a 286. These machines may be fine for some purposes, but you should be aware that they are limited by the standards of the newer models. For comparison, some older processors are listed near the end of the next chapter.)

There are a number of other considerations that influence overall performance, such as the bus speed (to be discussed later in this chapter) and the

| Table 5.1 | **Selected Microprocessors** | |
|---|---|---|
| **Chip** | | **Speed (MHz)** |
| Intel (IBM-Compatibles) | | |
| Pentium P54C | | 90–100 |
| Pentium P5 | | 66 |
| 486DX4 | | 75–100 |
| 486DX2 | | 50–66 |
| 486DX | | 25–33 |
| 486SX | | 16–33 |
| Motorola (Macintosh) | | |
| PowerPC 604 | | 100 |
| PowerPC 601 | | 66–100 |
| 68040 | | 25–66 |
| 68LC040 | | 25–66 |
| 68030 | | 25–33 |

speed of the individual components attached to the computer. Basically, the difference between data handling at 64- or 32-bits or clock speeds of 100 MHz and 50 MHz clock speed may not be exactly a factor of two, but it is generally true that the larger the word size and higher the clock speed, the faster the system will perform. In other words, all other factors being the same, a 486DX/50 (50 MHz 486 chip) should perform approximately twice as fast as a 486DX/25 (the 25 MHz version).

***Internal Versus External Values.*** The clock speed and word size given for a processor normally represent the rated values for *internal processing,* or how the processor performs while handling values internally in calculations or in making comparisons for logic decisions. A 100 MHz, 32-bit processor may work at those ratings only during internal operations. How it handles input and output of data and communicates with memory and the rest of the computer refer to *external ratings* and may be an entirely different story. The table below will illustrate this for the rated clock speeds of the 486 series of processors.

Notice that very similar processors such as the 486DX/50 and 486DX2/50 may have different *external* clock speeds, which can effect the overall performance of the system (see Table 5.2).

***Performance Ratings.*** Processors or components (sometimes entire systems) are often rated against some arbitrary standard. Values from these tests are useful for *comparison only* and do not normally provide any *absolute* measure of a processor or system's worth. One such standard for microprocessors is **iCOMP** (Intel **CO**mparative Microprocessor Performance), developed by Intel for its processors. The chart at left lists a number of recent and present Intel chips along with their iCOMP values.

iCOMP ratings are measured against a baseline of the earliest Intel microprocessor used in personal computers. They are derived from a series of complex computations and are not based just on clock speed

*Figure 5.2 Intel's iCOMP chip rating.*

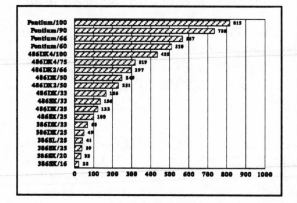

| Table 5.2 | **Rated Clock Speeds for 486 Processors** | |
|---|---|---|
| **Processor Designation** | **Rated Clock Speed (MHz)** | |
| | Internal | External |
| 486DX4/100 | 100 | 33 |
| 486DX4/75 | 75 | 25 |
| 486DX2/66 | 66 | 33 |
| 486DX2/50 | 50 | 25 |
| 486DX/50 | 50 | 50 |
| 486DX/33 | 33 | 33 |
| 486DX/25 | 25 | 25 |

but on word size (primarily internal), efficiency of operations, and other factors, which show why a 100 MHz Pentium outperforms a 100 MHz 486DX4.

If the selection of a processor appears complex, it *can* be, but it does not *have* to be. Except for the most demanding user's needs, any current processor will perform adequately in home applications. It should be remembered that a relatively small difference in performance is not likely to be noticed in day-to-day system response; an increase in performance by a factor of two or more is generally required to produce any significant difference in observable system response.

### ◆ Coprocessors

A **coprocessor** is a supplemental processor that works to assist the main processor in performing specific types of operations. Coprocessors usually add to the abilities of the main processor rather than increase its speed, although the latter may be the apparent effect. One of the most common coprocessors is the math coprocessor that works to increase the mathematical computing power of the main processor, usually by giving it the routines it needs to directly calculate values for various special, often advanced, mathematical functions.

Computers are increasingly being built with the features of popular coprocessors already built in. For example, most of the processors listed in the preceding table have built-in math coprocessors.

### ◆ Memory

There are **two** general types of computer memory: **RAM** (Random-Access Memory) and **ROM** (Read-Only Memory). RAM refers to the memory that is available to the user to store programs and data. This is the memory normally accessed by the user in everyday operation. Information placed here can be modified at will (thus, giving the user "access") but is lost when the system is turned off (or power is otherwise lost). ROM is preprogrammed memory that is available for use (or "reading"), but cannot be changed by the user. (For more on CD-ROMs, see page 84.) Microprocessors, coprocessors, display adapters, modems, and speech synthesizers are a few examples that have ROM.

In microcomputers, the microprocessor contains only a few memory locations that are used for the temporary storage of program instructions or data as they are being processed. The **main memory** into which programs and data are loaded for processing is separate. This is RAM. It is normally measured in terms of **bytes,** or the amount of storage space required for one unit of storage (i.e., a single character). Memory is often referred to as so many **K.** While 1 K = 1,024 bytes exactly, it is usually rounded off to 1,000 bytes. Thus 512 K would be exactly 524,288 (512 x 1,024), or approximately 512,000 bytes. One thousand bytes is also referred to as a **kilobyte,** or **kB,** and 1 million bytes is called a **megabyte,** or **MB.**

Most microcomputers now come with a standard memory of about 4 to 8 MB but are expandable to over 4,000 MB (equal to 4 gigabytes—GB); a total of 16 to 32 MB is adequate for all but the most demanding applications.

However, since early processors on MS-DOS machines could address only memory limited to 1 MB (1,024 K), this is referred to as **conventional memory.** It is this first 1 MB of memory that is normally accessible by the operating system and most programs. Further, most applications are limited to only 640 K of this 1 MB barrier, referred to as **base** or **user memory.** The remaining 384 K is called **system** or **upper memory (UMA).** It is most frequently used for DOS, video RAM, the system **BIOS,** the EMS page frame (Terminate and Stay Resident programs—TSRs), and various software drivers.

To access the memory above 1 MB requires either programs that are written to make use of it or special drivers that are now available on nearly all systems. Depending on how the software uses it, this memory can be used as either **expanded** or **extended** memory. The difference between these two is in how the memory is apportioned. With extended memory, all memory is available for use; with expanded memory, only certain segments can be used at any given time, those being accessed through a 64 K **page frame** in upper memory. How the memory beyond 1 MB is used is normally handled by the application program, with little or no action required by the user.

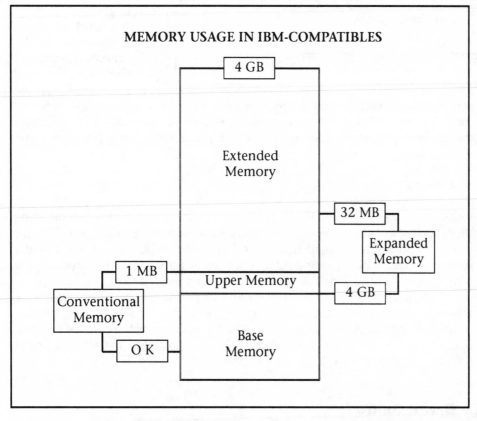

**MEMORY USAGE IN IBM-COMPATIBLES**

At left is a very simplified picture of memory allocation on an IBM-compatible machine running the MS-DOS operating system.

Note that the upper memory area can be used as expanded memory; this is a relic of early personal computers. However, despite the apparent advantage of expanded memory, using expanded memory is slowly disappearing in favor of extended memory.

The memory holds the operating system, the software programs that you are running, and the data to be processed. The amount of memory that you need will depend on what programs you will be running. If you intend to use a multitasking interface such as Windows, you will need much more memory, usually 8 MB minimum. Otherwise, go by the separate applications you will be running; the manuals normally give some indication of memory usage. This is usually a good estimate for average use, but if you anticipate working with unusually large files, you may wish to allow for a little extra memory. If you are still in doubt about the amount of memory you will need, make your best guess; you can always add more later.

***Cache Memory.*** In general, a **cache** is a special block of memory set aside to improve the operation (usually speed) of the computer. This may be a section of already existing RAM, but it is more often dedicated memory, either special high-speed RAM or on a **board** such as a **device controller** (see below).

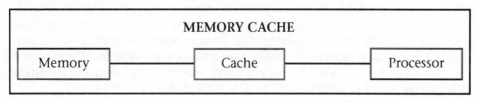

If it is in existing memory, it can be established by a software driver; however, here we are concerned with the type that involve supplemental memory.

There are basically two kinds of caches: memory and disk. A **memory cache** is a high-speed memory that acts between the regular memory and processor to speed the execution of instructions and processing of data.

This cache is achieved by installing special high-speed RAM memory chips. It normally ranges from about 8 to 256 K.

A **disk cache** works similarly except that the extra memory acts between the disk and the processor.

This kind of cache takes advantage of the higher processing speed of memory over disk. A disk cache can be

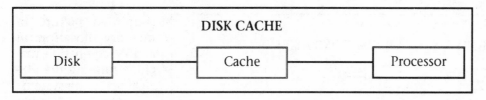

achieved by installing extra memory or established by loading special software for this purpose. It can be virtually any size that is convenient. Depending on the available memory, disk caches normally range from about 256 kB to several MB.

## ◆ Boards

As the processor is the heart of the computer, the board is the building block. Boards contain electronic circuits either directly printed or otherwise mounted on them. A board that has other boards mounted on it is called a **motherboard.** A board that contains prongs or pins and is designed to plug directly into another board is frequently referred to as **a card.**

All of the circuitry in the computer and its peripherals is on boards in one way or another. This includes the processor, coprocessor, memory, display adapter, ROM chips, and controllers. Even if you are not familiar with electronics or are not especially handy, you can probably install additional boards into your system if they are needed.

## ◆ Device Controllers

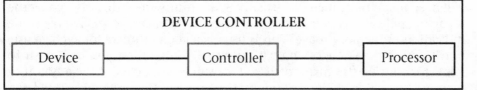

The term **controller** refers to a general class of equipment that acts to govern transferring information to and from the computer and a specific component. The controller may be built into the component or computer but is often on a separate board that plugs into the computer (into a slot); the component that it controls then plugs into the controller.

A typical computer might have a controller for the disk drive and video display. Controllers often come with the device, but sometimes they have to be purchased separately. If you have an IDE (Integrated Drive Electronics) disk and SVGA (Super Video Graphics Array) display, then the controllers must be the same type. The next section discusses display adapters, which are video controllers.

### ◆ *Display Adapters*

One of the most important boards you will need is the **display** or **video adapter,** sometimes referred to as a **graphics board** because it is the graphics display generated by the adapter that is usually of most concern. The term **graphics** refers to the ability of computers to generate and display noncharacter images such as pictures and drawings—in addition to the normal text display. The choice of a display adapter is inseparable from the selection of a monitor; if they do not have equivalent capabilities, then the two will work together but at the level of the less capable of the two. Refer to the section on monitors later in this chapter for additional information on selecting a graphics system.

All personal computers now support some type of graphics. Some come with the graphics built into the system, leaving you no choice about what you get. For example, some Macintosh systems include high-resolution graphics that provide a sharp display; others offer you a selection of display adapters that can be installed.

IBM compatibles usually offer you a choice of display adapters. You would be wise to select one that is considered as more or less standard and supported by the software you want. For IBM PCs or their compatibles, the most popular choices are the **VGA** (Video Graphics Array) and **SVGA** card. The former provides good graphics for many applications; however, the latter yields advanced, very high-resolution output but at a somewhat higher cost. Two display adapters for IBM systems that are roughly comparable to SVGA are XGA and **8514/A.**

*Resolution and Color.* Two of the main considerations in selecting a display adapter are the **resolution,** or the degree of detail that can clearly be dis-

| Table 5.3 | **Selected Modes for Popular Graphics Displays** | | |
|---|---|---|---|
| **Graphics System** | **Number of Pixels** | | **Colors Displayed** |
| | **Horizontal** | **Vertical** | |
| VGA | 640 | 480 | 16 |
| SVGA (VESA) | 800 | 600 | 65,536 |
| | 1,024 | 768 | 256 |
| | 1,280 | 1,024 | 16 |

played, and the number of colors that can be reproduced. Resolution is measured in the number of **pixels,** or dots, that can be displayed both horizontally and vertically. The more pixels displayed on the screen, the finer the detail. This is roughly comparable to photographic film, in which the finer the grain of the film, the sharper the image it will be able to reproduce.

Table 5.3 on page 77 summarizes some of the basic features of VGA and SVGA graphics, currently the most widely used graphics systems. Most systems provide a wide variety of operational modes far too numerous to list here. For example, a high-resolution graphics display must also be able to handle modes used by lower resolution software. The examples given in the table are either the most commonly encountered or the highest possible resolution and color combinations:

| Table 5.4 | **Extended Text Displays** | | | |
|---|---|---|---|---|
| Graphics System | 43 Lines | 50 Lines | 60 Lines | 132 Columns |
| VGA | Yes | Yes | No | No |
| SVGA (VESA) | Yes | Yes | Yes | Yes |

*The VESA Standard* (Video Electronics Standards Association). This does not relate to the resolution of the graphics but rather to an industry effort to standardize the various graphics systems. It is being increasingly used by manufacturers to help provide compatibility between video controllers, monitors, and multimedia applications. (Refer to the section on monitors later in this chapter for more details on selecting graphics.)

*Video RAM (VRAM).* Because of the large amount of processing normally required to produce high-resolution graphics displays, video adapters now come with their own, on-board memory. At a minimum, 512 K will be needed on the lower end boards, with as much as 2 to 4 MB or more required on the highest-resolution systems. Insufficient memory on the board can cause sluggish and inadequate performance, even failure to display properly with some applications.

*Text Modes.* Most graphics adapters permit some change in the traditional 80 column by 25 line display. In a few cases, you might want to reduce the amount of information displayed to the screen; this is done with a 40 column by 25 line mode available on all systems. However, normally the need is to be able to see even more at any given time. Table 5.4 gives some of the extended text modes found on common graphics systems.

Using smaller text can be tiring if viewed for extended periods. If you anticipate this as a possibility, you might find the savings in fatigue to be well worth the extra investment for a monitor with a larger viewing area.

### ◆ Graphics Accelerator

A **graphics accelerator** is a display adapter that is capable of performing, independent of the processor, much of the work necessary to produce and update the display. Graphics accelerators can significantly speed up the rate at which complex, high-resolution images are displayed to the screen as well as how rapidly and smoothly updating (as with motion in games) is achieved. They normally have at least 1 MB of VRAM on board with space for more.

### ◆ Slots

A slot is a position in the computer for attaching a board to increase or add to the capabilities of the system. This may be done to increase the memory, add graphics, or attach a coprocessor. Slots sometimes are of different types (such as 16-bit or 32-bit). If you anticipate adding any boards in the future, be certain the computer has the slots for them.

Also, just because a computer is advertised as having, for example, six slots, this does not mean you will necessarily have six slots for additions at a later time. Often, a computer requires some of the advertised slots for additional memory, disk controller, mouse, and display adapter, so you may actually have only two or three slots to use.

### ◆ Ports

A **port** refers to a position for attaching external auxiliary functions such as a printer, modem, or joystick to the computer's processor. Ports come in a variety of types. There are those dedicated to a particular purpose or function, such as a monitor, keyboard, or joystick (**game port**), whereas others are more generic in nature. The general-purpose ports are normally divided into serial and parallel, according to the way they transmit signals.

Serial ports are used for modems and other input/output equipment, whereas printers on IBM-compatible systems are most often connected through a parallel port. (If the printer is to be placed more than about 20 feet from the computer, a serial connection will be needed.) Apple and some other computer systems routinely use a serial port for the printer connection. As with slots, be certain that your computer has enough ports to satisfy present and future needs. (Unlike slots, additional ports can be added—provided you have a spare slot.)

### ◆ Bays

The openings within a computer case for disk and other drives are referred to collectively as **bays.** Bays are classified into two types, **internal** and **external**, depending on the nature of the drive to be held. If a bay is for a drive such as for floppy disks, CD-ROMs, or tapes that are inserted by you into the drive at the time of use, then it is an **external** drive bay. If it is to hold a hard disk within the computer, then it is an **internal** drive bay.

A computer has a limit to the number of components it can handle; however, it is usually the physical case that determines the limitation on drive bays. If you should run out of bays within your computer case, you can probably add a stand-alone, external drive, which attaches to the computer with a cable but has its own case and power supply. This would require using a slot (or maybe a port) and be more costly than using an internal drive.

### ◆ The Case

The choice of a case can be very important in selecting the proper system. This will be determined by the available space and the demands of your system requirements. For example, be certain any case has ample drive bays to accommodate both your present needs and anticipated future expansion plans (see display below).

You essentially have three options:

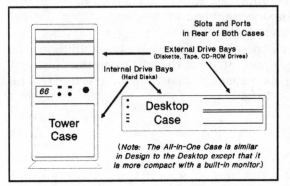

**Figure 5.3 Computer cases are available in many configurations.**

**Tower.** This is the largest and most versatile of the cases. Most IBM-compatibles are moving to the tower as the "case of choice." This configuration is a narrow, upright design with ample space for extra drives and other add-ons. The tower case can sit on a desktop; however, it is normally designed to sit on the floor adjacent to the worktable. If you anticipate a mid- to high-end system or want to allow for significant future expansion, this would be the best choice in a case design. (Smaller versions of the tower case are commonly referred to as **minitower** cases.)

**Desktop.** This is the traditional case for computers that sit on a desktop, often with the monitor on top. It is smaller than the tower, thus more limited in the size system it can handle. This would be a suitable design for low-end systems or where little or no expansion is planned.

**All-in-One.** The all-in-one case is a very compact design that often comes with a specific computer such as a Macintosh. Though more limited, it is a possible alternative when either space limitations or ease of mobility is a major consideration.

### ◆ The Bus

Although one of the most important parts of the computer, the **bus** is one component that you may not directly select. However, the speed and type of bus can significantly affect the overall performance of a system. Being knowledgeable about the bus designs of various systems can give you an advantage in making comparisons.

A bus provides a common link between all the components of a computer system for the transfer of data and instructions. In other words, the processor, memory, disks, printer, and other components are all connected through the bus.

All communications between components must pass through the bus. If you plug a new board into a slot or connect an accessory to a port, these will also be connected to and communicate through the bus. (The term "bus" is derived from a traditional passenger bus. Like a regular bus that stops at each point along the route, the signals on the electronic bus go to each piece of equipment connected to it.)

The bus will determine much about the performance of your system. Even if you have a 64-bit bus-capable processor, the bus may not transfer data at that rate; it may communicate with some or all of your boards as a 32- or even 16-bit bus. There are many factors that determine this, but the basic bus design and controller boards are the primary considerations. (A 32-bit bus can communicate only at 16-bits with a 16-bit board.)

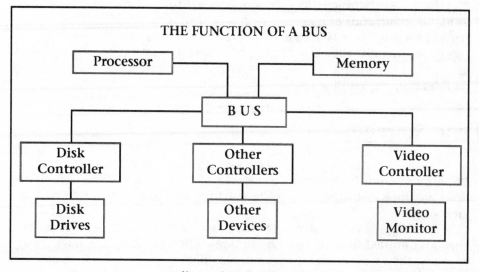

THE FUNCTION OF A BUS

The earliest microcomputers used an 8-bit bus; aside from the higher processor clock speeds, it is this increase in bus speed that accounts for much of the increase in computer performance. This means that a computer powered by a 100 MHz Pentium processor will not be just 20 times faster than an early model using a 5 MHz chip. Due to the increase in bus speed (as well as other factors), the difference will be significantly greater.

The bus is actually a very complex tool. It performs several functions and is really two buses in one: an **address bus**, which tracks where data is located in memory, and a **data bus**, which transfers the data. The address bus determines how rapidly the processor accesses memory as well as the maximum amount of addressable memory. It is normally fixed as a function of the processor, and you will have little or no choice in selecting an address bus; however, most computers are now capable of addressing more memory than will be needed.

As for the data bus, most computers have used the traditional **PC bus (ISA)** architecture; however, newer models are now employing the faster, competitive **EISA** and **Micro Channel** designs. More significantly, the **local bus** design has become increasingly popular; this is a bus arrangement in which a device (or controller) is connected directly to the processor, usually through a special socket on the motherboard; this bypasses the regular bus pathways and permits much faster processing. Two popular local bus designs are the **VESA Local Bus (VL-bus or VLB)** and **Peripheral Component Interconnect (PCI)**, which are popular on 486- and Pentium-based systems, respectively.

### ◆ *Expansion Capability*

It is just as important to be certain that a computer has the expansion capability to meet your future needs as it is to verify that it will do what you want it to at the moment. Research the expansion potential of the computer regarding total memory, disk storage, slots, ports, bays, and upgrade potential.

### ◆ *Operating System*

The operating system used by a computer can affect its performance beyond how it interacts with the user. The more user-friendly an operating system, the larger and more complex it tends to be. This means it usually requires more memory and time to execute instructions. The result of this may be a slightly more sluggish performance and somewhat less memory available to run your programs. This can be seen with the Macintosh as compared to most MS-DOS systems. Whereas the former are considered to be more user-friendly, they also tend to be slower and take up a larger percentage of the basic memory. (The same general effect can be seen on IBM-compatibles running Windows.)

# ▸ Data Retrieval and Storage

All systems come with some means of data entry other than the keyboard; these range from floppy disks to tape cartridges to CD-ROMs. The floppy disks and tape cartridges can also be used for data storage and retrieved at a later time.

Floppy disks have a relatively small storage capacity, and the tapes are very slow and limited in their retrieval options. Though CD-ROMs have a large capacity, they are a *read-only medium*, like ROM memory, which means that information can be accessed but the disk cannot be changed. Because of the limitations of all these media, hard disks are used to retain a large amount of data on a more readily accessible basis. Rather than being removable and portable as floppy disks are, these are usually fixed in a sealed system and are referred to as fixed disks or hard disks.

*Figure 5.4 The most popular sizes for floppy disks are 3½ inches (top) and 5¼ inches (bottom).*

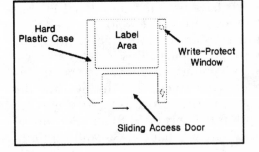

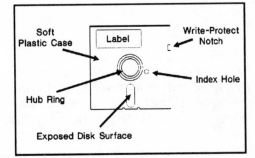

### ◆ *Floppy Disks*

The most common type of data storage (and entry) system used on microcomputers is the floppy disk (also called a **diskette** or **flexible disk**). These single, flat, flexible plastic disks are coated with a magnetic material on which data is encoded and stored as magnetic signals arranged in concentric circles called **tracks**. These disks come in three sizes: 8-, 5¼-, and 3½-inch diameter. The 8-inch variety is no longer used on home systems. Both the 5¼- and 3½-inch are common, but the smaller size is becoming increasingly popular.

The smaller, 3½-inch diskette (also called a **microdisk** or **microfloppy**) is not physically flexible like the bigger disks but has a rigid case that serves as better protection from environmental damage. (See the figure at left.) A typical 3½-inch diskette can store 1.44 MB of data, though the lower density 720 K format is still common. (A 2.88 MB format is becoming somewhat more widely used, but the 1.44 MB size is generally considered the workhorse for this particular diskette.)

The 3½-inch diskette reflects a complete redesign of the floppy disk. The 5¼-inch version (also called a **minidisk** or **minifloppy**) is little more than a reworked original 8-inch diskette. This means that the 5¼-inch diskette still retains most of the short-comings and vulnerabilities of the older diskette, especially the soft case and exposed disk surface. (See Figure 5.4.) A 5¼-inch diskette can hold up to 1.2 MB of data, but the 360 K format is in use by some older systems. Although the two diskettes have distinct physical differences, they are used in essentially the same way.

Most software is supplied on floppy disks, and all computers come with at least one floppy disk drive, normally a 3½-inch model. A number of systems also provide a 5¼-inch drive as well. If a system that you otherwise like does not have a 5¼-inch drive, and you need one for some reason (such as to exchange disks with a computer at work or school), a second floppy drive can usually be added for about $250 installed—much less if you can do the work yourself. Most computers now provide an extra drive bay for internally mounted second drives, but external hardware is also common, although somewhat more expensive.

### ◆ *Hard Disks*

Virtually all computers now come with a hard drive. Hard disks are similar in nature to floppy disks except that they are rigid and usually fixed and sealed in their mounts. Such disks can store much more data than floppies, and they are considerably faster. They consist of a series of metal platters coated with a magnetic material for the recording of data. Although a number of designs come and go, the most successful ones presently available are those based on the **IDE** and **SCSI** (Small Computer System Interface) technologies. The latter is used with most Macintosh machines.

Hard disks are also very convenient, since all active files are **online** and directly accessible without having to change and load from floppy disks. In the early years of personal computers, fixed disk systems were too costly except for the top-of-the-line models, but this is no longer the case. Computers containing both floppy and hard disk drives of 200 MB are now available for under $1,000, which is less than half of what a similar two-floppy system cost about 10 years ago.

Hard disks come in a variety of storage sizes beginning at about 100 MB (megabytes) and ranging up to several thousand MBs. (Reminder: 1,000 megabytes = 1 **gigabyte** or 1 **GB**.) There is no need to get the largest disk you can find, but be very careful not to err on the other side either. Plan what you think you will need and then at least *triple* it; you will always need more space than you think (sometimes quite a lot more). Tripling the disk space will not triple the price; larger drives are not substantially more expensive than smaller ones. If you are still unsure of what you will need, estimate 15 to 20 MB per application *before* you triple the value. Of course the "application count" should allow as much as possible for any future needs.

Other factors that affect the price of a drive include the **data transfer rate** and the **access time**. The data transfer rate determines how fast data is transferred to and from the disk. The access time is a little more complex but generally refers to an average time for the disk to find and retrieve something. There are no set values for these two parameters, but the transfer rate should be about one megabyte per second (MB/s) or greater and the access time no greater than about 15 milliseconds (ms). Remember that the higher the transfer rate and the shorter the access time, the faster and more expensive the drive. Generally, the larger the hard disk, the better these two values will be.

All computer manufacturers offer hard-disk drives to accompany their systems, but a number of independent companies also provide excellent drives. Many computers allow for at least one extra fixed drive to be internally mounted, but external drives can also be used. Also, some drives now come with a built-in tape-backup system as either standard or optional for those who want an alternative to floppy disks for backup.

### ◆ CD-ROMs

One of the most exciting accessories available for personal computers is the **CD-ROM** drive. This is a type of data retrieval device that employs compact disk (CD) technology. It is referred to as a **ROM** because it permits the data stored on the CD-ROM to be read only (**Read Only Memory**). Nothing can be "written" to the CD-ROM, meaning that you can't add or delete files as you can with a traditional disk.

CD-ROM drives may be found for either internal or external mounting. They can store huge amounts of information: A single CD-ROM can hold almost 700 MB of data (as much as 250,000 printed pages or well over 1,000 average books). Because they function differently, CD-ROM systems may appear a bit sluggish compared to traditional drives, but they offer additional features that were not so readily available before. For example, CD-ROM drives provide stereo-sound output jacks for connection to stereo speakers or headphones. (A separate sound board may be required—see page 107.) Also, most CD-ROM drives will also play audio CDs, either through headphones or a sound board. (Note: Even though they look identical, CD-ROMs will *not* play on an audio CD player!)

When looking for a CD-ROM drive, avoid the early single-speed models. Be certain that you are getting at least one of the double-speed, and preferably a quad-speed, drive; the data transfer rate should be no less than about 350 kilobytes per second. An access time of under 200 milliseconds is also desirable. The faster drives will not only access the software more quickly, but this will help to ensure continued compatibility with a rapidly advancing area of software development in which huge files are commonplace. Even now, the single-speed drives can encounter problems keeping pace with graphic-intensive software like that of many games and videos. At best, they may cause the images to move jerkily, or at worst, sometimes they can cause the entire system to lock up.

CD-ROM drives begin at about $150 for internal and $300 for external units. There is presently no universal standard for CD-ROM systems, although CD-ROM extended is probably the "safest" for future support.

### ◆ Tape Systems

Although tape systems are now used primarily for hard-disk backup (see page 85), they have a relatively large capacity (120 MB or more) and are well suited for the archival storage of data. Also, if a large amount of data (too large to be easily handled on diskettes) is involved, they might also find a use in the physical transfer of data between two computers.

Many of the early tape data-storage systems for microcomputers were much more unreliable than their disk counterparts and sometimes required several tries before a successful operation was achieved. Although the reliability of these units has been greatly improved, they still lack the flexibility and convenience of disks. Data recorded on tape is rigid and cannot be changed without rewriting the entire tape. Because of their inflexibility in data storage and retrieval options, tapes will never replace disks for daily use, but they will continue to be a valuable medium for some operations.

Whereas there are several tape systems to select from, the most popular format currently in use with personal computers is the ¼-inch tape cartridge (**QIC—Quarter Inch Cartridge**). These cartridges employ a ¼-inch wide tape in a cassette design but are not the same as a traditional tape cassette. They require their own drive system that, like a diskette or CD-ROM drive, fits neatly in a standard drive bay.

# ▶ Backup Systems

A backup system is basically a capability to make copies of any software (where the license agreement permits) or data files that you create. This is important because, like information stored on paper, the original files can be lost or damaged by unforeseen circumstances. A file backup method is recommended for any computer system and is essential for those that support a large or valuable program library.

It is necessary to keep a current backup of as many of your system files as you can, but since only a few files will likely be changed or created between backups, you actually need to back up only the new or altered files. The types of backup systems are relatively limited but are normally adequate. Your choice will depend on several factors, such as the size of your hard disk, the number of files that need to be safeguarded, how much and how often you use your computer, what you use it for, how much time you have to spend on backups, and how much money you can afford for a backup system.

## ◆ *Diskettes*

Floppy disks (or diskettes) are a commonly used backup method. If your computer has a small hard disk or your budget is very limited, then you may elect to use this method for all your backups. (Otherwise, you may use floppy disks in conjunction with tapes. This will be covered shortly.)

There are three basic advantages to using diskettes for backups. First, you will already have a floppy drive for loading software onto your system, so no additional hardware would be required. Second, a single file or a group of files can be restored easily and quickly to the main disk. This means that if you need to replace some information on your hard disk from a backup diskette, you can select and read the files that you need. With a tape you would have to scroll through all the files that come before the one(s) you want. (Some of the newer tape-backup software has improved on this annoying feature.) You can also overwrite single files on a diskette without disturbing the other files, which is not possible with a tape system.

Athough diskettes are faster and easier for working with a few files, they are very time-consuming and expensive for mass storage. For example, to back up a fully loaded 100 MB hard disk would take at least seventy 1.44 MB, 3½-inch diskettes. A 100 MB disk is quite small by today's standards; it could easily take well over 200 diskettes to backup the data on an average size hard disk. This would reflect a considerable investment in diskettes to simply keep as backups, especially if you use the "grandfather" method, which requires that two sets of disks be used alternately.

### ◆ *Tapes*

Tape systems represent the two extremes in convenience and speed for backup systems. Although somewhat awkward for handling individual files, tapes are ideally suited to working with large numbers of files or amounts of data. Fortunately, tape cartridges are now available with a relatively high capacity of 120 MB. This means that the 100 MB hard disk could be copied onto just one tape. Most hard disks could be copied to two or three tapes, especially if data compression is used, which can increase the amount of data that will fit on a tape by more than 50 percent.

The disadvantages are cost and flexibility. Although the tape needed to store the data from the 100 MB hard disk will be less expensive than the 70 diskettes, extra hardware is required to supply the tape system. Yet, aside from this initial hardware investment, most users will realize a significant savings in both time and money over the lifetime of the system over using diskette backups alone.

# ▷ Keyboards

The keyboard is the one part of a computer system that is frequently overlooked or just accepted as coming with the computer. This should not be the case. The keyboard is the part of the system with which you will interact directly and constantly, and you should be comfortable with it. Check the keyboard of any computer to see if it is satisfactory for you. This could help you decide between models that are similar.

Do not necessarily eliminate a computer that you otherwise like simply because you find difficulties with the keyboard. Nearly all computers come with a detachable keyboard. An increasing number of companies make separate keyboards, with some priced under $75. If you like a computer except for the keyboard, you might consider replacing it with the model you like better.

In general, examine the keyboard to be certain that it is well built and suits your needs, and you are comfortable with it. In addition, you should consider several other factors about keyboards.

### ◆ *Construction*

A well-constructed keyboard is essential if it is to receive much use. An inferior one will not withstand the many millions of keystrokes associated with heavy usage. Such keyboards may soon develop stuck, repeating, or otherwise malfunctioning keys.

### ◆ *Cord*

Some people like to rest the keyboard on their lap and sit back while entering data. Check to see if the connecting cord is long enough to permit you to move the keyboard about for more comfortable usage. This is even more critical with the newer tower cases that sit on the floor. Extension cords for keyboards may be an option, but they can tangle and get in the way.

### ◆ *Touch*

Keyboards come with a variety of touches. The **full-stroke** type has keys—similar to those on an electric typewriter—that have a definite give and slight resistance when pressed. There is often an audible **keyclick**, which may be turned off if desired. Full-stroke keyboards are found on most computers and are normally preferred by professional users.

A few computers, primarily laptop and notebook models, employ **limited-stroke keys**, which respond when pressed only very slightly. These keyboards are similar to those found on many pocket calculators. It is also possible you will encounter a **touch-sensitive keyboard**, which has the keys printed on its surface and responds to a light pressure on the appropriate spot. These types of keys are generally not found on the more expensive or professional systems and are considered unsatisfactory for frequent use; however, you may occasionally find that some full-stroke keyboards have touch-sensitive pads for special input applications.

### ◆ *Key Arrangement*

You shouldn't have any trouble finding the keys for the alphabet, ten digits, and the most commonly used punctuation marks placed in a standard typewriter arrangement on all PC keyboards. But not all typewriters are exactly the same in the arrangement of their keys, and neither are computer keyboards. If you are a touch typist or are accustomed to a particular key layout, you might want to consider a model with a similar arrangement. However, you will have several (perhaps many) keys on the computer keyboard that are not present on a typewriter, so some adjustment will be required for any layout.

***QWERTY Keyboard.*** Most people are accustomed to the familiar "QWERTY" key arrangement, which is found on most typewriters and keyboards. This layout gets its name from the first six (Q-W-E-R-T-Y) letters from the left in the top row of alphabet keys.

Amazingly, this keyboard was developed in the 1800s to *inhibit* fast typists in order to reduce jamming of the old mechanical type-

**QWERTY Keyboard**

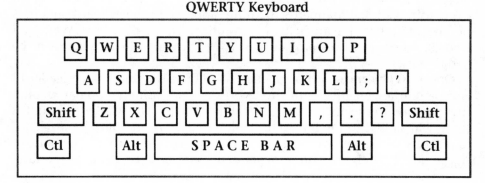

writers. Nonetheless, it lives on, and unless you specifically seek an alternative, this is likely to be the layout you will find on your keyboard.

***Dvorak Keyboard.*** Few experts dispute the inefficiency of the QWERTY design, and a number of alternatives have been tried, but none has met with wide acceptance. However, in recent years the Dvorak layout has become increasingly popular. This involves a reassignment of keys to place the most often used keys on the home row at the strongest finger positions, thereby minimizing finger action and errors along with increasing comfort and speed. This keyboard was named for its co-designer, August Dvorak (cousin of the composer Antonin Dvorak).

**Dvorak Keyboard**

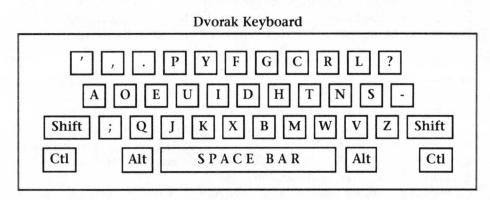

The five vowels (A-O-E-U-I) are placed at the strongest position for the left hand, and the five most commonly used consonants (D-H-T-N-S) are in a similarly convenient position for the right hand. The claim is that the Dvorak arrangement reduces wasted motion by 90 percent or more.

A comparison of the relative use of the three alphabet rows for the QWERTY and Dvorak layouts confirms that there is a substantial difference in the key action.

**Table 5.5**

## Key Usage

| Row | QWERTY | Dvorak |
|---|---|---|
| Top | 52% | 22% |
| Middle | 32% | 70% |
| Bottom | 16% | 8% |

This would appear to confirm the efficiency claims for the Dvorak design.

Although the Dvorak keyboard was originally patented in 1936, it has only recently become widely recognized as a more efficient design. In 1982, **ANSI** (American National Standards Institute) approved the keyboard layout. A number of keyboard manufacturers now offer a choice of either QWERTY or Dvorak. A few keyboards provide a switch to permit switching between the two layouts.

***Other Keyboards.*** Although the QWERTY is the undisputed leader in keyboard arrangements, with the Dvorak an increasingly popular second, these are by no means the only available choices. The **Maltron** design is somewhat similar to the Dvorak in basic philosophy and purpose. It claims to reduce stress, increase typing speed, and be easier to learn. It makes use of staggered key heights and independent left- and right-hand modules anchored by the T-H-O-R and A-N-I-S keys, respectively. It is shaped to conform to the natural position of the hands in an attempt to reduce occurrences of conditions such as carpal tunnel syndrome, a type of repetitive stress injury (RSI) that can arise from the repetitive, stressful motions of frequent keyboard use.

Persons who may be accustomed to the European **AZERTY** keyboard should be able to obtain this layout from most computer dealers or manufacturers. Alternately, special keyboard drivers or macros are provided by many applications that can remap the keys on a keyboard for alternate layouts. This might be of help to you if you will be using a different alphabet (i.e., Hebrew, Greek, or Cyrillic), or if you will be typing in a language that makes use of diacriticals and/or digraphs. (You may even find special keycaps or templates for your layouts.)

## Keyboard Discomfort

Much attention has been given in recent years to carpal tunnel syndrome (pain and numbness in the fingers), which is suffered by persons who spend lots of time working at a keyboard. If a keyboard you like (or the desk it is on) does not provide adequate wrist support for comfort, you might consider a wrist rest. This accessory fits under a keyboard, projecting toward the user to give a surface on which to rest the wrists while typing. They vary in their features and begin at about $15 for a simple rigid support. Also available are lightweight, molded plastic splints designed to support your hand and wrist. The splint prevents movement and supports the wrist in a neutral position.

If you have a special preference or need and cannot find it, check with the dealer or manufacturer. Although it will likely cost a little more, all but the most unusual requests can be fulfilled with specially-designed keyboards or software.

### ◆ Keypads

In addition to the standard typewriter arrangement of keys, most keyboards offer one or more special groups of keys (**keypads**) for performing special functions. The most common types of keypads are the **numeric** and **cursor control**. A numeric keypad offers an arrangement of keys similar to that found on an adding machine. Numeric keypads are especially useful if you are entering large amounts of numeric data.

Cursor control keypads are used to move the cursor (position marker) around on the screen and sometimes move about in a file. These always contain keys that move the cursor up, down, right, and left; however, they may also contain keys that do such things as clear the screen, move forward or backward in a file by a specific amount (i.e., one screen), perform simple editing functions, or jump to the beginning or end of the screen. This is a useful feature for many applications.

Most IBM-compatible computers come with both numeric and cursor con-

*Figure 5.5
A standard
combination
keypad found
on most
IBM-compatible
keyboards.*

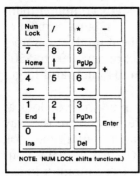

trol keypads. Many have one keypad that serves both functions. Some Macintosh computers do not have a cursor control keypad because they use a mouse to perform these functions. Other computers vary in the design of their keyboards in this respect.

*Figure 5.6*
*Standard 101 key*
*Enhanced keyboard.*

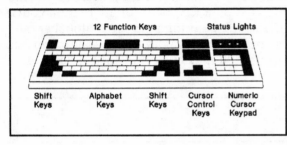

### ◆ Function Keys

Most keyboards have several keys that can be programmed to perform special functions. The number of such keys varies but is now usually twelve or more. Many function keys are capable of performing more than one task by using the Shift and similar keys. These keys are normally preprogrammed by the software package that makes use of them; however, some computers may permit these keys to be user-programmed directly from the keyboard. A standard 101-key **Enhanced keyboard** is pictured at the left. The keypads on page 89 have the function keys along the top.

### ◆ Special Features

Be on the alert for keyboards that offer special features. These may range from an extra key or two that perform useful functions to a touch-sensitive keypad or built-in track ball that can serve multiple input duty. This is an especially important point to consider should you decide to buy a separate keyboard or other input device.

## ▶ Monitors

*Figure 5.7*
*Most monitors*
*come standard*
*with multiple*
*controls to help you*
*adjust the screen*
*to your liking.*

A **monitor** (which looks just like a small television screen) accepts a video signal from a computer, converts it into an image, and displays that image on a screen. The idea is similar to television when it receives a broadcast signal from a local station or input from a cable company and converts it into an image that appears on the screen. A monitor, however, has no tuner to locate stations and is designed to process the input signals somewhat differently.

Since so much of your time is spent looking at a monitor screen, it is extremely important to choose the appropriate model. Many computer manufacturers offer a monitor with their systems, but a number of independent companies also make excellent products—sometimes at a substantially lower cost. Expect to pay $300 to $500 for an average 14- or 15-inch monitor; 17-inch and larger models exceed $1000.

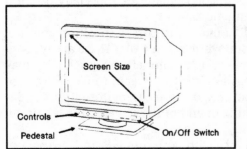

When looking for a monitor, keep in mind that you look at the screen of a computer monitor differently from the way you look at a television. When using a computer, you look intently at the image on the screen, whereas with TV your focus tends to wander. You should not select a monitor in the same way you would a television. View the monitors that interest you with applications that you intend to use on your computer.

## ◆ Controls

An often overlooked feature of monitors is the presence and placement of the controls. Although good monitors rarely need adjustment, when they do, it should not be necessary to fumble in the rear of the unit or some other inconvenient place for a well-hidden knob. Be sure that all commonly needed controls are in the front and readily available—but not placed so that they will be easily moved by accident. Conventional knobs, push buttons, or controls behind access doors are the least likely to be inadvertently moved.

Minimally, a monitor should have the four standard controls for horizontal and vertical adjustment, both size and position plus controls for screen brightness and contrast. In addition, there may be separate controls for the intensities of the three primary colors—red, blue, and green—that make up a color image. Some monitors offer an adjustment for the pincushion effect; this is the bowing-in of the screen on each side, the opposite of the barrel effect, in which the image bows out on the sides.

It is convenient to have an On-Off switch that is separate from the brightness or other control so that a setting is not disturbed each time the monitor is switched off and back on. Most better color monitors now provide a degaussing button that helps eliminate extraneous magnetic fields from the monitor; such fields can cause picture distortion if allowed to build up. A few top-line monitors have the ability to memorize one or more settings, so if the screen is changed, either accidentally or intentionally, your preferences can easily be restored.

## ◆ Screens

There are three general physical characteristics you should consider about monitor screens. First, what size do you want? With a few exceptions, most

| Table 5.6 | **Popular Monitor Sizes Compared** | | | | |
|---|---|---|---|---|---|
| Size | Height | Approximate Width | Area | Increase 12-inch | Compared to Previous |
| 12 | 7.2 | 9.6 | 69 | — | — |
| 14 | 8.4 | 11.2 | 94 | 36% | 36% |
| 15 | 9.0 | 12.0 | 108 | 56% | 15% |
| 17 | 10.2 | 13.6 | 139 | 101% | 28% |
| 20 | 12.0 | 16.0 | 192 | 178% | 38% |
| 21 | 12.6 | 16.8 | 212 | 206% | 10% |

*Figure 5.8*
*There are a wide*
*variety of screen*
*sizes available.*

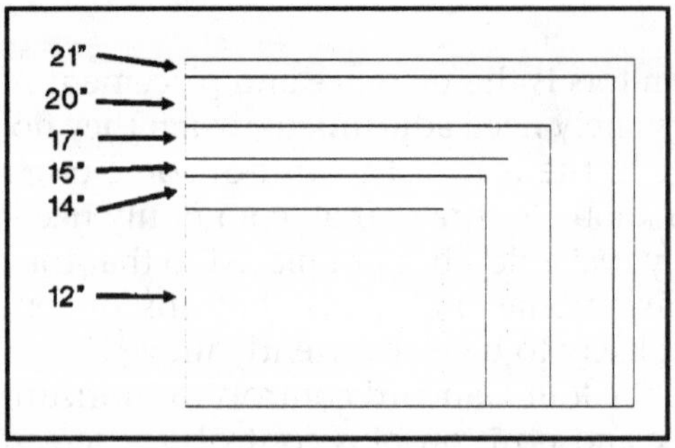

monitors come in screen sizes ranging from 12 to 21 inches (measured diagonally), with the most popular sizes being 14 to 17 inches. A larger monitor will make the images larger but not necessarily sharper. To get sharper images, you need a higher-**resolution** monitor. Table 5.6 and Figure 5.8 will help in comparing screen sizes.

(Note: (1) the actual image dimensions may be slightly smaller than the stated screen size, (2) rated diagonal measurements may vary slightly from one monitor to another and (3) a width-to-height ratio of 4 to 3 was used in calculating the above values, which may not apply exactly to all monitors.)

Second, a **flat-screen monitor** offers reduced screen reflections and glare, thus eliminating a substantial amount of eyestrain. These monitors also eliminate much of the distortion in an image that sometimes occurs at the edge of the screen.

The ability to physically adjust a monitor is often very important. Most monitors now come on some kind of swivel/tilt pedestal base. Try it out for height and vertical adjustment. Is the screen at eye level? Is the viewing angle comfortable?

### ◆ Resolution

Remember that the choice of a monitor must be matched to the display adapter. If you need 1,024 by 768 SVGA resolution, then *both* the graphics board and monitor must support this mode.

Generally, display adapters and monitors will support and display software designed for compatible, lower-resolution systems but not software aimed at higher-resolution models. That is, an SVGA system will run most VGA software but not vice versa. This means that your choice of graphics is going to be determined by your most demanding application. This is often games or multimedia software. (For further information on graphics, refer to the discussion of display adapters earlier in this chapter.)

### ◆ Dot Pitch

Another consideration relating to the monitor is the **dot pitch**. This refers to the size of the individual dots that make up the images on the monitor screen. The smaller the dot pitch, the sharper the image will be. A dot pitch of 0.28 mm or less will likely give a satisfactory result in nearly any situation.

### ◆ Persistence

If you have problems finding a monitor on which the image does not flicker, it may be that you need a long-persistence model. This is a monitor that holds an image on the screen a little longer, thus producing a more stable image. These will be slightly more costly.

From viewing your television, you know that voltage fluctuations in the

power line can cause the picture to jump. If the jitter is only slight or intermittent, you might try checking another monitor of the same model or examine it at another time or in another store. If the system is not protected from power-line surges, test one that is or return to the store in the evening, when power usage is decreased. However, remember that any problems that you see now may reoccur later. (For more on surge suppressors, see page 111.)

Beware, however, if this persists too long. This could result in ghosting (afterimages), especially with the kind of motion graphics that are common with action games.

### ◆ Interlaced Versus Noninterlaced

An **interlaced** monitor is one that paints only *half* the screen on each scan cycle. On alternating cycles, it will paint the image to the odd-numbered lines; then it will paint the even-numbered lines. Since this all happens in a tiny fraction of a second, it may or may not be noticeable. In situations involving animations or other motion situations, it can cause an annoying flicker.

**Noninterlaced** systems paint the entire screen on *every* scan cycle. These systems require twice the processing resources of the system, but they normally yield a much more stable and pleasing display. Of course, both the monitor and display adapter must be noninterlaced. Check the specifications carefully; sometimes, one or both might be noninterlaced in most but not all modes. Unfortunately, the modes that remain interlaced are usually those of highest-resolution where a noninterlaced display is mostly needed.

### ◆ Graphics Displays

Most computers display graphics images differently from the way they do text characters used for word processing, spreadsheets, and similar programs. Basically, text characters are displayed by **block-mapping**, which involves addressing an entire block of the screen at once. With this method, the computer can display only those characters that are stored in its video ROM. These are normally the standard 96 ASCII text characters (similar to those on an electronic typewriter) and sometimes the extended set of fixed graphics images. On the other hand, graphics are usually displayed by **bit-mapping**, which addresses each individual dot on the screen.

A notable exception to this is found with some Apple Macintosh displays that use bit-mapping to produce all screen images. This gives you a virtually unlimited character set for display, but it also causes the operating system to be somewhat larger and slower than its MS-DOS counterpart.

You need a monitor that can satisfactorily display images at the highest resolution. The basic considerations are color and sharpness. Even if the match seems right, watch the monitor with several graphics packages to see if you are satisfied. A monitor may perform adequately with some types of graphics but not with others. For example, you may want more or less persistence to help eliminate flicker or ghosting, respectively, with motion graphics.

Avoid monitors that have fuzzy or wavy displays. If you see lines across the screen, either fixed or rolling, this may be a sign of poor signal processing.

The black on a good monitor will be sharp and deep. Be certain that the colors are pure and the images well defined. Check the display for each of your major applications, especially word processing and graphics. However, always be certain that the monitor is properly adjusted (any problems can usually be corrected by the simple turn of a knob). Also, some apparent difficulties, such as weak or limited colors, may be the fault of the computer rather than the monitor.

# ▶ Printers

Most personal computer users select a **character printer**, which produces one line at a time like a typewriter. The very popular **dot-matrix** and **ink-jet** printers are of this type. However, **laser printers**, which produce an entire page at once **(page printer)**, are rapidly claiming an increasing share of the market as their price continues to fall. A complete test of printers is found in Chapter 8.

Printers for computers range in price from about $140 to $1,000. Aside from compatibility, you should be looking for adequate print quality, the features that you need or want (fonts, paper sizes, graphics, color), and a reasonable print speed. To get all three may cost more than you want or can afford to spend. Assess your priorities, and see where you can compromise.

Many computer manufacturers make printers, but you should not ignore the many fine models available from other sources. Sometimes you can find a printer from one of the independent manufacturers that will be closer to what you want and at a lower cost. However, verify that it will be compatible with your computer and software. Some companies make models designed especially for certain computers, whereas models for other computers may have to be custom interfaced by your dealer.

## ◆ *Impact Versus Nonimpact*

**Impact printers** were once the most popular type used with personal computer systems. These printers make an image on the paper by physically striking the paper through the ribbon, much like a typewriter. (A dot-matrix printer is an impact printer.) Impact printers do not require special paper, and they offer a good selection of print quality, features, and speed for their price range. **Nonimpact printers** produce an image by a nonphysical means such as a thermal, electrostatic, or chemical interaction with the paper and the ink material. (Laser and ink-jet printers are nonimpact.) These printers are usually quieter and faster than their impact counterparts, but they cannot make carbon copies and may involve higher operating costs in other ways as well.

## ◆ *Dot-matrix Printers*

Dot-matrix printers have been very popular with personal computer owners because of their relatively low cost, adequate print quality, durability, and versatility. They form characters by selecting and printing the appropriate dots from a rectangular pattern called a **matrix**. Matrix arrays range from as little as 7 x 9 dots to as many as 24 x 36. The more dots used, the better quality the print; a printhead will usually produce more dots for LQ (letter quality) or NLQ (near letter quality) characters than for draft-mode print.

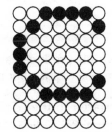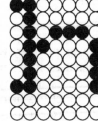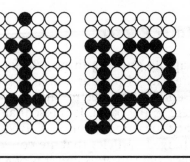

*Figure 5.9*
*The dot pattern*
*(magnified, in*
*this case) for*
*the four letters*
*of the word*
*"chip" as they*
*might be formed*
*by a 7 x 9 array*
*might appear*
*something*
*like this.*

Each solid circle (●) represents the dots that are used and each open circle (○) those that are not. Clearly, the more dots that are used to form each character, the better the overall shape and quality of the characters and print will be. (If you look carefully at a monitor screen, you will see that each character on the screen is similarly produced from a dot pattern.)

Dot-matrix printers produce characters by means of a **printhead** that consists of a series of small pins or wires that put the dots on the paper. For example, the four letters in "chip" might have been produced by a 9-pin printhead (a vertical column of 9 pins) that strikes seven times for each character. If the number of pins is relatively small and the pins large, then each dot tends to be distinct and the print undesirable. With a large number of tiny pins, the dots overlap and blend together. Many dot-matrix printers now use printheads with up to 24 pins to produce excellent quality print. Also, with a larger number of pins, the individual pins can be smaller so that each dot in the pattern is less distinct.

Many printers with 9-pin printheads can yield a reasonably good quality print by using multiple passes of the printhead coupled with a slight shift in the position of the dots. In other words, in subsequent passes the dots are shifted vertically or horizontally by half the width of a dot. This means that a less expensive 9-pin dot-matrix printer can produce reasonably good print quality but at the cost of speed; the multiple passes cause the print speed to be reduced dramatically.

### ◆ *Ink-jet Printers*

These increasingly popular (and decreasingly costly) printers are dot-matrix in nature but employ a series of tiny electrically charged particles of ink rather than having a printhead with a series of pins that physically strike the paper. Since ink-jet printers are nonimpact, they are quiet to operate. The speed is comparable to a fast dot-matrix printer, and the print quality is generally good to excellent. Also, there are ink-jet printers that print in full color, and they are not much more expensive to buy than their black-and-white counterparts. Older models required using special paper that was expensive and not aesthetically pleasing, but many of the new models can print on standard paper. Now that some early technical problems have been more or less overcome and ink-jet printers are relatively reliable to operate, they are worth considering if you desire laserlike quality but don't want to pay the initial up-front cost of a laser printer. Ink-jet printers typically cost about 6 cents per page to operate, compared to 3 cents per page for laser and dot-matrix models. However, that difference in cost may be covered in the lower price of the ink-jet, depending on use.

### ◆ Laser Printers

Rapidly growing in popularity is the laser printer, which produces an entire page of print at a time. A laser printer uses toner in place of a ribbon and employs an electrostatic process that causes the tiny toner particles to adhere to the paper. It is essentially a copy machine interfaced to the computer. (The name "laser" is derived from using laser beams to create a pattern of charged particles that are converted into an image.) This still creates an image from tiny dots, but it is of a very fine resolution and gives the appearance of good print quality.

The first laser printer was introduced by IBM in 1975 for use with its mainframe systems. A model suitable for use with a personal computer did not appear until about ten years later, with the advent of the Hewlett-Packard LaserJet. Until recently, the high cost kept laser printers out of the reach of most personal computer users. However, they are now becoming affordable, with the low-end models competitive in price with the upper-end ink-jet printers.

Laser printers are quiet, fast, and very versatile, and offer print capabilities not found on other printers, including nearly unlimited control over fonts and graphics. Nearly all software now supports laser printers, some exclusively. If you intend using a desktop publishing system or top-of-the-line word processor to generate professional reports, newsletters, manuscripts, or other special applications, you may find that you need a laser printer to achieve the quality you desire. Also, laser printers use common, inexpensive copier paper.

Some laser printers offer **PostScript** compatibility, which is a device-independent method of preparing output. In other words, once a document has been formatted for PostScript, it can be sent and read by another printer, typesetting machine, or film recorder with PostScript capability.

Exciting new laser printers are beginning to appear that can serve multiple functions. A few companies are now offering printers that not only serve in that basic capacity but can also act as a FAX machine, copy machine, or even scanner. Presently, these are relatively expensive, but like any new technology, the prices should come down as the novelty wanes and the competition grows. However, even now the cost is probably less than the sum of the individual components, especially when convenience is considered.

### ◆ Print Quality

Even the most inexpensive printers now provide a fairly nice-looking type. Most printers provide a choice of two or more modes of print quality. Laser printers can even produce "camera-ready" output, including special print styles and graphics images, that appears to have come directly from a print shop.

A draft-quality print should be sufficient if you use a printer only for rough drafts, informal reports or letters, and other work that does not require superior print. If you need to print formal letters or reports, you will want a printer that produces **near letter quality (NLQ)** or **letter quality (LQ)** print much like an electric typewriter. That's a "given" with lasers and ink-jets. Printers that permit various special print effects are also available. Nearly all printers now have graphics capability.

### ◆ *Printing Speed*

Most character printers have speeds from about 25 characters per second **(cps)** to around 400 cps. Many printers offer more than one speed, depending on the quality of the print being produced. In general, the better the print, the slower a character printer will produce it. You can expect such a printer to work in **correspondence** (NLQ or LQ) **mode** at about one-third to one-fourth its speed in **draft mode**. Thus, a printer with a draft speed of 240 cps will likely offer better-quality print at about 60 to 80 cps. Normally, printing graphics will cause the print speed to drop substantially.

The speed of a page printer is measured in the number of pages per minute **(ppm)** it produces. Typical speeds for such printers that might be used with a home system range from about 1 to 8 ppm. For laser printers, the speed is not directly tied to the print quality or type; graphics will print nearly at the same rate as text. It will, however, depend on the size of the paper being used.

The rated speed for a printer may not be the actual speed that you see in use. If a manufacturer rates a character printer at 160 cps, this may not include such things as the time to advance the paper between lines, return the printhead, or print enhancements (boldface, italics, underline, and so forth). In reality, this might cause the 160 cps value to be more in the range of 120 to 140 cps.

Unless you anticipate having a very large amount of printing each day (say, hundreds of pages), you will find that the extra cost to get the higher print speeds may not be justified. If you will be printing only a few pages at a time or have larger printouts only occasionally, you should not find the slower speeds too inconvenient. Print speeds of under 200 cps (in the draft mode) or 4 ppm are adequate for most home users.

### ◆ *Print Buffers*

Most character and all page printers have a print **buffer** or temporary memory for storing data to be printed. If this buffer is sufficiently large, it can expedite printing jobs. Once the document to be printed has been received in its entirety by the printer, the computer will then be free for other tasks. If your word processor or other software does not have a **print spooler** (see Chapter 4), this is a real time-saver. Although it depends on what is being sent to the printer, a buffer of 8 K (kilobytes) should hold about two pages of information.

### ◆ *Variable Pitch (Character Printers)*

**Pitch** refers to the number of characters that are printed per inch (**cpi**). Standard "pica," or print size, is 10 cpi, whereas elite is 12 cpi. Many printers offer a choice of several different pitches.

All of these fonts would produce the same *height* type; it is the *spacing* or *size* of the individual letters that would change. Some printers do offer double-high characters, but the character height is now normally altered by using scalable fonts (as described in the previous chapter).

It should be noted that **condensed** (or **compressed**) print is not always set at 17 cpi but commonly ranges from about 15 to 20 cpi. Notice that three of the sample pitches shown at left represent double-width characters for three others.

Some printers allow you to mix pitches or set your own spacing. For example, you might be able to print with the smaller elite characters but maintain the pica spacing; this would have the effect of slightly increasing the spacing between adjacent letters.

### ◆ *Proportional Spacing (All Printers)*

Most printers provide proportional spacing, which allots space to a character according to its width. This means that a narrow letter such as *I* or *l* will not occupy as much space as an *A* or *m*.

| | |
|---|---|
| **Standard spacing:** | `Mary had a little lamb.` |
| **Proportional spacing:** | Mary had a little lamb. |

*Figure 5.10 Standard spacing vs. proportional spacing.*

### ◆ *Print Enhancements*

Most printers now provide some types of print enhancements. Commonly available enhancements include **boldface**, *italics*, underlining, superscripts (such as $5x^2$ and $98.6°F$) and subscripts (such as $H_2O$ and $D_{max}$), and overstrike (such as piraña and fiancée). Usually most of these can be combined with one another or with the various pitches and fonts. For example, you might print *STOP!* or $Co(NH_3)_6)^{+3}$.

### ◆ *Variable Typefaces and Fonts*

Printers come with at least one resident typeface; Courier, Helvetica, Sans Serif, and Times Roman are common examples. Some of these are shown on page 99.

Usually several fonts, or variations on a typeface are also provided. For example, a printer may be able to print in Courier and Times Roman, and in addition have the ability to print them in fonts such as italics, boldface, expanded type, compressed type, and so on. The printer may be restricted to certain available combinations of pitches and fonts, or virtually unlimited varieties may be permitted through downloaded, scalable (such as **TrueType**)

```
This is Courier typeface.
```
This is Helvetica typeface.

This is Sans Serif typeface.

This is Times Roman typeface.

*Figure 5.11*
*Various*
*typefaces*
*available from*
*most printers.*

fonts. With some applications, it may be possible to extend the ability to print fonts on a dot-matrix printer by using graphics mode.

Many printers, particularly laser printers, allow you to add many typefaces and fonts (as do desktop publishing languages such as PostScript) by plugging in cartridges and cards. Some printers and programs (the Windows operating system, for example) allow you to design your own fonts or use **downloadable** fonts. Remember, however, that not all available fonts and typefaces are interchangeable, and many printers will not offer all of the same font variations for each typeface or print quality. (Fonts are discussed in more detail in Chapter 4.)

### ◆ *Downloadable Characters and Font Buffers*

Printers with the capability to accept downloadable characters have an additional memory buffer to temporarily hold special characters that are sent to it from the computer. These may range from a single character, such as a letter of a foreign alphabet or a mathematical symbol, to an entirely new font or alphabet. This memory is optional for a character printer and is usually in the range of 16 to 64 K when present. But laser printers may require extra memory and can need as much as one or more megabytes added for proper operation.

### ◆ *Selection Mode*

The selection of a print pitch, font, or enhancement is usually simple when you can select from the word processor or other program (referred to as being **software selectable**). However, there will likely be times when you want to use a particular pitch or font but you are not using a program that lets you designate it. Many printers have a control panel for this purpose that permits you to select your pitch or font mode directly. This is called **hardware selectable**.

### ◆ *Carriage Width (Dot-Matrix)*

Most dot-matrix printers come in one of two carriage widths: "standard" for paper widths up to $9\frac{1}{2}$ inches and "wide" for paper up to $14\frac{7}{8}$ inches. Before the various pitches were available, this was a relatively simple choice. If you needed more than 80 characters on a print line (pica was usually standard), you needed the wide carriage. Today, you can get the same number of characters on a line with a standard carriage by using a condensed print mode. The table that follows gives the number of characters that will fit on a line for both carriage widths for a number of commonly provided pitches.

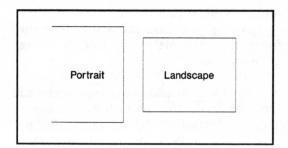

***Figure 5.12
Printing
orientations.***

Other pitches may be available, especially as condensed print. Also, there may be a slight variation between wide carriage printers in the total number of characters that they will print on a line.

Before rejecting the wide carriage model in favor of a slightly less expensive narrow carriage printer, consider two other factors. (1) Will you need to print on envelopes larger than a standard #10 business size? (Also, narrow carriage printers are designed to always print in **portrait**, or lengthwise, format.) (2) Will you need to print in **landscape**, or sideways, mode (such as for signs, posters, or charts)? If you answered either question "Yes," then you should select a wide carriage model or a page printer.

### ◆ Color

Some printers offer color capability. This may be a simple two- or three-color system that works from a single ribbon much like a typewriter that uses a multicolor ribbon. Others offer many colors, but the degree of manual assistance that is required varies.

Color ink-jet printers are becoming more affordable and popular for the home user. However, they sometimes disappoint because they may not offer good reproduction of the colors on the screen. You may spend time trying to match available screen colors to those supported by your printer. Also, the cost of operating a color printer is normally higher. The ribbons or cartridges are expensive and usually have shorter lifetimes; once one color is exhausted, the ribbon must be replaced.

| Table 5.7 | **Characters Printed per Line** | |
|---|---|---|
| **Print Pitch (in cpi)** | **Carriage Width** Standard | Wide |
| 5 | 40 | 68 |
| 6 | 48 | 81 |
| 7.5 | 60 | 102 |
| 8.5 | 68 | 115 |
| 10 (pica) | 80 | 136 |
| 12 (elite) | 96 | 163 |
| 15 | 120 | 204 |
| 17 (condensed) | 136 | 231 |
| 20 (compressed) | 160 | 272 |

## ◆ *Graphics*

All printers now offer some type of graphics capability. On dot-matrix printers, this is usually a **dot-addressable** method, in which each dot in the matrix array can be individually printed. This means that the smaller the pin size (or the more pins in the array), the finer the detail of the image produced. Some printers can now produce graphics resolutions of several hundred dots per inch in which the dots blend together so well that the patterns appear to be solid and rival comparable images from plotters (covered later in this chapter). A resolution of at least 300 dots per inch (**dpi**) is needed to obtain this result.

## ◆ *Tractor Versus Friction Feed*

Laser and ink-jet printers use a feeder tray much like a copy machine; to change paper size, change the tray. A similar option known as a sheet feeder (see below) is often available for dot-matrix printers, but in general, there are two ways to move paper through a dot-matrix printer: a **tractor** (or pin) feed for continuous forms and friction feed for separate pages. All dot-matrix printers provide for both methods; however, a tractor may not be standard equipment and may need to be purchased separately.

Most standard carriage printers have pins on either side of the platen (a cylinder that supports the paper) that are used for pulling and guiding continuous forms through the printer. This type of paper is normally fed from either the rear or the bottom of the printer and continues through as you print. You then tear off what you have printed.

A tractor has a series of pins for better paper feeding, but it can also be adjusted for different paper widths. A tractor is necessary for a wide carriage printer and is recommended for any printer when you have a large printing job (or throughput). This is because the tractor's additional pins hold the paper more securely, reducing paper jams.

If you will be using individual sheets, check the friction feed. Be sure that the paper feeds through easily and remains properly aligned. If you will be using both friction and tractor feed, check to see if feeding single sheets is possible without having to remove the tractor. Most printers permit you to use friction feed without having to completely remove the continuous forms. Friction feeding is slower (unless you have a sheet feeder described below) because you have to stop to insert each page, but this method permits you to use various paper types that are hard to find or unavailable as continuous forms. This enables you to print directly on letterhead or preprinted forms.

## ◆ *Sheet Feeders (Dot-Matrix)*

If you plan to do a large quantity of dot-matrix printing using friction feed, you might want to consider a **sheet feeder.** (Page printers come with a tray feeder system.) These attach directly to a dot-matrix printer and feed the individual pages into the friction feed system of the printer. Sheet feeders can feed one set of pages or more than one type of page, plus envelopes. Sheet feeders can greatly speed up friction feed operations; however, they can be quite expensive (as much or more than the printer itself), are not available for all printers, do not function with all types of paper, and can be very difficult to operate.

### ◆ *Ease of Use*

Sometimes a printer that is excellent in every other way can make you wish you had a degree in engineering when you try to load the paper or change the ribbon. You might want to check on the ease of accomplishing these two tasks, especially if you are not mechanically inclined, before making a purchase.

### ◆ *Emulations*

There is no universal standard among printers for the codes that are used to communicate with the computer. However, several commonly accepted printer types are accepted to serve as unofficial standards and as emulation modes. These are often employed by printer manufacturers to increase the appeal, versatility, and compatibility of their products. The most frequently encountered of these are IBM and Epson for dot-matrix printers and Hewlett-Packard for ink-jet and laser printers. (Note: Do not buy a page printer without the proper "Window drivers.")

## ▶ Cables

The individual components of a computer system are connected together by cables. Sometimes the cables are permanently wired to one of the components, but more often this is not the case. One or more ports are provided for this purpose. (Ports are female and cable ends are male.)

There is a certain amount of standardization in cables and ports, but this does not prevent variety. You might encounter anything from the small, round RCA phono-style or BNC coaxial design to the long, flat RS-232-C serial or Centronics parallel designs. Most computers have at least two or three different ports, thus requiring as many differing cable types. For example, the printer will most likely use a 36-pin Centronics port on its end and a 25-pin RS-232-C port on the computer end. The monitor may make use of a high-density 15-pin DB-15 connector, and the mouse may need a simple 9-pin RS-232-C port. (A diagram of two common varieties of RS-232-C cable ends is provided in Chapter 7.)

Individual components may not come with cables, in which case the proper cables need to be purchased separately. In general, the type of port that the components will use for connection will determine the type of cable that will be needed.

Two components to be connected may not always use the same type of port. Also, if a cable has one end and a port is of a different type, it may be possible to find an adapter if the two designs are not too dissimilar. The length and quality of printer cables vary with the source, so this should be checked, along with the type and any special requirements. (More information on cables is provided in Chapter 7.)

# ▸ Documentation

All hardware and software should come with documentation, which is explanatory material to describe their functions and uses. This may be supplied in the form of manuals, booklets, tutorials, files on disk, or even demonstration disks or programs. Often, a combination of several formats will be used. Examine the documentation that comes with every item that you intend to purchase. Sloppy documentation may indicate the same in a product or, at the very least, make learning to use the products difficult and frustrating.

In the past, computer manuals were not very well done, most often as result of rushing a product to market or having the programmers or engineers write the manuals, either of which is a prescription for disaster. Computer professionals have a term for these often incomprehensible manuals—**RTFM** (Read The Flaming Manual), which expresses the tendency to consult that document only as a last resort. (As you might imagine, somewhat more colorful versions of RTFM have been used.)

However, manufacturers are becoming more aware of the need to produce accessible and helpful materials to accompany their products for first-time users. Many companies have tried to improve and supplement their documentation by supplying tutorials, call-in 800 numbers, demonstration programs, and/or online help facilities. If, however, you discover that you have an item of software or hardware with documentation that you find to be inadequate, check your local bookstore. There is a wide selection of how-to books on nearly every popular model of computer or type of software package.

# ▸ Modems

**Modems** are used to establish **telecommunications** links with other computers in order to access bulletin boards, electronic shopping catalogs, online services, and public service information data banks. They may also be used to link one computer directly to another, such as your home computer to one at school, work, or a friend's home. One of the most recent uses for modems is to send and receive FAX messages using models equipped with that capability.

Most people visualize modems in the older **acoustic coupler** design, in which the telephone handset fits into a cradle on top of the modem (probably because this is the type most frequently pictured in movies and on TV). Today, internal modems are in the form of a board that fits into a slot inside the computer to which the phone line directly connects. External modems are usually flat and about the size of a small book, and connect directly to a serial port and the telephone line. (Technically, a communications link can be established using any **data communications channel**, such as telephone lines, microwave relays, and communications satellites. However, since few homes have access to either of the latter two methods, virtually all home computer systems use a telephone line for this purpose.)

As with most other computer equipment, the price of modems has dropped significantly over the past few years. You can now get a model adequate for most home uses for under $100, but those that offer the most advanced and greatest choice of features can cost several times as much.

With a wide choice of features and capabilities, modems are available from a number of companies. Check to see if the systems that you intend to link with require any special **protocols** (the signals or commands needed to establish communications and transmit data) or other capabilities. You can then look for a modem (and telecommunications software) with these particular abilities. Otherwise, there are four basic areas that you will want to consider.

### ◆ Transmission Rate

This refers to how rapidly data is transmitted from one place to another. It is usually measured in **baud** or bits per second. For most systems, this means that to transmit one character per second normally requires a rate of 10 baud. (It is 10 rather than 8 because there are usually 2 "control" bits transmitted with each character.) Common transmission speeds between microcomputers range from 300 baud up. If you use the regular telephone lines, you will want to use at least 2,400; however, this will also be determined by the capabilities of the modem on the other end.

Table 5.8 summarizes the transmission times required for sending or receiving a file of 57.6 K (about fifteen printed pages) at the most commonly used rates.

Most modems offer a selection of speeds. The table shows how higher speeds can substantially reduce transmission times. This means that a somewhat greater initial investment for a model with a higher transmission rate may be more than offset by the eventual savings in long-distance charges when accessing other systems.

| Table 5.8 | **Modem Transmission Times for Common Rates** |
|---|---|
| **Rate (baud)** | **Time for 57.6 KB File (min:sec)** |
| 300 | 32:00 |
| 1,200 | 8:00 |
| 2,400 | 4:00 |
| 4,800 | 2:00 |
| 9,600 | 1:00 |
| 14,400 | 0:40 |
| 19,200 | 0:30 |
| 28,800 | 0:20 |
| 57,600 | 0:10 |

### ◆ Auto Modes

Nearly all modems now offer either or both **auto-answer** and **auto-dial** (**AA/AD**) capabilities. This means that the modem will answer any incoming calls to your system or permit you to dial a call directly from your computer without ever touching a telephone. Other models offer additional automatic modes such as automatic transmission rate selection. This means that your modem will automatically match that of the modem of the computer you are calling. (Of course, that rate must be within the capabilities of your model.) Your telecommunications software must also support these features.

### ◆ FAX Capability

If you need FAX capability, you may find a FAX modem to be right for you. Such a board is similar to a standard modem, except that it permits files to be sent to or received from a traditional FAX machine or another computer equipped with a FAX capable modem. FAX modems come with a variety of features, including many automatic modes, regular modem transmission, remote retrieval of documents, and direct input using a scanner for "reading" and then sending the printed documents. A FAX modem can be preprogrammed and set to transmit or receive in basically the same way a regular FAX machine can.

The advantages of a FAX/modem are convenience and ease of use. In order to send a document, it must be in the form of a file within your computer. Also, in order to receive a FAX, your computer must be on and set to receive. FAX modems are considerably less costly than regular FAX machines, beginning at just about $100 for simple models.

### ◆ Compatibility

A modem must be compatible with the software that establishes the link as well as the communications protocols. There are several systems in use, but the most frequently used reference standard is that pioneered by Hayes. A **Hayes-compatible** modem should satisfy most needs, but you should check to see if you need any other special compatibility.

## ▶ Other Input/Output Devices

The following accessories are used for data input, cursor control, and information output.

### ◆ Joystick

A **joystick** is used to control the cursor or some other screen motion by the back-and-forth, left-and-right movement of a vertical lever. There is usually a "fire" button to initiate certain types of screen action. Joysticks are most frequently used with games, but they have many other valuable uses that can add much pleasure and flexibility to your system. Joysticks are inexpensive; good ones can sometimes be found for under $15.

### ◆ Mouse

A mouse is a small palm-sized device with a ball on its base. It is operated by moving it around on a flat, smooth surface; the motion of the ball indicates the direction, which is translated into the desired screen action. That is, move the mouse down or toward you, and the cursor on the screen moves down. As with a joystick, there are usually two or three buttons to initiate additional action such as capture and release.

A mouse is most frequently used with graphics-based applications; however, because of their rapidly growing popularity, many types of programs are now providing mouse support. These programs allow you to highlight an icon by "clicking on" the mouse and then "dragging" whatever was highlighted to a different part of the screen. A number of computers even come with a mouse as standard equipment; the Macintosh line has made the mouse an integral part of its operation. A mouse for most computers goes for as little as $25, but the more popular models cost $75 or more.

### ◆ Track Ball

A track ball functions the same as a mouse. It also uses a rolling ball to maneuver the cursor on the screen similar to the mouse; however, with the track ball, the ball rests on top of a fixed base and is moved with the fingers, the palm, a pencil eraser, or any other convenient method. As with the mouse, the ball's movement will determine the action on the screen. Like a mouse, track balls are most often used with games, graphics, or other applications that require fine screen movements. (Other variations on the basic mouse design are also available.)

### ◆ Light Pen

A light pen consists of a light-sensitive stylus that is connected to the monitor by means of a cable. It is used to enter, delete, change, or move values on the screen by simply touching the tip of the pen to the proper spot on the screen. This can include anything from selecting a menu item to drawing. These are most frequently employed with software packages and utilized by a wide variety of users. They not only simplify and standardize the interaction with the system but are much faster than a traditional keyboard.

### ◆ Tablet

A **tablet** is a touch-sensitive membrane connected to the computer for data input. A tablet is used by moving an instrument such as a pen (or perhaps even a finger) across the surface with a slight pressure. Freehand drawings can be done or paper diagrams placed over the membrane surface and then traced. The tablet senses the position of the touch and transmits this to the computer. Although tablets are most frequently used for detailed graphics applications, they can be used for other input tasks as well. Tablets are not often used on home systems because they are relatively costly.

A tablet is also referred to as a **digitizing tablet,** or a **digitizer;** however, it is only one of a wide variety of digitizers that include the mouse, track ball, light pen, and scanner. The term digitizer more generally applies to anything that converts continuous values such as motion or temperature into digital data for computer processing. There are two basic differences between tablets and mouse-type systems. One is that a tablet provides more precise information; the other is that the values returned by a tablet are absolute and reproducible rather than being relative to the point at which the mouse was first placed on the desktop.

### ◆ Sound Board

Using sound boards has added an entirely new dimension to computers. Now, the former world of computer "beeps" has turned into one of every possible sound imaginable. A sound board permits the computer to reproduce virtually any sound from a Beethoven symphony to a monsters' growl in your favorite computer game.

Although sound boards may be used independently with games or any software that supports them, they are more and more often being paired with a CD-ROM drive or MIDI (Musical Instrument Digital Interface) or both. The Sound Blaster is the most commonly emulated standard, but the Adlib is also frequently supported. Sound boards frequently have built-in ports for a joystick and MIDI device as well as headphone jacks, microphones, stereo speakers (with surround-sound and subwoofers), or other audio equipment.

### ◆ Speech Synthesizer

A **speech synthesizer** is quite different from a sound board. A sound board reproduces prerecorded sounds such as a melody, a speech, or various sound effects. It can reproduce speech, but only if it is previously recorded and programmed for output to the sound board. A speech synthesizer is designed to read text (with the aide of software called a **screen reader**), and using phonetic rules, to simulate human speech as it does so. A sound board can reproduce a truly human-sounding voice because it is a recording of a human voice; speech synthesizers normally sound like a "computer" reading.

Some sound/speech synthesizers are internal boards that fit into a slot, and others are external that plug into a port. Features vary widely, as does the accuracy of the speech reproduced. Low-end models may generate speech that is not easily understood or controlled. Top-line products often offer a choice of voices and good reading management features. The market for these is limited, and they are still relatively expensive. Considering the necessary software, one that will give really good results will cost at least $1,000.

### ◆ Access Hardware

The speech synthesizer makes it possible for many visually impaired persons to use computers. There is also access (or **assistive**) equipment available, ranging from large print keycaps to special hardware (and software), to assist persons with disabilities.

Check with your local dealer about having the system specially equipped. If the dealer is not knowledgeable about what is needed, contact your state's department of rehabilitative services; they should be able to help you find a computer representative who can help you meet your special access needs.

### ◆ MIDI Device

**MIDI** is a system that is already familiar to most music enthusiasts. It is a standard for the exchange of musical information in digital format, and makes music an ideal medium for processing by computers. The musical information can be entered into the computer in a number of ways, including a MIDI keyboard, a live recording, or a direct transfer from an instrument or synthesizer through a MIDI interface.

MIDI allows not only for the operation of both instruments and synthesizers but also for the synchronization of notes; it accounts for virtually every parameter that is needed for writing and editing music. This means that music recorded and stored as a file can be easily edited by simply altering the appropriate parameters. Thus it is an easy matter to change an entire score by altering a few characters or control codes in the MIDI file.

Many sound boards are equipped with a MIDI port.

### ◆ Label Printer

**Label printers** are small, usually dot-matrix, printers designed exclusively for printing labels. These printers are substantial time-savers for processing mailing lists. Costs begin at about $150 and go up.

### ◆ Plotter

Some of today's graphics printers are very good and produce high-quality images of pictures, graphs, and drawings that require fine detail. If you need more detail than you can get from even very tiny dots (as in matrix), you might consider a **plotter.** Plotters do not produce normal printed output but rather are designed to draw images with continuous lines. They come in a variety of designs, including models that move an ink-filled pen under the paper and those that move the paper under the pen. This is another advantage of plotters; they can produce continuous plots of graphs using roll paper without the need to break for a new page.

Color is more or less standard with most plotters; however, the degree of automation in its use varies widely. Plotters are available at prices that are competitive with the less expensive graphics printers, but the more sophisticated models cost several thousand dollars. With the increased quality of printers, the use of plotters has declined; however, plotting devices are still very much in demand for many medical and scientific applications needing uninterrupted output, such as monitoring of vital signs or tracking earthquake activity.

### ◆ *Scanner*

Basically, a **scanner** is any mechanism designed to scan and read printed, drawn, or other material and convert this into a computer usable format such as a disk file. These range from relatively simple **optical mark readers (OMR)**, which detect the presence or absence of a mark and are commonly used with standardized tests, to complex digital scanners, which can read the fine details of engineering or other design diagrams. Also included in this category are optical character readers (OCR), which can read printed material provided it is written in a font and size that the OCR is programmed to recognize.

Scanners popular with home systems come in a variety of models ranging from simple, inexpensive hand-held units to more complex and costly models capable of scanning a full page at once. A good scanner is priced under $200 but, depending on its capabilities, a complex, full-color scanner could cost $2,000 or more.

## ▶ Protection and Convenience Devices

Several items that you might want to add to your system can provide both convenience for you and/or valuable protection for your equipment and data. In some cases, the relatively modest investment can more than pay for itself in savings of time, annoyance, and repair costs.

### ◆ *Dust Covers*

It is wise to use a dust cover for your computer and the other major components of your system. Covers are available for most "standard"-size components but are sometimes unreasonably expensive. Consider making your own from plastic or some other heavy, nonporous material.

### ◆ *Glare Screens*

If you have to work in a room with bright lights that produce a glare on the monitor screen, you might try a glare reduction attachment. These usually fit directly over the screen and reduce the reflected glare (as well as the screen intensity). They are available in most common screen sizes and cost from $20 to $50.

### ◆ *Monitor Turntables*

Many monitors come with a turntable base that permits them to be tilted and rotated. This allows you to adjust the position of the screen for the best viewing angle for your height and sitting position. If the monitor you select is not equipped with a turntable, they are available for standard-size monitors for about $25.

### ◆ *Mouse Pads*

If your desk top is plastic, polished wood, or some other smooth surface, you may find that your mouse does not track as it should. This is because there is insufficient friction to cause the ball on the base to turn properly with the sliding motions of the mouse.

Mouse pads are flat, rectangular mats that sit on the desk top and provide a nonskid surface that will cause the ball to move with the mouse. These pads are generally very inexpensive, sometimes even given away for free as promotional gimmicks. No-frills pads can be purchased for less than $5, but ones with colorful designs or images are often higher priced.

### ◆ *Printout Basket*

If you will be producing long printouts, you might want a printout basket to give some order to the mess that can otherwise result. These are often attached to the rear of a printer and catch the paper as it comes through. They do not fit all printers and may not be usable at the same time with a sheet feeder or sound baffle, so be cautious before you buy.

### ◆ *Sound Baffle*

Also called an **acoustic enclosure**, a sound baffle simply fits over the top of a noisy printer to reduce (but not eliminate) the noise. Baffles occasionally can get in the way, but some have access doors to help ease the inconvenience. Check to see that the paper path and cables will be unobstructed. There should also be adequate ventilation.

Sound baffles can be expensive and even difficult to find because of the increasing use of laser printers. Moving the printer to a more remote location may be a preferable option.

### ◆ *Static Guards*

One of the most common causes for data loss and even equipment damage is the static discharges that everyone has experienced in cooler weather. A touch to a computer or disk can result in a spark of static electricity that is fatal to data or a chip. Many products, ranging from mats to sprays, are available to help protect against such damage and are generally a relatively low-cost investment, considering the possible alternative. (These little sparks can also damage stereos, VCRs, and anything else that contains a microprocessor.)

### ◆ *Noise Filters*

Electrical disturbances called "noise" are always present in the AC power lines but are usually at such a low level that they are not noticeable. You have seen the effects of this noise as distortion in the television or radio—it usually appears as an audible hiss in the sound of a TV or flicker on the screen.

Computers are just as vulnerable to this problem, only the effect is usually a loss or distortion of data.

Noise filters, inserted between the computer and the power line, will eliminate all but the most severe noise. They are not usually found as separate items but are most often incorporated into a power conditioner (see below) or as part of a protective piece of equipment.

### ◆ *Surge Suppressors*

Another hazard with AC lines is voltage surges, or spikes. Small voltage spikes are not uncommon and can occur whenever there is a disturbance along the power line. They can also damage data and, if large enough, your computer hardware. Nothing will protect against the massive surges that can result from a nearby lightning strike, but even simple voltage suppressors can eliminate most other spikes. These are separate items or obtained as part of a more complex device offering more general protection.

### ◆ *Power Conditioners*

A power conditioner usually combines both surge and noise protection. They come in a variety of styles, ranging from a small unit that fits between the computer's power plug and the AC outlet, to large, multiplug models with complex switching arrangements. They cost from about $10 up. (If a modem is part of your system, you would be wise to purchase a power conditioner that provides protection from surges along the telephone lines as well.) Surge suppressors and power conditioners are available for about $20 and up, with the price increasing with the number of outlets and the amount of protection provided.

### ◆ *Power Strips*

This is the familiar arrangement of usually four to eight electrical outlets in a strip. There is normally a master switch and a circuit breaker. Power strips may or may not be power conditioners; read the packaging to check before purchasing. They are priced from about $10 and up.

### ◆ *Power Directors*

A power director is basically a power strip on which each outlet has its own switch. All of the components of a computer system can be plugged into it and each turned on or off using its switches. They start at about $50.

### ◆ *Uninterruptible Power Supplies (UPS)*

Most computers have a **volatile RAM**, which means that they will lose whatever is in their main memory should the electrical power be cut off.

Under certain conditions some systems can even experience more serious and permanent problems, such as damage to the files on a disk when the process of writing data to the disk is interrupted in mid-operation, possibly resulting in the loss of information on the disk.

An uninterruptible power supply is a power conditioner that contains a battery backup system so that it will cut in and supply power to your computer should the normal AC power be interrupted. These are not intended to run a computer for very long but are designed to provide power for a sufficient period to permit an orderly termination of any jobs and the shutdown of the system. The price will depend on the power output requirements and could run several hundred dollars. If you live in an area where the power is erratic, this could be a wise investment. After all, it takes only a blink of the power to clear the computer's memory.

### ◆ Switch Boxes

A switch box is a simple switching mechanism that permits more than one computer or component to share the system resources without having to add more hardware to accommodate them. For example, one computer could send data to several different printers without requiring the addition of more ports. The signal is sent through the switch box, which directs it to the selected printer via a single switch; hence the name switch box. (On some newer models, the "switch" has been replaced by pushbuttons.)

These boxes are valuable if you need both a laser and label printer but find that you are short a port. A switch box would connect both printers to a single port. The trade-off is that you will be able to use only one printer at a time (which would probably be the case anyway).

Alternately, in another design, more than one computer might share the same printer without needing a network setup.

Selecting which component or computer will be active is again accomplished by simply flipping a switch on the box. Should you acquire additional computers in the future, such a switch box might permit you to avoid the duplication of some system components, especially printers.

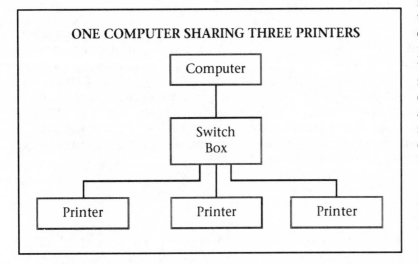

ONE COMPUTER SHARING THREE PRINTERS

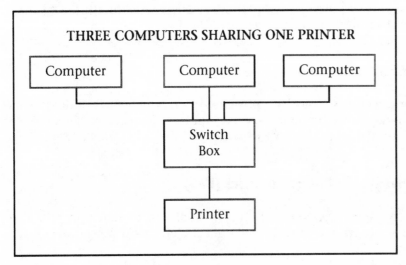

THREE COMPUTERS SHARING ONE PRINTER

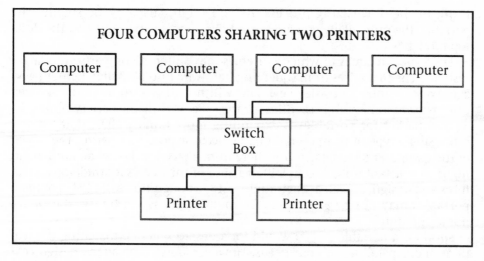

**FOUR COMPUTERS SHARING TWO PRINTERS**

Although most switch boxes are very simple in design, more complex models are available that can simultaneously connect multiple computers to several components. For example, four computers might share access to two printers.

While there is theoretically no limit to the number of components that could be connected through a switch box, generally eight computers and four printers (or other devices) is considered to be the practical maximum. (The more complex boxes are normally found in schools or businesses and are rarely needed by home users.)

Care must be taken when selecting a switch box to see that it has the correct configuration for the number of computers and components involved. It is fine to have extra positions for connecting components or computers, but if there are not enough, it will not function as needed. Also, the type of ports (cable ends) that will be used must match *exactly*. The switch box in Figure 5.13 connects four components to a common unit, all using standard 25-pin serial connectors; however, boxes are available with virtually any kind of cable end you might need. Cable adaptors to change from one type of connector to another are also available for most common combinations. Additional cables will also be needed, and these must be properly matched as well.

Switch boxes are considered by many to be one of the best buys around for what they can return in over-all savings. Switch boxes generally cost about $25 to $75, depending on the number and type of available connections. Auto-switching models are somewhat higher, depending on the features offered, but the convenience may be worth the extra cost.

**Figure 5.13 Diagram of a switch box.**

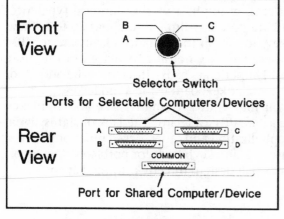

### ▶ Portables

**Portable** is a very general term applied to a computer that is small enough and light enough to be moved from place to place. The selection of portables is abundant and rapidly increasing. The most common classification of portables is the **notebook** computer. A few so-called **subnotebook** or **palmtop** computers have even appeared on the market. These names are roughly descriptive of the intended size of each type of system.

Portable notebook computers are about the size of a ream of paper, and they can weigh from 5 to over 8 pounds. Many offer all the features and capabilities of their larger, desktop-sized cousins, but others must sacrifice something in the downsizing process. As you might suspect, the smaller the portable, the more likely you are to find differences between it and the desktop models.

There are two areas in which portables may suffer in comparison to larger systems. The first arises from squeezing hardware into a smaller, lighter package. For example, a full-size keyboard will not fit within a notebook-sized case. The second involves sacrifice for the sake of available battery power.

The market for portables is expanding more rapidly than that for any other single type of computer, probably because portables permit the power of the computer to go nearly anywhere from a physics class to an airplane in flight to a distant hotel room. Still, because of the necessary trade-off in features and design, as well as their high cost (although this will likely change), portables may not be as suitable for many users as a primary, stationary home computer.

Shop for a portable as you would for a desktop model, matching the features and capabilities to your needs. However, due to the added design cost for the portability of these machines, you should expect to pay more for a portable than for a desktop model with the same computing power.

There are some special considerations unique to portables. Here are some of the most important points to investigate.

### ◆ Keyboard

Because of the smaller size of the "box," it is not possible to fit a full-size keyboard into a notebook-size package. For this reason, keyboards for portable computers usually offer only the basics—the standard typewriter section and function keys—and are normally limited to about 80 to 85 keys (as compared to the 101-plus keys found on the enhanced keyboard for IBM compatibles). Unfortunately, these keys are not always placed in the more familiar arrangements or styles. Numeric keypads either must be added, or otherwise simulated within the smaller keyboard using a mode key.

If you have large hands, you may find the smaller size and tight key arrangement of many portable keyboards awkward. The lack of status signal lights on some keyboards (for capitalization and other locked functions) can be a minor annoyance for some users. Many keyboards for portables now incorporate a mouse (usually as a track ball design) directly into the keyboard.

### ◆ Display

Probably the most disconcerting problem associated with portables is the unusual, often hard-to-read display. Since it is not possible to run a traditional-type monitor off a portable battery, alternate designs had to be found. Most rely on some type of **liquid crystal display (LCD)** similar to digital watches and calculators. The ease of reading such displays often depends on the intensity and direction of ambient light, which is not always ideal. This is especially true when you're working on a portable while traveling.

Many models incorporate improved LCD designs such as **dual scan**; most employ backlit or sidelit displays. A few top-line models come with "active" **thin film transistor (TFT)** screens that are very readable but come with a substantially higher price tag. These advanced displays do, however, normally eliminate **submarining**, an annoying feature of many LCD screens in which the moving cursor will temporarily disappear.

The size and format of the display are also different. Portable screens are smaller but still display the same amount of information as a normal monitor. This means that letters and other characters are compressed to fit the screen. The shape of the screen is not critical for text, but graphics will show up better on the squarer designs. On portables that use monochrome displays, colors are shown in shades of gray. However, most portables now come with color screens.

When considering a portable, it is very important to examine a wide variety of displays under as many different light conditions as possible to see which might be best for you. Remember that most portables do provide a port for the connection of an external monitor. If you think a portable will best suit your needs but find the display unacceptable for prolonged periods of use, you might consider acquiring a separate, full-size monitor for use with the system when it is at your home or office.

### ◆ *Data Entry and Transfer*

Most portables come with a 3½-inch floppy disk drive, but a few of the smallest subnotebook pocket models may lack even this. This can cause problems in transferring data between the portable and other systems.

To solve this problem, some portables have an assortment of software preloaded in ROM. Others permit the entry of programs from small cartridges. A few provide a special feature for downloading data to a desktop system. The latter process is basically equivalent to the **null modem** concept of directly linking two computers for information exchange and can be done with nearly any two computers having serial or parallel ports. It requires only the proper cable and the appropriate software. A modem might be used to transfer data to or from a portable and another computer such as the one at your home or work. Most portables can be equipped with a modem.

### ◆ *Add-ons*

Manufacturers of portables are well aware of the unavoidable shortcomings created by the smaller and lighter designs. To help compensate for this, most provide the capability to attach full-sized components such as standard keyboards and monitors. In addition, they also provide ports for keyboard enhancements, additional disks, printers, modems, and other peripherals. This ability to attach add-ons often preserves the ease of movement of the computer while maintaining its overall power and features when stationary (an important consideration for many potential professional users).

### ◆ *Battery*

In order to be truly portable, a computer must be equipped with a battery to provide power when you cannot be near a regular AC outlet. The power provided by such battery systems varies widely, but at the very least it should last for several (3 to 6) hours. As a general rule, the more built-in devices the battery powers, the shorter period of time it will run between recharges. That is, a computer with a backlit screen and hard disk will not run as long on a charge as one without these features.

If the computer is used for extended periods on battery power (such as during long flights), check to see if the battery is removable and if extra battery packs are available at reasonable cost. Calculate how much time is required to recharge a battery and if it can be done while the computer is being used (while plugged into an AC outlet). Since the computer will temporarily "die" and your work can be lost when the battery runs out of power, verify that the computer provides an adequate low-power warning system (usually special lights or an on-screen display). Other helpful signals are a battery charging indicator and warning signal in case you forget to turn the system off. A useful feature is an auxiliary battery, which temporarily preserves the memory when the power is lost.

### ◆ *Ruggedness*

By its general nature, a portable is subject to more knocks and potential damage than a traditional laptop. For this reason, it is especially important to ensure that your portable is transported in a case (sometimes sold separately) that can protect it from most normal hazards.

### ◆ *Weight and Size*

The trade-off with portables is weight and size versus power and features. If you intend to carry the computer only from your home or office to your car and always use it near an AC outlet or for short periods, then weight is not as critical. However, if you'll be carrying your system from class to class across a large campus, or on long treks to get to and through airports, weight should be a primary consideration.

When testing the weight of a portable, check to see if it is with or without its battery pack and carrying case. The higher the battery capacity or the larger the hard disk, the more that will be added to the overall weight of the computer. Also, remember that any accessories that you may add (like extra battery packs, the AC adapter, or a modem) will increase the carrying weight.

# ▸ Multimedia

**Multimedia** technically refers to systems that are equipped with a variety of storage/retrieval media; however, the term has come more generally to refer to a computer equipped with sound and CD-ROM capabilities. With the introduction of high-capacity CD-ROM drives, high-resolution graphics, sound boards, and stereo sound to the personal computer market, a new era for computing has arrived. This is reflected in computers that employ these new features in addition to traditional text and graphics displays and accessories such as hard drives or floppy disks.

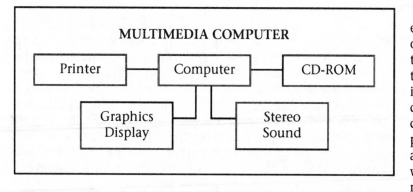

MULTIMEDIA COMPUTER

Printer — Computer — CD-ROM

Graphics Display — Stereo Sound

Multimedia systems are well suited for those needing extensive, online reference—either general or technical—as well as special applications that were previously very limited or nonexistent on personal computers. Encyclopedia sections can be highlighted not only by still photos and drawings but also with audio and video clips. For example, while researching spaceflight, you might hear Neil Armstrong's first words from the moon or see a video of the *Challenger* explosion. None of this takes into account the enhanced entertainment value that these additional capabilities can provide in leisure activities such as playing games or pursuing a hobby.

But the potential goes much further. Not only are the methods for presenting information different and more diversified, but the way you interact with the program itself is often different with multimedia. Traditionally, online help took the form of text that popped up on the screen when a certain key was pressed or icon clicked. With multimedia, a recorded human voice and/or animation actually *explains* a concept or procedure to you.

The downside of multimedia is the cost in hardware resources. Processing the graphics, audio, and video files usually associated with a typical multimedia presentation will push even the most powerful systems to their practical limits. Meeting the minimal requirements often proves unsatisfactory (if not immediately, then in the future when the more demanding applications exceed today's minimums). Considering the explosive rate of growth of multimedia, the caution here is to allow plenty of room to grow and handle future needs.

Anyone looking to this type of system should investigate the standards carefully; presently the **MPC (Multimedia PC)** standards are probably the best for continued future support. Also, if feasible, it would be wise to purchase the entire system as a unit assembled by a single manufacturer as opposed to buying it one component at a time from a variety of companies. The standards are still so uncertain that independently assembling the various components can be a nightmare even for an experienced technician.

# ▶ Specially Designed Systems

### ◆ *Upgradable Systems*

An increasing number of computers are being designed to be easily upgraded as your needs grow. With these computers, you can simply unplug the present processor and insert a newer, more powerful one. For example, if you would like a Pentium processor-based system but your finances will not permit it, you might consider an upgradable system equipped with a 486 processor and move up to the more powerful chip at a later time.

### ◆ *Turnkey*

Some companies provide what are called **turnkey systems**, which are complete computer systems, including hardware and software, that are designed to do certain jobs such as office management, desktop publication, or patient care. Turnkey systems are more than preloaded systems. They are intended to be very user-friendly, are set up with all the necessary application software, and are ready to use when you get them. Although most are designed to be self-contained within their specific applications, the computer dealer may arrange it so you can expand the system for other uses. The disadvantage is that turnkey systems tend to be more expensive than other similar systems.

## Preloaded Software

Many computers, especially those bought at discount stores, are now coming preloaded with software. Aside from the operating system, this normally includes a selection of application software. This may include everything from an integrated package that gives you several capabilities (such as word processor, spreadsheet, and data base) within the same program as well as access to games and software for an online service. There is often a shell or interface to make using the system easier, and a tutorial that may explain anything from how to use the computer to how it actually works.

Preloaded systems allow the beginner to avoid much of the initial setup, which can be very trying for the uninitiated. Such systems are often no more expensive than similar systems that are not preloaded. But beware, and read the software descriptions carefully. Sometimes the software provided for a particular application is only a shareware or demonstration version intended to entice you to purchase the full-featured package. Also, if that particular model has been on the market for a while, some of the software releases may be outdated.

### ◆ *Multiuser*

Nearly all personal computers are single-user models. Few people have the need for a computer that supports more than one user at a time. There are, however, several microcomputers that can and do support multiple users at once. This is usually done by using a multitasking approach, which divides the resources of the microprocessor among the users. A few systems have used multiprocessing by employing more than one microprocessor. The latter approach is losing out to the former due to the increasing power and lower cost of competing one-processor systems. (This may reverse again in the near future.)

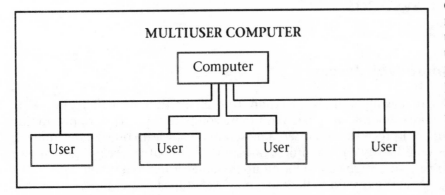
MULTIUSER COMPUTER

Keep in mind that the number of users any multiuser system can adequately support depends not only on the number of ports provided but also on the applications to be run on the system. For example, a system can support more users doing relatively nonintensive tasks, such as word processing or personal finance management, without a noticeable degradation in performance than it can with users running very intensive tasks (such as data base manipulations or large graphics applications).

Most multiuser microcomputers are not capable of handling more than a relatively limited number of users. Models that are powerful enough to adequately support more than a few users are normally very expensive. If you need to have more than one user with simultaneous access to the various components of your system, you might want to look into such options as networks and multiplexors before making a final decision.

## ▶ Networks

A network consists of a group of computers connected together and organized in such a manner that they can share certain common facilities, including printers, disk storage units, data base managers, and other hardware and software components. The obvious advantage is that it permits each member of the network to have access to the common facilities without actually having to purchase additional resources. Of course, there may be a fee for this use, and a particular item such as a printer may not always be available when you need it.

There are many ways to organize a network. One of the most common for microcomputers is the local area network, or **LAN.** This involves computers within a small area such as a room or building connected together with cables. A typical LAN arrangement is shown here.

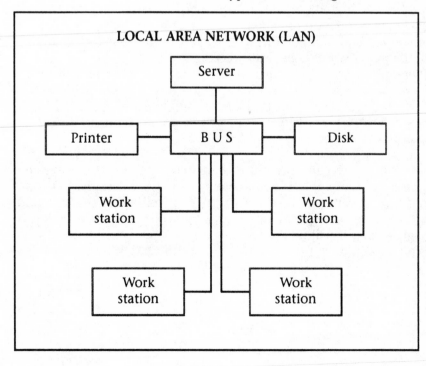

The server is a high-performance computer that is dedicated to controlling the operations of the LAN. It will run the software that governs its procedures. The bus performs the same basic function as in a single computer (described earlier in this chapter). Each client is a stand-alone workstation (normally personal computer) that can access the resources of the network, such as retrieving data from the disk or sending output to the printer, but otherwise performs its own computing chores. This is an important distinction between a network and a multiuser system; in the latter, each workstation is normally a simple data entry terminal with no independent computing power.

The server may perform a number of functions, such as controlling the network disk or printer, in which case it is called a disk server or print server, respectively. A print server will accept commands for print jobs and send them to the network printer as it becomes available, freeing the workstations for other tasks. As a disk server, the power of a network is even more apparent.

LANs are often used in schools and businesses to avoid the duplication of less frequently used components such as printers and to permit access to a common storage unit. Other networks permit remote access using a modem. Some users find it to their advantage to either join an existing network or organize a new one in order to reduce overall system costs yet maintain or even increase capabilities.

## ▶ Computer Furniture

There is an almost unlimited variety of computer furniture available. Some of these units have been constructed to fit a particular model or type of computer, whereas others are modular in nature, allowing you to mix and match components to create the arrangement that best suits your individual needs.

Keep the following questions in mind when looking at computer furniture:

──◆ Is it sturdy enough to hold all your equipment without any danger of falling?
──◆ Is there adequate room for all parts of the system and ample work space?
──◆ Will the keyboard be at a comfortable height?
──◆ Will the monitor screen be at eye level?
──◆ How adjustable are the components?
──◆ If space for a printer is provided, is there storage for both blank paper as well as the printed output?
──◆ Is adequate ventilation provided?
──◆ Can you reach all components without getting up from your chair?
──◆ Will the power switches be readily accessible?
──◆ Is there sufficient room in the rear so that cables and power cords are not crimped?
──◆ Is there ample storage space for manuals, supplies, and diskettes?
──◆ Will you be able to conveniently position a phone, light, and other accessories as needed?

Computer furniture can cost more than many parts of your system. Carefully research your choices. Before buying, sit at the desk (with a computer in place, if possible) and see how it fits you. Verify that the keyboard and monitor will be in comfortable locations and that the construction is rigid enough so that it will not collapse or topple over. Let the others who will be using the equipment try it out for their comfort as well.

# Buy Intelligently

*W*<sub>here</sub> you buy a computer system is as important as *what* you purchase. Be cautious and check out the store as thoroughly as possible. Before making any purchase, know the dealer's policies and reputation (ask friends or family members). Check also the Better Business Bureau or the state attorney general's office to see if there are any complaints against the store.

## ▸ Buying Software

When you buy a software product, read the features listed on the outside of the package and verify that they match your needs. Be certain that the program is written for your particular computer, operating system version, and system design, as applicable. What runs on an IBM compatible does not run on an Apple Macintosh and vice versa. If you plan to run more than one operating system or more than one version of the same operating system, check to see that the product is compatible with what you will be using. The description on the package will also give any special memory and disk requirements. Verify that this is satisfactory as well.

### ◆ *Version/Release Numbers*

Software often comes in more than one release. Version or release numbers are usually indicated as something like "v2.3" or "v4.21." These are normally preceded by the word "Release" or "Version" or perhaps only an abbreviation such as "Rel" or "Ver" or just "v" (or "V"), as used above. Release numbers are easy to interpret. The digit before the decimal indicates the number of major versions or revisions that have been released. The first digit after the decimal counts the minor revisions to the last major release. If there is a third digit, this indicates very minor corrections to the last minor revision. Thus, v2.3

would indicate the third revision of the second major release; v4.21 means that there has been one correction to the second version of the fourth major release. To confuse things a bit, you may find a package with *both* version and release numbers, such as Ver. 3.3 Rel. 1.3. The interpretation is the same as above. This would mean release 1.3 of version 3.3. (Note: Version and release numbers are not found on many games, onetime releases, and software for some types of computers or may appear in somewhat different forms from the description here.)

The version of one package has nothing to do with that of another; you may have an operating system that is v6.2 and run a word processor that is v5.0 or spreadsheet that is v2.3. But you can know something about the product from the release number. A package with v1.0 means that this is the first version to be released and is more likely to contain bugs than one that carries a number of, say, v3.2. This is not to say that you should avoid purchasing first releases; these have likely been well tested and are usually reliable. But given a choice, higher release numbers indicate more testing and actual user experience and feedback, which should improve the product. You would be well advised, however, to avoid anything with a number beginning with a zero, such as v0.9; these are often test packages and may not work well.

### ◆ Registration Cards

Most software comes with a registration card or **license agreement** that you should complete and return as instructed. This permits the company that produced the package to inform you of any problem with their product and how to correct it. Most companies are willing to assist registered owners who have received a defective copy of a program. Many will also send you information on new and, it is hoped, improved versions of your software that you can order, often at a special reduced price since you already own an earlier release. Such offers are sometimes as low as 20 to 25 percent of the actual retail price. You may also receive information on other products offered by that company, sometimes with the option to buy at a reduced price. The license agreement also gives information about the actual ownership of the software (some software is leased rather than sold), any permissible copying, other legal uses of the software, and your legal rights.

### ◆ Renting Software

Some companies rent software packages so you can test them before actually purchasing them. The rental fees are usually a fraction of the full purchase price, but you will likely have only a relatively short time to examine the package. If you do rent with the idea of possibly purchasing the material, ask if the rental fees apply to the purchase price. Also, you probably will receive a used copy for inspection; if you decide to purchase the software, return the used copy and ask for a replacement. This costs you more in shipping charges but carries a smaller risk of receiving a worn, defective, or incomplete package. (Don't count on building up your software library by illegally copying rented packages; many are copy-protected while others are on CD-ROM format.)

### ◆ *Computer Viruses*

The danger of **software viruses,** hidden programs that can alter or destroy data, is an increasing concern to all computer users and will be discussed in detail in Chapter 7. Since viruses are spread intentionally, either as a not-so-funny joke or as a very destructive prank, there is no certain way to always avoid them. In a few cases, the original manufacturer's distribution disks have been infected, although this is extremely rare.

Use caution when acquiring software. Buy from established dealers or from those who have tested all disks for viruses. Dealing with questionable sources or third parties can be risky. Also, renting, borrowing, or pirating software carries significantly increased dangers of infection. To be safe, never accept a disk if you are not sure of its history. If in doubt, ask if it has been tested for viruses. If you are still unsure, look elsewhere.

## ▸ Buying Hardware

Although you should select your software first and then the hardware that can handle it, circumstances may dictate that the hardware will determine where you buy your basic system. A basic familiarity with hardware brand names leads people to look for hardware and then try to fit the software to it.

### ◆ *Tested and Name Brands*

Be cautious when it comes to products that are new to the market. This includes both computers and accessories that are either from a manufacturer who is just entering the computer business or represent a new concept or technology. Such equipment may be fine, but it will not have experienced the user testing of older models and may be less reliable. This is not necessarily the fault of the manufacturer. Whereas most products are thoroughly tested before release, problems are often found only after actual use.

Many people are also more comfortable with a brand name that they recognize. You can often find as good or even better products from less well-known companies, sometimes at substantially lower prices. You should not necessarily eliminate these from your choices, but if you do not know certain manufacturers, check to verify their reputation and determine how long they have been making microcomputers or accessories.

To perform a fast check, first look for any current reviews of the company or its products which may have been done by *Consumer Reports* or many of the major computer magazines. Then compare these to similar reviews from the past several years. (Back issues of the same reviews should be in the local library.) Look for any trends either up or down. Finally, a good indication of the financial stability of the company can be obtained by making a spot check of the financial section of the newspaper for the past few years.

### ◆ *"Too Good to Be True" Usually Is*

Be careful of unusually low priced or vaguely described products. Some retailers try to get the competitive edge on prices by removing certain standard accessories such as manuals, cables, or even the operating system, which they then offer to you at an additional cost as required extras. Beware of "quality" products. These may indeed be of fine quality, but they may also be cheap imitations. Unusually low prices may also indicate reconditioned or refurbished equipment, although such products may be fine, especially if they have been factory rebuilt and are backed by a good warranty. Normally, the warranty on such equipment should be similar to that on an equivalent new system. Very low priced systems may indicate one or more inferior components or substitutions for the manufacturer's original parts.

### ◆ Used Equipment

Be very cautious here. You may not be protected by a warranty, and you could end up with out-of-date equipment for which it is difficult to find software or service. Most computer stores do not deal in used systems, but a few may have a trade-in or demonstration model to sell as used, or know of other customers who are ready to upgrade and need to sell their present system. If you buy a used system through a dealer, try to get the same warranty and benefits that come with a comparable new system. There is, however, a ready market for private sales between individuals.

### ◆ Warranty Cards

As with software, be certain to complete and return any registration or warranty cards that come with your hardware even if your system will be serviced locally. You can never be sure when conditions will change. You may move to another city, or your local dealer could stop local service or go out of business entirely. Registration with the manufacturer and your sales receipts will help you verify your qualification for service under the warranty should it be needed.

Look carefully at the manufacturer's product specifications. These are valuable when checking on the general capabilities of a given product as well as when comparing similar products. This can be tricky and deceiving. One printer may advertise a print speed of 120 cps (characters per second) while another claims only 60 cps. Are these for the same type of print? The latter could be faster for your needs if it is for **correspondence** (letter quality) mode while the former is for **draft** mode.

## ▶ Buying Supplies

You will need printer paper, floppy disks, tapes, printer ribbons, storage units for disks, and other odds and ends. There are many more sources for this material than for your hardware or software. You may wish to purchase your supplies from your dealer, but there is no good reason why you should not seek out the best buys for such items.

Wherever you purchase your supplies, be certain of two things: First, check to see that the specifications for an item match those suggested by the hardware or software manufacturers. For example, if your computer's floppy disk drive uses 3½-inch, double-sided, high-density (DS/HD) disks, be sure the disks you get are marked as such. Or when buying a printer ribbon, check both the brand and model number for a match.

Second, computer supplies can be misleading. Very tiny differences in quality can make the difference between success and failure or a satisfactory or unsatisfactory job. Be careful about buying sensitive items such as disks and tapes that are either very inexpensive or manufactured by an unknown company. These items might be satisfactory for occasional backup work but may have a higher failure rate in heavy use. Likewise, the quality of the paper or ribbon that you use could make a significant difference in the appearance of your printouts.

# ▶ Types of Retailers

Several types of retailers offer a varying range of services and support both before and after a sale. In general, the number and variety of services offered is usually directly related to the prices charged; that is, the larger the discount, the fewer services will be available. But there are considerations other than cost that may also be of concern in making your decision.

## ◆ Full-Service

These stores offer a complete range of support and services for the systems they sell, including promising a well-trained and knowledgeable sales staff, the availability of special training, post-purchase support, and local service. All of these services may not be free with every purchase but, if needed, can be obtained through the dealer. Many dealers will even deliver your new system to your home, set it up, and check that everything is working properly.

It is in this type of store that you are most likely to receive the most detailed, one-to-one help in making your selections or designing a system to fit your needs. You may be able to actually try out a custom system similar to one you are considering. Full-service retailers are normally small, local computer or electronics stores. Many of these stores have a limited inventory or may specialize in a certain type of system but may not offer a very wide variety of products from which to choose.

Full-service retailers also tend to be the most expensive because of the extra services they provide to their customers. They normally price items near or at the full manufacturer's suggested retail price, and with potential extra costs for training, support, or maintenance contracts, a total system cost can balloon significantly. However, some offer free post-purchase support and maintenance for a limited period (usually from as little as thirty days to as much as one full year), the value of which should not be overlooked.

## ◆ Limited-Service

Here you will find a number of services available, such as a reasonably knowledgeable sales staff or service department. Training or post-purchase support may not be offered. Prices may be somewhat lower than at a full-service store because of the fewer services available, but often the services that have been eliminated are the ones that cost extra in the first place.

Most chain computer stores are of this type, as are many electronics, some department, and a few discount stores. They often carry a much larger inventory than the smaller, full-service dealers. This permits them to provide a larger variety of demonstration systems for you to try. Whereas specific system customization is usually possible in these stores, it is more often due to the wider selection of components available than to direct, one-to-one counseling.

### ◆ Over-the-Counter

This arrangement provides that you simply buy whatever you want directly off the shelf without the benefit of a sales staff or a demonstration. There may be systems or individual components set up for you to examine, but you will be on your own. Normally, no extra services are offered, although most provide an exchange or sometimes even a refund for defective merchandise. The selection is very good at some of these stores, especially for some types of software. Some department and discount stores as well as warehouse clubs and many mail-order services are of this type.

### ◆ No-Frills

Here you may not even have a store to browse through in making your selection. Most of these stores sell by mail and have little or no actual computers on display in the store. You will likely get the best prices from these retailers, but you take the highest risk as well. The wide selection offered is extremely tempting to buyers who are looking for bargains or hard-to-find items, but do your research elsewhere before trying the "no-frills" approach.

### ◆ Direct from Manufacturer

An increasing number of manufacturers, including Compaq, IBM, and Zeos, are now offering their products through direct-to-consumer sales, a trend pioneered by Dell and Gateway. Most offer a wide variety of choices, some even very detailed customization options. This does not necessarily get you a cheaper price. Although many bargains are available this way, such sales are frequently near or at the product's suggested retail price. By ordering directly from the manufacturer, however, you may be able to obtain certain advantages that are not available from a retailer, such as a trial period or on-site service.

### ◆ Mail-Order

This is an increasingly popular way to acquire computer equipment. The variety of retailers is mind boggling, ranging from dealers who will work with you to customize a system much like a full-service dealer to those who want to just take your order and ship the boxes and bill—not necessarily in that order. You can get virtually anything by mail-order that you can get locally; likewise, the same cautions and common sense approach should apply.

If you are willing to shop around, you will likely find the lowest prices through mail-order, but this could also be a high-risk option. Before you order, do your homework and know what you are going to get. Also, not only do you risk an item's being damaged in shipment, but there is the difficulty of dealing with a seller by long distance. Should there be a problem with a product and you do not feel the store is treating you fairly, you do have certain very specific rights as a mail-order customer, but an uncooperative retailer can make life miserable until you force a resolution to the situation.

## ▶ Your Local Market

Your local retailer is likely to be very important to you in two ways: (1) It may be a very significant source of information as you are gathering data and deciding on a system, and (2) Most people eventually purchase their equipment from a local dealer. The lure of the lower prices offered by mail-order companies entices many people away from their local store. Before buying by mail, you should consider that in return for the reduced costs you may sacrifice some degree of support, carry-in service, or other benefits or conveniences that are provided by local stores.

There is generally a trade-off between services and price. If you want a fully staffed store that offers a wide range of support, then you are likely to have to pay extra for it. If you feel that you will need this type of assistance, then the extra cost may be worth it to you in the long run. If you tend to be a do-it-yourselfer, and believe that you can get your system up and running by yourself, then you may be happy with an over-the-counter or no-frills dealer. Of course, you do not have to purchase everything from one source. You could very well purchase the hardware and basic software from a full-service store and some of your extras from a less expensive source. You could also shop around and assemble your system from a variety of places to obtain the best value.

There is one very significant advantage in purchasing all the major components of your system from one dealer, especially if it is a complex system or one that you intend to expand. If one dealer sells you your entire system, then it *should* be able to ensure compatibility and service for the individual components. If you purchase a computer from one store and a printer from another, and then discover that they do not communicate properly, each store may very well blame the other and send you back and forth between them. Also, should you decide to expand or upgrade, your dealer should have a record of your system and be able to assist you so that you can maintain your system's integrity and internal compatibility.

If you go to a certain dealer to gather information and find the staff to be very helpful, straightforward, and honest, you might be well-advised to consider that store for your purchases. Many buyers make the mistake of looking at the stores that provide information freely and then going down the street to buy their system from a discounter for a few dollars less. They later wonder why they have problems getting assistance or service when they need it.

If you would like to deal with a local full-service dealer, but cannot resist the temptation of the lower prices of a discount or mail-order store, ask your local proprietor if he would agree to cut his prices if you agree to waive some of the benefits that go with the sale, such as support and training. You may find that some of the smaller, locally owned retailers are willing to deal in order to make a sale and boost their business.

There are now a number of nationwide chain stores that carry computer systems. These stores offer some advantages over locally owned dealers, such as lower prices, a larger inventory, and continuity in case you move. However, you may find that the local retailer is better equipped to provide the individual support and service you need. The chain store may be a more stable dealer, but the local retailer might be able to give you more personal attention. Again, take someone with you who has purchased a computer system for their own personal use to lend support.

## ▶ Assessing the Need for Support

Even the most experienced computer user needs help at some time, which is one reason many companies provide telephone support lines. Before selecting a dealer or computer brand, it is very important for you to consider carefully the level of post-purchase support you might need.

Some companies provide a minimum level of assistance free of charge; however, you may find that you have to pay a hefty amount for any intensive or extended support. Classes or other special training sessions are almost always at additional cost. If you decide that you want extended support, then carefully comparison-shop for that as well.

Do not forget to include your need for service in your considerations of support. Clearly, everyone wants to have service available, but there may be many levels ranging from shipping an item back to the manufacturer to on-site service. Again, the more convenience or support you receive, the likelier you are to pay for it.

## ▶ Gathering Information

Research and gather information about the computer dealers that you are considering. When you visit a store or talk with a sales representative over the phone, consider the following points and make inquiries where necessary.

*Helpfulness.* Is the sales staff willing to assist you? Can they and do they answer your questions?

*Demonstrations.* Can you see and use a demonstration model of the system you want before actually making your purchase? This may not be as important when all components are supplied by the same manufacturer. However, compatibility is sometimes not universal, especially when brands are mixed and the system relies on so-called plug compatibility.

*Competency.* Do you feel that the sales staff is well qualified and competent? Do you have confidence in what you are being told? If not, seek another opinion. It is a good idea to ensure that you will be satisfied with the service and support staff as well.

*Honesty.* Do you feel that you are being treated honestly? If you have the impression that you are being pressured to buy additional equipment or a larger system than you originally planned, then you might need to reconsider this dealer. Beware of fast-talking salespersons and substitute components.

***Competitiveness.*** Are the prices competitive with other stores of a similar type? Don't avoid a local full-service dealer because he cannot meet the prices of a discount or mail-order store. A variation of a few dollars in the price of an item that may cost several hundred dollars should not be considered significant if all else is satisfactory.

***Reputation.*** What do you know of a store's reputation? Aside from prices, a retailer's reputation for overall business practices is very important when considering any significant purchase. If you are unsure of a store, check it out with the Better Business Bureau or other sources. This is especially important when considering a purchase from a mail-order dealer.

***Support.*** Will the dealer provide support for your system should you need it after the sale? If so, is it free? If not, what are the rates and conditions? Exactly what does this support cover? It should cover everything you purchase from the dealer. If it does not, be careful; unsupported items can serve as a loophole to void or avoid support, or even service, for otherwise covered components.

If you are purchasing part or all of your system from a mail-order dealer or directly from the manufacturer, don't forget to check on any promised support from these companies. Don't assume that your worries are over just because you are provided with a toll-free telephone number to call in case of trouble.

Do not assume just because the person on the other end of the phone represents a major company that he or she is accurate. You might be surprised to learn how much misinformation is given out by support personnel over these toll-free lines. When you call a number, try to have a few simple test questions to ask the person answering the phone.

***Training.*** If necessary, inquire about special training to learn how to operate your new system properly. Ask when it will be available and at what cost. Find out how many hours it will take and what it will cover.

***Service.*** Does the seller service all parts of your system after the sale? If not, where can you get service? Most modern microcomputers are very reliable and usually operate for a long time (often years) between breakdowns, but should a problem occur, you don't want to have to ship a component to a service center in another city if you can avoid it. Some regional service centers are notorious for their long delays (sometimes months) in returning items.

***Service Contracts.*** If you purchase a complex or expensive system that will see heavy use in demanding or sensitive applications, you *might* want to consider a service contract. Such contracts frequently run about 10 percent or more of the total cost of the insured components per year. (Some dealers will not sell contracts, whereas others will issue them only on entire systems.)

If you think that such a contract might be for you, *be sure that you know exactly what you are getting.* Some contracts include *parts only* or apply to *carry-in service only.* Many others may not apply if the failure is of a certain type or from certain causes. Or, you may have to pay a fee if no problem is found or if the difficulty is discovered to be because of your error in operating the system. Still others have tricky "void" clauses.

Service contracts are probably not a wise investment except possibly for those engaged in the most intensive and critical applications (such as in certain businesses), and then they should be entered into only with a company that has a good reputation and that has earned your confidence. The bottom line: read the fine print.

# ▶ After the Purchase

***Understand All Charges on an Invoice.*** Be sure to get an *itemized* bill that shows each item purchased along with its cost. Any charges for less tangible things, such as support, training, service contracts, shipping, processing, and taxes, should also be shown. Verify its accuracy before issuing any payments. Keep a copy of all sales transactions for future reference. If there is a problem or you have to make a claim for warranty service, then you may be asked to prove when and where you bought the item(s).

***Know What to Expect.*** If you are to receive any post-purchase services, whether free or paid, be sure you understand when, where, how much, and to what extent each will be provided. This also applies if any part of your system is to be supplied at a later date.

***Report Equipment Problems.*** At any time, especially within warranty periods, it is very important to report problems to your dealer or local service center as soon as you discover them. Most such places record only the date that the problem is reported rather than sourcing it from the date it actually occurred, if different.

# ▶ Private Sales of Used Computers and Components

You may get lucky and find a real gem such as an almost new, state-of-the-art system for a bargain price. But, in general, you should search for used computers in the same way you would anything else, thoroughly checking each component and feature as to its suitability for your individual needs. Remember that you are buying a system that someone else has decided to discard for some reason.

Nearly everything you find available will fall into one of three general categories.

First, there will be those systems that no longer function, either totally or in part. This is the biggest pitfall. You would be well-advised to avoid anything that is not in good working order, even if you believe that the repairs are minor. Often, even a seemingly insignificant part for an older system can be very difficult, if not impossible, to locate. You may end up searching for other used systems just for parts or upgrading the entire system, eventually paying more than you would have for a new system.

Second, there are many systems, such as early models of Commodore, Apple (not Macintosh), Atari, Radio Shack, Texas Instruments, and many CP/M based systems, that still function but are no longer supported by software or hardware manufacturers. Although primitive by today's standards, some of these computers have much to offer and may serve adequately in some situations, but further expansion, or even repair in the case of a serious failure, may be impossible. (One resource for older computers is through the few remaining user's groups that still exist to support these systems.)

Third, there are literally millions of older models of IBM, IBM-compatible, and Macintosh systems that are up for sale for one reason or another. Maybe the system has a defect or possibly the present owner simply needs a more powerful system. In any case, it will generally be true that the various parts of the system will not be the latest technology. The processor or graphics may be one or two or more steps behind what is presently offered in the computer stores. This is not in itself a reason to avoid a purchase, but be warned that many older systems will not run some software programs written for the newer, faster processors and higher-resolution graphics.

Tables 6.1 and 6.2 are provided to assist you in comparing many of the older processors and graphics displays to more up-to-date systems.

Sometimes, you can find a feature in an older component that may inexpensively serve your needs. For example, if you need good quality print but neither need the versatility nor can justify the cost of a laser printer, you might look at a used **daisy wheel** printer. This type of printer works much like an electronic typewriter, with interchangeable printing elements called **printwheels.**

There is one special precaution relating to older dot-matrix printers. Some older (before about 1985) models may be disappointing to you in more than just the overall print quality. Some models do not print true **descenders,** which are required for several lowercase letters such as *p* and *y* that extend below the line. Here is a comparison of a line printed with and without descenders.

With descenders: Now, jump quickly and be gone!

Without descenders: Now, J̇umP ꟼuicklУ and be ꝶone!

| Table 6.1 | **Selected Older Processors** | |
|---|---|---|
| **Chip** | **Speed (MHz)** | **Word (bits)** |
| IBM–Compatibles | | |
| 8086 | 4–8 | 16 |
| 8088 | 4–8 | 16 |
| 80286 | 6–16 | 16 |
| 386DX | 16–40 | 32 |
| 386SX | 16–25 | 32 |
| 386SL | 20–25 | 32 |
| Apples and Others | | |
| Z80 | 1–4 | 8 |
| 6502 | 1 | 8 |
| 65C816 | 3 | 16 |
| 68000 | 8 | 16 |
| 68020 | 8–16 | 32 |
| 68030 | 16–40 | 32 |

Such print may be acceptable if you do not plan to print very much in lowercase. However, it can be very annoying to read. Many professionals such as publishers discourage or reject this or any other type of poorly produced print, and you will likely find it unsatisfactory for any text-oriented uses such as word processing.

***The Sale.*** Almost everyone has participated in some sort of private sale transaction, yet the courts are jammed with cases involving people who have been burned, robbed, and ripped off. Here are a few simple guidelines for private sales:

◆ Exercise caution. If it doesn't "feel" right, leave it and move on to another seller.

◆ Ask why the item is for sale. Get a sense as to whether or not the reasons given are feasible and believable.

◆ If it is a software package, do not accept a duplicate disk unless you know that it is public domain or shareware material. Selling duplicates of copyrighted software is against federal law, and you could become implicated should the seller be caught doing anything illegal. Also, since you cannot be certain of the origin or history of any such disks, there is the added concern of one or more being infected by a virus.

◆ If it is a local sale, insist that you see and check out the equipment. If it is a through-the-mail deal, insist on a ten-day return privilege. If either

| Table 6.2 | **Selected Older Graphics Displays** | | |
|---|---|---|---|
| **Monitor and Graphics Card** | **Number of Pixels** **Horizontal** | **Vertical** | **Colors Displayed** |
| Monochrome | | | |
| Hercules | 720 | 348 | 2 |
| MDA | 720 | 350 | 2 |
| Macintosh (early) | 512 | 342 | 2 |
| Color | | | |
| CGA | 320 | 200 | 4 |
| MCGA | 320 | 200 | 16 |
| EGA | 640 | 350 | 16 |
| PGA | 640 | 480 | 256 |
| Apple II e/c | 280 | 192 | 6 |
| Apple IISG | 320 | 240 | 256 |
| Apple (double-high) | 560 | 192 | 16 |
| Macintosh II Series | 640 | 480 | 256 |

request is refused, you should proceed with extreme caution, if at all.

◆ *Know exactly what you will be getting.* If you are still uncertain about what you may be getting, ask to see the manuals and specifications for the hardware and software to resolve any questions you may have. (Having the system checked out by someone knowledgeable in computers is also a possibility.)

◆ Bring someone along who knows something about computers—someone you trust.

◆ The conditions of the sale, in writing, should include an exact statement of all provisions: what you will receive, what you will pay, any warranty or return privilege, the signatures (with addresses and phone numbers) of all involved parties, and the date.

If you are interested in this type of venture, you can consult the classified ads of your local newspapers for possible buys. Some national magazines such as *Computer Shopper* are also valuable sources of possible sellers. With the increasing number of used systems becoming available from both individuals and businesses wanting to upgrade, national exchanges are beginning to appear that attempt to match the needs of the buyer with the seller.

# Set up, Use, Maintain, and Care for Your Computer

Most of what you should do to maintain your computer system and your data files in good condition requires only a little more than common sense; however, computers do present a few unique needs and sensitivities that you should be aware of and understand.

## ▶ Setting up Your System

Your computer and all of its components will need access to a reliable supply of electricity. If you use a multiplug power strip or conditioner, a single outlet is usually sufficient. However, this outlet should not be shared or on the same line with electrical equipment, such as an air conditioner, refrigerator, electric dryer, or power tool, that draws a strong current and cycles on and off. If you find this to be a consideration, a good, heavy-duty power conditioner should help to eliminate power fluctuations. (Most large computers in business and industry are placed on a separate, dedicated line to prevent any such interference.)

If you will be using a modem or FAX board, you need to have a telephone jack nearby. If you will be transferring a large amount of material by this method, you may want a separate line; otherwise you should be able to use an extension of your regular phone line. With auto-answer/auto-dial (AA/AD) modems, it is not necessary to have a telephone by the computer, although it is often convenient.

All printers make some noise, but some can be very distracting or painfully loud. Under certain conditions, you might possibly run a long cable and place the printer in a secluded place, but this would not be very convenient for most uses. A better solution might be to use a sound baffle, an attachment that fits over the top of the printer and suppresses much (but not all) of the printing noise.

Personal computers do not require the rigorous environmental controls that their older and larger ancestors demanded. As a basic rule of thumb, if you are comfortable, your computer probably is as well. Extremes in temperature and humidity should be avoided whenever possible. A much greater hazard is physical contamination. Besides dust, possibly the greatest potential gremlin for computer equipment is cigarette (or other) smoke.

Today, computers are generally very sturdy. Precaution and prevention are the best maintenance procedures. If you have several options for placing your computer, it would be wise to avoid rooms that have many open windows or an active fireplace. Try to locate your system away from windows or direct drafts. The continuous humidity from a large window, kitchen, or bathroom could eventually cause a problem, as could the airborne particles produced by food preparation. Find a spot where the system is permanently set and placed out of the usual traffic patterns, in order to avoid any physical damage from being accidentally bumped or knocked over.

If you buy your computer system from a full-service store, it is possible that they will set up and test it for you. You may also receive training. However, an increasing number of people are buying their equipment from stores, or via mail order, that offer a lower price and consequently fewer or no services. If this is the case, you'll find yourself with a number of boxes, manuals, and sometimes all-too-confusing and inadequate instructions. When you unpack, assemble, and test the system, take your time and be organized.

### ◆ Unpacking

As you open each box, remove the contents very carefully. Check all of the packing materials, especially any Styrofoam supports, for accessory items such as power cords, connecting cables (some components may have more than one of these), papers (such as warranties and supplemental or updated instructions), printer ribbons, demonstration or test diskettes, and small items such as extra fuses and screws. Many manufacturers are ingenious at concealing small but often vital components in little pockets in the Styrofoam packing or hiding them in the bottom of the carton. Nothing is irreplaceable, but some items can take an annoyingly long time to get. It is not a bad idea to keep a list of what you find in each box for future reference in case of loss.

Double-check to verify that all items are exactly what you thought you were getting regarding manufacturer, model, features, and capacity or size. Be on guard for words such as "rebuilt" or "refurbished" on items you thought were new.

### ◆ Inspection

Check everything very carefully for damage or defects. Internal damage within a box can occur during shipment even if there are no apparent external signs of mishandling.

Do not rely on an invoice, itemized sales receipt, or packing list to check if the system is complete. Consult the manuals for the components. These usually list the specific contents, including all standard items but possibly not those that were added after the manual was printed, such as corrections or additions to the manual itself.

Do not discard the boxes and shipping materials. These are essential if you need to ship a component to a service center. Even if your local store does this for you, it is still better to use the original cartons for shipment. Should you move, packing the computer system will be a lot easier if you hold on to all of the original shipping materials and boxes.

## ◆ *Read the Manuals*

It cannot be emphasized enough that before you connect the various components, you must read the manuals. These will tell you exactly how and where to connect the various cables. There may also be certain DIP (described later in this chapter) or other switch settings that must be made before a component will function properly. Disks may need to be **formatted** or possibly **partitioned** before they can be used. Also, the operating system may have to be installed. The instructions for all of these tasks are found in the system manuals.

You may wish to install auxiliary boards now, but if they are not essential to the operation of the system, it would be best to verify that the basic system functions properly first. Install the boards later and check each, one at a time. Should a problem arise, the fewer items you have to check and eliminate, the easier it will be for you to locate the offending component.

## ◆ *Cables*

Your computer may come supplied with all the connecting cables you need, or your dealer may make them for you. If some or all the cables come with your system and you discover one is missing, damaged, or even too short, don't panic. Check with the store where you bought the system and see if they can help; in most cases they should be able to assist you. If that fails, you might contact the manufacturer and ask for a replacement. This could take some time.

If neither of these sources proves productive or practical, contact any local dealer who handles that model computer to see if they can provide a replacement. If that is not successful, any computer (and almost any electronics) store with a service department should be able to make a new one for you. They will need to know the type of ports, pin configurations, and communications protocols, which should be in your manuals. If you cannot find the right information or are in doubt, bring the manuals for each component to be connected to the service department.

## ◆ *Assembly*

Once you are sure that each part of the system has been properly set up, you are ready to make the necessary connections. Check that each cable is plugged into the proper port and that it fits securely. If there are screws or clips to secure the connection, *use them.* Most components have a separate power cord. These should first be connected to the equipment and then plugged into the AC power outlet.

### ◆ Testing

Now you are ready to turn on each part of the system and see how it functions. If your computer comes with a special test or demonstration disk, that is a good place to begin. Otherwise, you need to use one or more of your software packages. It would probably be better to start with the simpler and easier packages to eliminate additional complications in case of a problem.

Check to see that each component of the system functions properly. In addition to verifying that all the hardware is in proper working order, you should also check to see that all software loads and runs properly. This does not mean that you need to verify the proper operation of every feature of every item; there will be time for that later. Perform basic checks to see that each component works in a general manner. If an item appears not to function, recheck everything and try again.

### ◆ Report Damage

If you find any damaged items or any that do not work properly even after going through all available checks and troubleshooting procedures, *report the problem immediately* to the retailer where you bought the item. If you delay, it could adversely affect the action your seller will take. Nearly any seller will replace a damaged or defective item if it is reported promptly after the sale. However, if you wait weeks or months to inform the seller of the problem, he may then (with justification) decide to treat it as a breakdown that occurred after you received the item. In the case of software where there is no warranty or where the warranty has expired, you may have to replace or repair it at your own expense.

# ▶ Start-up

Don't expect to do everything at once. Take it slowly. Learn the basics first, so that you understand how your system operates. This way you will be better able to discover the causes of any problems and resolve them. When the computer and all its parts are up and running, the operating system, the applications software you are using, and the printer or other additional components will be interacting together simultaneously. Sometimes the source of a problem is immediately clear, but other times it is very difficult for even a trained service technician to discover the offending part. The better you know your system, the easier it will be for you to diagnose problems and serve as your own service person, saving on unnecessary service charges.

*Don't try to install or run all your application software at first.* Concentrate on one or two programs. You can then test each program in turn as you become comfortable with the ones you have tried. If you are not familiar with the computer's operating system, that should probably be the first task to tackle.

Start simply. Turn on only the computer. Study some of the operating system commands, such as how to list the contents of a directory on an IBM-compatible (folder on a Macintosh) or change from one drive to another. Read your manual. It will instruct you on the importance and procedure of making immediate backups of your system disks. You should do this *immediately* before doing any experimenting on your original disks. Once you are comfortable with the operating system, you can then begin to look at some of your other software. This one-step-at-a-time approach also applies to the hardware. The printer can wait until you know what you are doing with the computer and the software that will be addressing it.

## ◆ *System Boot*

A system boot is merely the process of bringing the system into a condition where it is ready for use. When you turn on the computer, it initiates what is known as a system boot. The computer reads from the disk and brings into memory the part of the operating system (the **bootstrap**) that is necessary to make the system function. Please note that a few computers maintain their bootstrap internally on a **ROM** chip and boot without a disk. On most computers there are normally two ways to accomplish a boot: the **cold boot**, which is the type of boot that occurs when the computer is turned on from a power-off condition, and the **warm boot**, which is done while the computer is on. The warm boot can usually be accomplished directly from the keyboard or by using a special Reset button located somewhere on the computer. The latter is a nice convenience but is sometimes not effective in error conditions.

You may expect a pause between the time you first turn on the power and the time the system is actually ready to use. This pause, which depends on the system, is caused by several factors: The boot disk has to be "brought up to speed" before being addressed. The computer has to load the bootstrap into memory. Most systems go through a series of self-tests and diagnostics before they release control to you. There is often a **batch file** (see following) that loads additional commands into memory.

A disk must be present in order to boot the system in nearly all computers. If you use an internal (hard) disk for this, as most computers do, this is usually automatic when you turn on the system. If you use a floppy disk (or wish to boot your hard disk system from a floppy), you must have a floppy disk in the drive (and the drive door closed on 5¼-inch drives) when you boot the system. Also, this disk *must* contain the bootstrap. Most application software does not come with the operating system already on it. In fact, there is often no room to add it. For this reason, if you will be booting from a floppy, you need to have handy *at least one* **boot diskette** that contains the operating bootstrap. You might wish to add to this disk any other operating system files that you find useful—such as those for formatting or copying disks; copying, renaming, or deleting files; checking the disk status; and so forth.

As your computer comes to life, it makes some noises that will soon become familiar to you. These beeps, whirs, and rumbles should not concern you unless one day you hear something unusual or clearly alarming. You will know that the boot process is complete when you see the **system prompt** on the screen. The nature of this prompt varies from one type of computer to another and may even be different for two computers of the same type if one has been customized by the dealer. But in general the prompt ranges from a simple symbol such as **A:>** or **C:>** to a full-screen **menu.** Once the prompt appears, you are ready to proceed.

## ◆ *Batch Files*

Many new computer users initially feel that batch files are only for computer experts, and they are not likely to have much use for them. That is a misconception. Batch files are simple to write and can be helpful to even the most inexperienced user.

A batch file is a special type of file that causes one or more operations to be performed by the computer in a specified sequence. Whereas there are times when a batch file is used to perform a single operation, normally it is used to do more than one. The procedure is simple. When the file is run, the computer executes the first job in the file. When that is completed, it returns to the batch file and executes the second job, and so forth until all the jobs in the file are completed. In this manner the computer can be instructed to perform a series of tasks without your having to be physically at the keyboard to type in each one as the preceding one is completed.

Batch files can usually be executed anytime the computer is operating. Probably the most common example is the file that is used to add instructions or programs to memory at the end of the boot procedure. This type of file is provided for nearly all types of computers; it is referred to as the AUTOEXEC.BAT file on an IBM-compatible system, and we will use that as an example.

Perhaps you wish to check (or possibly set) the time and date when your computer is turned on to ensure that they are correct. You can do this manually by typing DATE and TIME at the prompt. Let us assume you have three programs that increase the efficiency of your memory, disks, and printer operations, and you wish to load them into memory to make your system work faster. This might be done by typing MEMORY, CACHE, and SPOOLER at the prompt. Perhaps you have a shell program that shows you all the programs on your disk and assists you with routine operating system commands. We will call this SHELL. In order to accomplish all of this, you have to type all six commands every time you boot the computer. A batch file prevents you from having to do that repetitive task.

All you have to do is type the programs *once* into a file called AUTOEXEC.BAT, as you would if you were doing it manually at the prompt. You can do this with any word processor that can create ASCII text files or a simple editor. The file would look something like at the left:

```
SPOOLER
DATE
TIME
MEMORY
CACHE
SPOOLER
SHELL
```

If this file is placed on your boot disk (in the root directory), it will be run routinely every time the system is booted. These six commands are then executed for you automatically, and you never have to type the sequence again. The system will still pause for you to check and, if necessary, correct the date and time just as if you had entered these commands manually. You may, of course, change the file at any time. This is an example of a batch file.

Other batch files can be created and placed on any disk and named almost anything. They can be made to pause for your instructions at various points or to accept variables such as file names, switches, or other parameters for processing. With some imagination and experience you can become proficient and creative with batch files and save yourself much time and many keystrokes. Refer to your operating system manual for details on writing batch files for your system.

## ◆ *Menus*

A **menu** on a computer is a list of what you may do under that particular program. Many application programs operate from menus. You may even elect to run your entire system from a **shell** program that permits you to control your system directly from menu options. You will often find that you have to move through several levels of menus before you get to the function you want. Opinions regarding the usefulness of menus vary, but beginners normally find them much more user-friendly than trying to remember a series of individual commands.

Here is a simple example of a **menu-driven** program with an **integrated package** on your system that performs several different tasks. When calling up a program, you are presented with an initial list of options available in the form of a menu that might look something like at the left:

```
GENERIC SOFTWARE
1. Work with Document
2. Work with Spreadsheet
3. Work with Data Base
4. Work with Graphics
5. Access Phone with Modem
6. Use File Utilities
7. Customize Options
8. Exit to System
Enter Number or Letter of Selection: _
```

From this menu you can see the program functions that are available. All you do is select the number or emphasized (or "bold") letter of the option that you want and enter it. For example, to enter a data base, you'd either type in the number "3" or the letter "B." (Some menus may provide only numbers or letters but not both.)

One of two things will then happen. Either you will be taken directly to that function, or you will be presented with a second menu. For example, if you select Option 2 (or **S**) above, you would then see the traditional spreadsheet screen ready to receive data. In the case of "5" (or "M"), your modem would be initialized for use, and you would be ready to make a call to another computer

If you choose "U" (or "6"), you would be presented with a second menu that lists the available file utilities. This second menu might look something like this:

```
FILE UTILITIES
1. Print File
2. Copy Files
3. Rename a File
4. Delete Files
5. Import file
6. Export file
7. Return to Main Menu
Enter Number or Letter of Selection: _
```

Clearly, menus could go through many levels, but if you find a program that goes beyond three levels, it is probably unnecessarily complex, and there is likely a better choice.

Some menus might make use of a highlighted bar that you can move along the option list using the arrow keys until you find the option you want. You can then indicate your choice by hitting the ENTER (or RETURN) key. Many permit the selection to be made with the mouse or track ball pointer. Other menus might make use of a split screen to offer more than one menu on the same screen or alternately a **window** to show useful information, possibly about your disk or the job you are currently doing. Still others may present a combination of these features or even more exotic display options.

One popular type of menu worth special mention is the **pull-down** (or **drop-down**) menu. This works the same in principle as any menu; however, it looks somewhat differently on the screen. Pull-down menus make use of a **menu bar** across the top of the screen. In the example of the menu for the integrated software labeled "GENERIC SOFTWARE," a menu bar might look something like below.

Because of space limitations, options are often designated by somewhat more cryptic entries on the menu bar.

| Document Spreadsheet DataBase Graphics Phone Utilities Options Exit |
|---|

A selection is made in the usual manner by using either the keyboard or mouse. Then, a second menu "drops down" from the selected option. As above, if we select "Utilities," the new menu might appear as follows:

The dots (. . .) that appear after three entries ("Print," "Import," and "Export") indicate that there is yet another menu level below this one. This is also frequently indicated by a pointer similar to ▶ or → at the right of the menu item.

| Document Spreadsheet DataBase Graphics Phone UTILITIES Options |
|---|

Print file . . .
Copy files
Rename file
Delete files

Import file . . .
Export file . . .

The line between "Delete files" and "Import files" is simply a separator line to group items with similar functions. Although not shown here, keyboard commands are often included next to the options on pull-down menus below the menu bar level. With the possible exception of the menu bar itself, all pull-down menus disappear once a selection has been made.

(Unfortunately, sometimes, the most attractive thing about certain programs is their menus. Never select a program simply because of an impressive menu display. Nevertheless, become comfortable with menus—they are pervasive among software today.)

### ◆ Running a Program

Running a software program is usually a simple matter. If possible, select a program that does not require an installation or configuration program to be run beforehand. Installation and configuration programs are normally used either to assist you with a difficult or lengthy installation or to transfer copy-protected software to your hard disk and to make some special modifications to the program. Such programs are sometimes long and involved and would best be avoided until you are more experienced and confident with your computer.

Once you have selected a program to run, make a backup copy before you try to run it. Instructions for making a backup are found in either your program manual or in your computer's operating system manual. When this is done, place the backup copy in the floppy disk drive. You may need to copy the program files to your hard disk, but sometimes you can run it directly from the floppy. (Programs run from a floppy disk may be very sluggish compared to those that are run from a hard disk.)

A program can usually be run just by entering a single command or making a single entry from an operating system shell menu. You will then get the program's menu or request for a command. If it is a menu, you can probably make some sense of it. If it is a request for a command, you will surely have to look at the manual for help. But in any case, reading the manual is always a good idea. (If you are in doubt, consult the disk label, disk directory, or manual for information on what to enter to start the program.)

You may be tempted to just experiment, but this is not always the best choice for a beginner. It is not likely that you will do any irreversible harm, but the chances of becoming frustrated and discouraged are at their peak at this time. Even a very small error may seem insurmountable to the novice user.

You will find that many programs perform several different functions. You may not be interested in all of them. Explore the available options one at a time. Learn about what interests you the most and become comfortable with those features of the package, then go on to another program. You can return later to explore the advanced and optional features after you have become more familiar with your system and the basic operation of all your other software. This approach also allows you to test and become acquainted with as much of your software as possible in the least amount of time.

### ◆ *Online Help*

Many programs now offer an online help function that provides varying degrees of assistance directly on the screen by just hitting a certain key or selecting a menu option. Help is usually in the form of a menu or block of text that appears somewhere on the screen until you hit another key to make it disappear. The amount of help varies with the program: It can be minimal and almost useless, or excellent and nearly as good as the manual itself. Also, such help may be available only at certain points in the program or may be found at nearly any time. Some programs have "smart," or **context-sensitive**, help that automatically gives you the proper help screen for whatever you are doing. Always check for help; it can be invaluable if available.

## ▸ Troubleshooting Hardware Problems

If your system is ready to go but you find that part or all of it doesn't work, don't panic and call for help (especially if you will be charged for it) until you first check a few simple things. The problem may be a loose connection or another simple oversight that is easy for you to correct once you locate it. Any experienced service technician can relate stories of systems that were "down" because a cable was loose or the power plug was disconnected. Service contracts or warranties do not cover problems that result from user carelessness.

You should always be alert for any unusual, erratic, or poor performance by any part of the system and check it immediately. Many of the manuals that accompany the hardware and software items offer suggestions for troubleshooting their products. Here are some additional guidelines.

***Isolate the Problem.*** If only part of the system works, then the first thing you should do is try to isolate the problem to a particular component. This will greatly simplify your troubleshooting tasks.

***Power Plugs.*** Be sure that all power cords are securely plugged into the power line and firmly attached to their respective component. In the latter case, sometimes the cords require a little extra push to become properly seated and make contact.

***On/Off Switches.*** Check that everything is turned on. Verify not only that the individual components are turned on but that the switches on any power strips are on as well. Many devices have a "power on" indicator light, and a few even beep when turned on. If in doubt, turn a component off and then back on (remembering to wait a few seconds in between).

***Fuses and Breakers.*** If all plugs and switches check out but there is still no sign of power, check for loose or bad fuses or thrown circuit breakers. These are found on most individual components as well as on all good power strips. If after replacing or resetting an offending fuse or breaker it continues to fail, do not persist; there may be a short somewhere. If the problem is with a piece of equipment, then it may be defective. If a power strip is the problem, you could be overloading it. Check the sum of the rated power requirements of all items plugged into it against its rated capacity.

***Proper Mode.*** Many components have one or more mode selection switches, buttons, or other controls. For example, most printers have an Online/Offline indicator that must show Online in order for them to receive data for printing. Verify that the proper modes are set.

***Drive Doors.*** If you are using a 5¼-inch floppy disk drive, be certain that the drive door is closed when it is in use; it will not function otherwise.

***Connectors and Pins.*** Check all connecting cables to be certain they are plugged into the correct ports and the connections are secure. You should be able to feel the cable slip into the port. Use the little screws or clips when available to secure the cables in place. If you are using RS-232-C or another type of connector that employs pins at the ends of the cables, check to see if any of the pins are bent or broken. Match the pattern against the one shown in the manuals to see if any pins are missing or possibly in the wrong position.

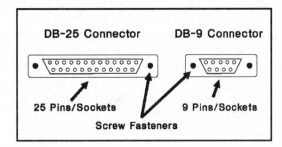

*Figure 7.1*
*The pin/socket*
*arrangements for*
*the most common*
*RS-232-C connectors.*

***Keyboard Lock.*** Many computers provide a key to lock the keyboard, preventing unauthorized access. If the computer has power but appears not to recognize the keyboard, check to see if it is locked out.

***Hardware or Software.*** It is very important to determine if the problem originates in the software or in the hardware. For example, if a printer fails to print with one package, try it with another before concluding that the trouble is the printer. It could be that the software is faulty, or it might be a communications problem between the two; possibly you need only to "tell" the software about your system or printer by using the **configuration program** or **setup menu** (described on page 147). Testing components directly from the operating system is the most effective way because it is less likely to encounter communications problems.

***Error Messages.*** Sometimes you may get an error message displayed on the screen or a control panel that can help you determine what the problem is. The key to these messages is usually found in the manual that accompanies the component. Keep a record of these messages. They may be the solution to the problem, but sometimes the message does not recur and is then lost.

***Reboot.*** If you get a persistent error message (especially from the computer itself) or another indicator of trouble, try a reboot or restart of the system by turning it off for a few seconds and then turning it back on and beginning all over. Occasionally your system may experience a **glitch**, which is a problem of unknown origin that does not recur. Also, computers sometimes "lock up," and you must reboot them to regain control. Please note that anytime you turn off an electronic component, always wait at least 15 seconds before turning it back on. Restoring the power immediately carries a small risk of causing a circuit failure.

On most systems, you may reboot in either of two ways: the cold boot from the power-off condition, or the warm boot from the keyboard or a Reset button with the power on. A warm boot is usually sufficient to eliminate error conditions, glitches, and locked systems, but in some cases the problem is not resolved until a cold boot is performed.

***Diagnostics and Test Patterns.*** You can often generate a helpful error message by using diagnostic routines or test patterns. If the problem appears to involve part of the computer or disk units and your computer comes with diagnostic routines, run these and see if you get an error code. If a component such as a printer or modem seems to be malfunctioning, look for an error code or light on its control panel. Many of these products have a self-test pattern that can sometimes be of help.

***Boards.*** If you have installed any extra boards in your computer, double-check all of these to be sure they are firmly seated in the correct slots. Be certain that none of the prongs or pins along the edge of the boards are bent, broken, or missing. If you can find no other obvious problem, remove the boards that you inserted and try the system without them. If it works, replace each, *one at a time,* and recheck the performance until you find the trouble.

***Communications.*** The computer and a peripheral must both be set to communicate at the same **baud** (see Chapter 5). For example, if a computer is set up at 9,600 baud for the printer port and 2,400 baud for the modem port, then the printer and modem must also be set to 9,600 and 2,400 baud, respectively. (The proper baud is usually determined by the peripheral and explained in the corresponding manual.) Other settings may have to be adjusted as well.

***Figure 7.2***
***A simplified drawing of a set of DIP switches.***

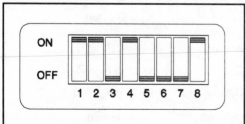

***DIP Switches.*** DIP (Dual In-line Packages) switches are commonly used to select various features, such as automatic modes, alternate character sets, emulation modes, bauds, and other communications protocols. Sometimes two or more switches are used to set a feature. These switches are normally located either at the rear of the unit, on or under a control panel, or under some other cover. The key to the numerous switch combinations is found in the operating manual for that component.

Many components have DIP or other switches that must be properly set. DIP switches are usually found in sets of eight in a row, each of which can be set to either On or Off. Sometimes several panels of DIP switches are present. See Table 7.1 for a simplified example of a typical DIP switch selection chart for a printer.

If you wish to use a parallel connection with Epson emulation and the standard ASCII character set, you would set the first three switches to Off, Off, and On, respectively. If you are uncertain about or don't understand some of the switch settings, leave them at the factory preset default positions since these are preferred by most users.

# ▸ Troubleshooting Software Problems

If your system hardware checks out and functions properly with some of your software packages but not with others, then the problem may well be with the software. This does not mean that it is necessarily defective; there are a number of possible problems and solutions.

***Error Messages.*** Note and record any error messages. These are usually listed and explained in the accompanying documentation. The presence of an error message is often an indication of a problem but not a defect, and it can be the clue to the source of the trouble and its solution.

***Reload.*** If a program does not load properly, try reloading it. Some computers or programs (or a particular combination) tend to be "temperamental" and may occasionally require more than one attempt to load. Reloading is a possible remedy anytime you experience a software failure.

***System and Version.*** If your computer runs more than one operating system or more than one release of the same operating system, be sure that each application software package is compatible with the operating system or version that you are currently using. (This is not a consideration for most computers and programs.)

If a program loads but does not appear to function properly, it is probably a communication problem, either between you and the software or between the software and part of the system. Software packages should run properly the first time on your computer. If you are having a consistent problem with most or all of your programs, then you may have a more seri-

| Table 7.1 | **DIP Switch Selection Chart** | |
|---|---|---|
| **Switch** | **Function if ON** | **Function if OFF** |
| 1 | Serial Mode | Parallel Mode |
| 2 | IBM Emulation | Epson Emulation |
| 3 | Standard ASCII Set | Extended ASCII Set |
| 4 | 8 1/2" Page Default | 8" Page Default |
| 5 | Automatic Line-Feed Advance with Each Carriage-Return | No Automatic Line-Feed |
| 6 | Skip 1/2" Space at Perforations | No Skip |
| 7 | Paper Out Signal | No Paper Out Signal |
| 8 | Print DEL Character | Ignore DEL Character |

ous difficulty. Either you are not performing the installations and operations of the programs correctly, or there is a compatibility problem somewhere within the system.

***Commands.*** Verify that commands are being entered correctly. For example, some programs require that all commands be entered using only uppercase letters. Also, do not confuse similar characters such as *0* (zero) and *O* (oh) and *1* (one) and *l* (el), which may be interchangeable on a typewriter but not on a computer keyboard.

***Responses.*** Be certain that your responses to program inquiries are proper. If you do not give a proper response to a question, some programs may not know what to do, usually resulting in unexpected (and possibly unwelcome) results.

***Protocols.*** There could be a difference in the way a program tries to address a part of your system, such as the printer or the monitor screen, and the way that components expect to be addressed. For example, the codes that a program sends to a printer to initiate different print fonts, pitches, and enhancements may not be the same as those that the printer requires. If this is the case and your software package does not have a configuration program (see following) that will solve the problem, contact the manufacturer to see if one has become available. If that fails, ask your dealer about having the software **patched**, or modified, so that it will use the proper codes.

It also could be that you do not have all the hardware required by the software. For example, if a program makes use of sound and your computer does not have that capability, then you cannot make use of that feature. The hardware and software must be compatible. If you have a VGA graphics board, for example, then the software must honor that graphics system. This cannot be patched.

***Configuration.*** Many of the professional-level packages come with a configuration or installation program that permits you to customize the specific package to your individual hardware. They allow you to specify things such as the type of terminal or printer you are using, communications protocols for modems, screen highlights (such as design and color), and specific codes for printer protocols. Unfortunately, even the best of these programs cannot anticipate and handle all users' needs and you may find that an installed version of a program still has some communications difficulties and may need to be patched. (In some cases, the configuration is accomplished through a "Setup" or "Options" menu selection within the main program.)

***Write-Protection.*** Another possibility is one that is more likely to occur after you have used your system for a while. This involves trying to write data to a disk or file that has been write-protected. If the problem seems to occur only when you attempt to save a file, check to see if the diskette has a write-protection tab in place or is otherwise guarded. Also, examine the file directory (see the next section) to see if it lists the file that you are working with as "R" or "R/O" (or some other designation for read-only) or another protected status.

***Re-install.*** As a final resort before returning a package or calling for support, try re-installing the program. It is possible that an error was made during installation or that something unexplained caused a fault to occur.

# ▶ Files and Data Organization

A computer stores information in a manner not too different from how you might do so in an office. As you read this section, think of an office (your computer) with a huge file cabinet (disk drive) containing many drawers. This cabinet is where information is placed for permanent storage. Your desk is much like the computer's main memory (RAM, or "on the board" memory). It is where you take a file (information) from the file cabinet to examine, replacing it when you are done. The file you put back in the file cabinet, like the computer file you save back to your disk, will contain whatever new information you've added. One advantage to a computer file, however, is that a copy of the file is always left on the disk (much like leaving a photocopy of an entire file in the file cabinet when you take it to your desk to work). If you should forget to save your changes to a computer file, you at least still have the previous version on the disk.

## ◆ Files

Your computer will store programs and data in **files** that designate collections of related information.

Your list is made up of the information on each person to whom you send a birthday greeting. The data for each person is referred to as the **record** for that person. The record for Nancy would be: Nancy—July 4—43. The record is, in turn, composed of **fields**, which are the basic facts about the person. In this case, there are only three fields: the name, date, and age.

Files are normally stored on a disk and then brought into the main memory when needed. Sometimes the entire file will be loaded, and at other times only a part—possibly only a single record—will be retrieved, but the basic idea is the same. If you make a change in a file, you must save the file back to the disk or your changes will be lost when you exit the program or turn the computer off.

| Name | Date | Age |
|------|------|-----|
| Nancy | July 4 | 43 |
| Robert | October 31 | 32 |
| Marilyn | December 13 | 11 |
| Barbara | June 16 | 24 |
| Charles | August 26 | 41 |
| Janice | March 8 | 19 |

*Figure 7.3*
*An example of a file of a birthday greetings list.*

## ◆ Directories

On any system, you can generate a list of the files on the disk or a particular section of the disk. This is referred to as a **directory** on an IBM-compatible computer and a **folder** on a Macintosh. Although the procedures for obtaining the file list and the on-screen appearance is quite different on the two systems, the concept is exactly the same. An IBM-type directory will be used here for an illustration, but all the concepts presented apply to Macintosh folders as well.

The information displayed with a directory can vary with the system or

**Figure 7.4**
***This shows the list of files on the disk, their size, the date and time each was last saved, and how much of the disk is in use.***

user-interface, but a typical directory listing might look something like Figure 7.4.

Often, you can create multiple directories or **subdirectories** on a single disk. This permits you to better organize your files. In such case you might think of your disk as comparable to a file cabinet, with each directory representing a single drawer containing files for a particular purpose.

For example, you might have directories for word processing, games, graphics, a spreadsheet, and your data base, which you might name (in order):

```
Volume in drive A is CLUB INFO
Volume Serial Number is 1A37-527E
Directory of A:\

ACHIEVE  REC    28,474   09-22-95    6:52p
AWARDS   DAT   110,220   03-31-93    2:49p
CHANGE   LTR     4,281   11-27-95    7:17a
FINANCE  REC    57,902   12-30-95   10:02a
LOCAL    LST    15,360   12-05-95    8:03a
MEETING  LTR     5,646   10-26-95   11:04a
NATIONAL LST   445,696   11-06-94    1:11p
REPORT95 TXT    32,351   01-12-96   12:18a
        8 file(s)         699,930 bytes
                          755,200 bytes free
```

WP
GAMES
GRAPHICS
SPREAD
DATABASE

Just as file drawers are labeled according to their contents, directory names are usually descriptive of either the directory's purpose or the program contained in that directory. These directories may also have subdirectories to permit you to further organize your data. A word processing directory may have subdirectories for personal correspondence, business letters, work reports, and schoolwork. This "branching" effect into more and more subdirectories is often called a **directory tree**.

In a directory tree, a directory that is immediately above another is called a **parent directory**, whereas the one that branches off is a **child directory**. For example, WP is a parent with four children: PERSONAL, BUSINESS, REPORTS, and SCHOOL. A child can also be a parent if it has children of its own, such as BOARD.

This should give you an idea of the concept of directory organization. A "how to" for creating and working with directories can be found in your operating system software manual. (The "ROOT" directory is the branching point for all other directories. It also normally contains certain files necessary for loading and running the operating system.)

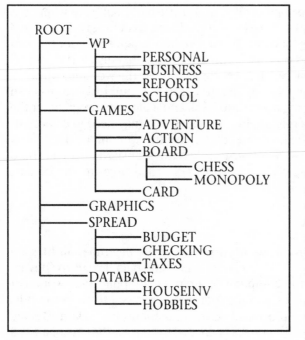

**Figure 7.5**
***An example of a directory tree.***

It takes reasonably little effort to establish an orderly disk directory structure, but the time saved in the future when your disk becomes crowded with many different applications will be well worth the initial effort. Also, often different applications may have files with the same name. If you attempt to put such applications into the same subdirectory, they will interfere with each other and one or both will not function properly.

# ▸ Understanding Basic Operations

You may also need to become familiar with many of the operating system commands and **system utility** files. These are used for formatting and copying disks; creating, changing, and displaying directories; deleting, renaming, printing, and copying files; making backups; and checking the system status. All of these processes are the same in principle for all systems, but the commands required to achieve them vary widely. Also, some models do not require some of these operations, such as creating or changing directories and checking the system status. Here is a brief description of some operations.

## ◆ *Formatting*

Disks must be prepared to receive data. This process initializes a disk and sets it up to record data in the format used by the system. *Any data already on a disk is erased when it is formatted.* Formatting is usually done using a system utility program and a simple command. Different types of disks, even on the same computer, may require slightly different commands. Normally, you will use this only for floppy disks (see page 163). Tapes may also have to be formatted before use, but this will require a different command that is supplied with the software that came with the tape system.

## ◆ *Backups*

You need to make a backup copy of all your diskette-based software where it is permitted. Not all software can or should be copied, and sometimes only selected parts of a package are available for copy. Check your license agreement for the software to be copied for the rules on this. Normally, the original disk is then **write-protected** and kept in a safe place. The new copy becomes the working copy.

In many cases, you can simply copy the files onto a second diskette. You can copy either individual files, using a formatted disk and a file copy program, or the entire disk, using a disk copy program. In a few cases, you may need to copy separate files from floppies onto the hard disk, then make the appropriate floppy disk backups. CD-ROM-based software (other than what is transferred to your hard disk) is normally not backed up because it consists of such a large amount of data.

## ◆ *Types of Files*

Files are classified according to their purpose. For the beginner, all files are roughly divided into two very broad groups: program and data. **Program files** are those files required to make the computer or a particular application work. For example, all the files that are necessary for your word processor to accomplish its various functions compose the program files for that application. **Data files** are those files that contain information typically created by you. In the case of a word processor, the letters, reports, and other documents that you write will be the data files. Normally, you will be able to create and change data files, but changes in program files are not recommended. Even an apparently innocent change, like the name of the program file, can prevent the program from operating properly.

### ◆ *File Commands*

Once you have files on your disk, you will need to be able to handle them properly. Here are some of the most common file operations and what they mean. (Note: The words used to describe each command are descriptive of what the command does and may be different on your system or within a particular application program.)

**COPY**
To copy a file is to make a duplicate image of the file in a second location. This is what is done when you make a backup of your files.

**DELETE**
Deleting a file will remove it from the disk. More accurately, it simply marks the file as unused and frees that disk space for further use. This means that if a mistake is made and the wrong file is deleted, the process may be reversible if the file space has not been overwritten by another file.

**ERASE**
This is the same as DELETE.

**LOAD**
This command loads a file from the disk into memory for execution or processing by another program. Usually, loading a program requires only typing the name of a file at a prompt. To load a data file, you must be using the program for that file. For example, you must be in a word-processing program to load a word-processing data file.

**MOVE**
To move a file places the file in a different location, removing it from the original site. The difference between COPY and MOVE is that COPY creates multiple copies of the same file, whereas MOVE simply relocates the original file.

**RENAME**
This command simply changes the name of a file, leaving it otherwise unaltered.

**RETRIEVE**
This is the same as LOAD.

**SAVE**
This command saves the updated copy of a file that is already in memory or creates a new file. If the file already exists, the old version will be replaced by the new one. If the file does not exist, it will be created, and you must choose an appropriate name for it.

**STORE**
This is the same as SAVE.

**TYPE**
This command displays the contents of a text-type file to the screen or sends the file to another output device (such as a printer) or a disk file.

**VIEW**
This is the same as TYPE.

File commands may be issued directly from the operating system. However, a large number of programs now provide utility functions, and many computer users find it easier and more convenient to issue file commands from within these programs.

### ◆ Directory Commands

Remember the file drawer analogy for directories. There are several functions that you may find convenient, even necessary, in working with directories:

| | |
|---|---|
| **CHANGE** | This command permits you to change your location on the disk from one directory to another (similar to closing one drawer and opening another). |
| **CREATE** | This command creates a new directory on the disk. |
| **GRAPH** | This is the same as MOVE. (Remember the "tree" image of the directories.) |
| **LIST** | This command will list or display the contents of files contained in a directory. Normally, this is directed to the screen, but it can often be sent to the printer or a disk file. |
| **MAKE** | This is the same as CREATE. |
| **MOVE** | This command will move a directory, together with all the files within it, to another position on the disk. |
| **PRUNE** | This is the same as REMOVE. (Once again, compare to the "tree" analogy.) |
| **REMOVE** | This command removes or deletes a directory from the disk. Often, a directory cannot be removed until it is empty. |
| **RENAME** | This command allows the name of a directory to be changed without affecting the files within it. |
| **SORT** | This command will permit you to sort the files within a directory into a specific order, such as by name, date, or size. |

Similar to file commands, the names for the directory commands describe their function; they may be different on your system or within a specific application.

## ▸ Getting Acquainted

Once you are satisfied that everything (including all software) is in working order, you are ready to become acquainted with your new computer and learn all about what it can do. Take your time. A single software package can take days or even weeks to master, and there may be features you never need. Work with a program until you understand and feel comfortable with it. Don't try to memorize all the commands; they will become familiar with regular use.

### ◆ Read Your Documentation

When you select a program to run, first scan the accompanying documentation. This usually tells you how to begin and provides a brief description of the available features and commands. Some have a "quick start" section. There may also be sample sessions, a tutorial section (or separate manual), or a demonstration disk to help you learn about and use the program. You can then study the manual in detail as you learn each feature and capability.

### ◆ Try Everything

Don't be reluctant to try things. *The only way you will learn is to do.* You cannot physically harm your computer's hardware with any command from the keyboard. Also, if you exercise reasonable care and common sense, the chances are remote that you will accidentally damage or destroy any software or data files that you have created. Think before you use the keyboard. *If you do not know what a particular command will do, then don't use it* unless you have some assurance that whatever it does will be harmless. Should you accidentally lose a program or data file, you should be able to restore it from your backup copy. If it is a protected program that you cannot copy, most companies will replace damaged disks at a minimal charge.

### ◆ Ask for Help

If all your attempts to solve a problem or master a particular program fail, ask for help before you give up in frustration and disappointment. Some good places to start are local full-service dealers, other users, computer clubs or users' groups, or computer professionals who have experience with your model computer and the particular item that is giving you trouble. Also, most major software companies provide telephone support for their products, but this is often available only to licensed owners and only during normal business hours.

### ◆ Report Problems

Sometimes a problem is not discovered until you have used a product for a while. If you cannot resolve it, consult your dealer or the manufacturer. They should be able to give you possible solutions and, in the case of some software, perhaps even provide a free corrected version.

# ▶ Misrepresentations

If you did your prepurchase homework and were careful in selecting your system and dealer, you should have no unpleasant surprises. However, if you find that a product has been misrepresented or does not perform according to its reported standards, immediately discuss your concerns with the retailer from whom you purchased the item. It's possible that you are not using it properly or have misinterpreted something. If there is a gap between performance and claims, however, you do not have to accept an inferior product. Certain remedies are available.

First, ask your dealer to make an appropriate adjustment. If this fails to resolve the problem to your satisfaction, there are several things you can do or sources you can contact for possible assistance. Try a letter or phone call to the manufacturer, or contact the local Better Business Bureau or Chamber of Commerce. The Better Business Bureau offers a mediation or arbitration service and is very useful in resolving such disputes. Your local or state Department of Consumer Affairs can provide you with information on local laws and your rights regarding cash refunds, merchandise exchanges, implied warranties, fair advertising practices, and so forth. (This information may be valuable *before* making your purchase.) If you have a local television or radio station or a newspaper with an active consumer "watchdog," this can be an especially powerful medium because of the potentially adverse publicity for the dealer or manufacturer.

A company is sometimes less cooperative when it has all your money from the sale. If you paid for your purchase by credit card, you may be able to stop or delay part or all of the payment. There is usually a time limit on this sort of action, however, and if you do not prevail, it could cost you extra interest charges. If the problem involves a mail-order sale, you have very specific rights with this sort of purchase. Consult the U.S. Post Office (or other shipper) for information. If the problem involves a substantial amount of money and you feel you have really been wronged, you might consult an attorney for advice and possible legal action. In all cases, your complaints should be documented and your letters should be copied and sent via registered mail.

# ▶ Preparing for Work

A system that is handled and maintained in a sloppy manner is a disaster waiting to happen. You may experience a serious problem such as losing data or equipment damage that could have been prevented by taking a few precautions. Here are a few suggestions that might help you avoid future difficulties.

## ◆ *Establish Good Work Habits*

It is a very good idea to establish basic guidelines for using your system. Everyone who uses your computer should be familiar with the basic start-up and shutdown procedures as well as any software packages. If several people regularly use the disks, it is normally better for one person to take charge of disk "housekeeping" chores and making backups. This is safer and has less potential for a misunderstanding that might cause a backup or other job to be left undone. This same person might also be the troubleshooter for any problems. Routine maintenance such as changing paper and ribbons in the printer should be shared by all except very young children.

The environment you provide for your computer equipment can make the difference between years or only months between breakdowns. Establish rules relating to food, beverages, smoking, pets, chewing gum, open windows, use of sprays, and other potential hazards to your system. Be sure that each user understands the possible damage from such hazards. Simple chores, such as replacing dustcovers and putting diskettes away properly, can make a difference in how reliably your computer will run, especially if your system exists in a dusty environment. Routine dusting and other external cleaning duties should be shared by all users.

### ◆ *Get Organized*

Arrange your materials in an orderly fashion. Keep all of your documentation and other written materials, including printed copies of files, neatly organized and ready for quick reference. No matter how many times you use a particular software package, you may still occasionally need to consult the manual. Your active diskettes should be kept up-to-date with labels and conveniently stored for quick access. All diskettes or tapes used as backups should be carefully labeled and arranged in a similar fashion.

You should keep the contents of any disk free of unwanted or unnecessary files. Whenever a file is no longer valuable, delete it from the disk. You can always save a copy of it on a backup diskette until you no longer need it. Take advantage of the ability to create different subdirectories and organize your disk according to its major uses (one directory for games, one for word processing files, one for spreadsheet work, and so forth). You can always change or delete the directories as necessary, files can be moved from one to another, and a program in one directory can use a data file in another.

### ◆ *Plan a Backup System*

It is important to maintain a current backup copy of all your software (where it is permitted) and the files that you create. Without this, you may not be able to recover lost data. The backup system and procedures you use are to a great extent a matter of personal choice, but there are a few general suggestions that you might find useful.

You need to keep a permanent backup copy of your operating system and application software, but there is generally no need to recopy these files every time you do a backup unless they have changed. Most backups involve only files that have been created or changed since the last backup. This can be done manually, but the selection of the files that have been created or changed since the last backup can be tedious and time-consuming. There are software packages for performing backups that will automatically back up only those files that are new or have been modified since the last backup.

For all but small hard disks (under about 120 MB), you might consider using a tape system for major backups of the entire disk, and diskettes for backing up selected files. If certain files are very important, or would be extremely difficult or impossible to replace, it would be wise to make two backups and keep one in a physically separate location. Thus, if the room where the computer is kept is damaged, perhaps by fire or a storm, you would still have a copy intact.

Try to avoid making a backup copy on the tape or diskette that contains the most recent prior backup. If there was a failure during the copy procedure (rare but not unknown), both the original and the backup copy could be lost. Use some type of alternating system that makes use of two or possibly three tapes or diskettes that are used in rotation. (Using two copies in this way is known as the **grandfather system**.) Carefully label each with the date and contents as it is made.

How often you make a backup will depend on how often you use your computer, how much data you generate, and how sensitive and irreplaceable your data is. There is no rule that will apply to all users about when to make a backup, and each person has to establish a schedule for their own system, but the following rule of thumb is a good guideline: If the system is used constantly (all day), daily or alternate-day backups are probably needed. If the computer is not used every day, then weekly or biweekly backups are probably sufficient. If the computer is used only occasionally, then monthly or bimonthly backups should be sufficient. Clearly, if you generate important files, then you will need to perform backups as needed to protect the files as they are generated. There will be little need for backups if the computer is used constantly but only for playing games, which produce no new files.

### ◆ Formatting Disks

It is strongly recommended that you keep some or all of your extra floppy disks formatted in advance. (You should always have some spare blank diskettes on hand.) You may need a diskette to save a file and will not be able to stop and format one without losing your work. This situation can occur if you try to save a file on a disk that does not have enough space left to hold it; this is not an uncommon occurrence with floppy disk systems and could also happen with a hard disk. Many users routinely format all diskettes as soon as they get them and most are sold already formatted.

### ◆ Naming Files

Naming your files is very important to the proper organization of your work. A file should be given a name that gives an indication of its purpose or use. Compare the two directory listings in Figure 7.6 for the same six files.

Judge for yourself. If you were not sure exactly what was on this disk, which listing would be more helpful?

Notice that in the second directory, the file names are in two parts. The first part is the actual file name; the second three-letter *extension* tells something about the nature of the file. Whereas extensions may not always be required, it is a good idea to always use them because they can provide addi-

```
     Volume in drive A has no label
     Volume Serial Number is 31C2-3885
     Directory of A:\

   AR                    15,533      08-21-95     11:16a
   C                    174,281      10-18-91      3:43p
   E                      8,044      12-31-94     11:07a
   FK                       933      09-14-93      3:10p
   O1                    12,010      11-30-95      7:48p
   O2                    12,339      12-19-95      2:32p
            6 file(s)         223,140 bytes
                              989,184 bytes free



   Volume in drive A is HEALTH CLUB
       Volume Serial Number is 3396-1A3B
       Directory of A:\

   ACCIDENT  RPT         15,533      08-21-95     11:16a
   CALORIES  LST        174,281      10-18-91      3:43p
   EXERCISE  LST          8,044      12-31-94     11:07a
   FIRSTAID  KIT            933      09-14-93      3:10p
   OWNER1    LTR         12,010      11-30-95      7:48p
   OWNER2    LTR         12,339      12-19-95      2:32p
             6 file(s)        223,140 bytes
                              989,184 bytes free
```

*Figure 7.6*
*The top directory uses unclear file names, whereas the lower directory (titled "HEALTH CLUB") is much clearer and easier to read.*

tional information about the file from the directory listing.

With a few possible restrictions, you can usually name a file anything you want. You may be limited to a certain number of characters (eight was assumed in the sample), and some symbols might not be permitted (such as an asterisk, question mark, colon, and period). Some files require that you specify it as a certain type, such as BAS for a program written in BASIC, BAT for a batch file, WP for a word-processing file, DBD for data to be processed by a data base manager, and COM or EXE for command or executable files. Sometimes these are supplied by the system or software. Many times, however, you can select the type as well as the name, in which case you should try to make it meaningful by using something like DAT, LST, LTR, or RPT for a data file, a list, a letter, or a report, respectively. (The three-letter file type is technically known as the **file extension.**)

The simpler or more user-friendly the system, the less you will need to specify or name a file. In some systems you have to do no more than supply the basic name, and all other needed items such as an extension are handled automatically. However, with other systems or software packages you may have to supply additional parameters for a complete **file specification.** With such programs, you may have to add an indicator to tell which drive or part of a drive you are using as well as a directory or account designation.

## ◆ A Word about Passwords

The new computer user is often tempted to attach passwords to everything possible. This is normally not only unnecessary but unwise. The general rule of thumb is that if there is no good reason to secure it with a password, *don't!* Adding passwords has proven to be the nemesis of many experienced computer users because the password is forgotten and/or lost.

Before you decide to add a password to anything, ask yourself some basic questions such as *why* you feel you need to secure the file, program, or system and from *whom* you feel it needs to be secured. Be absolutely certain that you are not just adding the password for the fun of it. This might be okay for experimentation, but *never add an unnecessary password to any files containing important data!* Unfortunately, it is sometimes not possible to recover from a forgotten or lost password.

If you do elect to add a password, possibly to your financial records because children or nonfamily members may have access to the computer, be wise in your choice of a password. Do not choose obvious things like your spouse's name or your birthday. The trick is to pick something that you will *remember,* but not something that's easy to guess. Some good ideas (before they appeared here, that is) are the time of your birth, the name of someone important from your childhood, a grandmother's maiden name, or your favorite flavor of ice cream or pie. Some people feel more secure by typing the password backward, but this is needless (and borderline paranoid) if it was carefully chosen in the first place.

# ▸ Caring for Your System

The key to taking care of your investment is to know and understand your system's vulnerable points. Generally, both computer hardware and software are very sturdy and will not fail because of any environmental problem. However, sometimes minor matters can cause major headaches.

### ◆ *Hardware*

Your manuals will recommend ideal temperatures, humidity ranges, and maximum altitudes for the optimum performance of each product. Good ventilation is essential at all times for adequate air circulation and proper cooling of circuits. If the humidity is high enough to form moisture on surfaces, then this moisture is probably inside your system as well. If you are aware of pollution in the air or on surfaces, your system may even be far more sensitive to this than you are. A dustcover is both useful and recommended, especially for systems in rooms with open windows, but it is not a cure-all.

The read/write heads on a disk drive may ride as close as a few millionths of an inch above the disk surface and scan it at speeds in excess of 100 miles per hour. (This has been compared to a jet plane flying only a few inches above the surface of the earth.) The gap between the head and disk surface is many times smaller than such tiny particles as those found in smoke or the thickness of a fingerprint. Larger, visible dust particles would be enormous to such a system. For this reason, most high-speed, high-capacity disk drives are now fixed in a sealed unit, the most popular of which uses the **Winchester** technology originally pioneered by IBM. However, a few hard disks and all floppy disks are not sealed and are thus open to contamination from the environment.

Although nonsealed disk units do not have small **head gaps** or operate at high speeds, they are still sensitive to foreign substances. A dust particle can be ground between the disk and head, causing permanent damage to both. Less visible obstructions, such as fingerprints and very tiny particles from smoke or sprays, can be even more damaging as they build up over time. There is always the possibility that a large particle will be knocked out of the way; however, the smaller ones tend to be more tightly stuck to the surface and are more likely to be ground or smeared under the head and on the surface of the disk.

A few diskette drives will not have a good protective panel over the opening in the front of the unit. If you have one of these drives, a simple way to protect the unit is to place a blank diskette in the drive when it is not in use. This will cause the drive to "close down," leaving a smaller opening for contaminants to enter. (On 5¼-inch drives, be sure to physically close the drive door by flipping down the little lever.)

Cigarette smoke is one of the greatest hazards your system faces. Smoke particles are very small and can get into places where larger particles cannot. This has the potential to damage not only the disk drives as described above but also many other parts of the system as well. One very sensitive item is often the keyboard. Sometimes very tiny particles get under the key caps and, in time, interfere with the contact, causing a key to skip or repeat erratically.

One reason smoking around a computer is a significant risk to the system is that the smoker tends to blow the smoke forward and directly at the system. Any smoke can be harmful to your equipment, but if you smoke while using your computer, it would be better to direct the smoke away from the system. It would be even better if you arranged to take a break when you want a smoke.

Sprays pose additional hazards. Some aerosols, such as cleaners, polishes, room fresheners, and personal grooming products, can cause a thin film to form on surfaces. The gummy buildup of these substances can be as damaging in time as the grinding from solid particles. *Never spray anything directly on your hardware that is not designed for that specific use, and never under any circumstances expose disk or tape surfaces to any sprays.* It would be best to avoid, if possible, spraying around unprotected equipment. If this is not practical, then cover your computer and take further precautions to minimize the system's exposure.

There is also the potential hazard from electrical disturbances. These normally come from two sources: static electrical discharges and power surges or noise. We have all experienced a shock when we touch things during cold weather. This can be disastrous to a computer. Such sudden charges can destroy chips and the data on disks or tapes. You can buy nondamaging sprays or other products that will help eliminate this problem. Also available are antistatic mats that can be placed under your computer or on the floor under your chair and feet.

Power surges and noise from the AC power line can be equally deadly to equipment and data and often occur without any indication. Power strips and the like are available at a reasonable cost and can provide protection from such interference except in extreme cases, as in a nearby lightning strike. It is strongly recommended that every system be protected by one of these. Your entire system should be isolated; unprotected components can send a surge back through a connecting cable, thus damaging elements you thought were protected. If you have a modem, don't forget that the telephone line should also be isolated.

## ◆ *Software*

Software can be damaged when a disk is physically scratched, or the data affected without any actual physical damage to the medium on which it is recorded. Practically anything that can harm your hardware—heat, humidity, dust, smoke, sprays—can also be a hazard to your software. Dust and other airborne substances are probably the most common sources of physical damage to diskettes and tapes. Never leave diskettes in a closed car on a hot summer day. Never leave software out of its storage container, and always store your software, preferably with diskettes upright, in a closed area. A contaminated diskette or tape frequently damages drive heads.

A few special precautions are needed for the less protected 5¼-inch diskettes. Because there is an exposed surface, never leave one of these diskettes out of its protective jacket. Because of the softer covering, never place anything on top of a 5¼-inch diskette because this can damage the recording surface. Tiny particles that have accumulated may grind and mar the delicate magnetic material. A diskette can become crimped or bent if left lying around on a table. When you label a diskette, never use a sharp pen or pencil or press down hard; use only a soft-tip pen or marker that requires little pressure to write.

The pattern of magnetic images on a disk or tape can also be damaged, and your information can be lost (without any actual physical harm to the surface). This can even occur from excessive heat and humidity. If these conditions are severe enough to disturb the data, however, they will usually harm the surface as well. There is one notable and very important exception: magnetic fields. Static sparks are an example of this effect. A disk or tape exposed to a magnetic field can have part or all of its data erased, and you may not even be aware of it until you try to use it.

Magnetic fields are fairly common in the home. Any electrical piece of equipment generates one to some extent, but fortunately magnetic fields are generally fairly weak and not strong enough to cause a problem except around certain appliances or other electrical units. There are two considerations: how large the current is and how close to it one gets. Televisions or monitors, transformers, large speaker magnets (in stereos), vacuum cleaners, compressors, and some power tools generate substantial magnetic fields. Software has been lost simply by placing it on top of a monitor. Even the transformers in stereo amplifiers or other power supplies have been known to cause similar damage. Never place any magnetic media on or near an electrical unit that is not designed for it. Don't forget about permanent magnets such as those that decorate the refrigerator.

### ◆ Supplies

Treat your extra supplies with the same care you give to the ones currently in use. Store items in a cool, dry, and clean place until needed.

### ◆ Cleaning Your System

Computers require relatively little physical maintenance. For most systems, a good screen cleaner and a small vacuum or soft brush is all that is needed to maintain the external surfaces.

A few simple cautions should be observed when cleaning your system's external surfaces:

⎯⎯◆ Never clean your computer with any part of the system turned on. To help avoid generating static charges, always turn off the entire system at least five minutes before cleaning any surfaces.

——◆ Never use a wet cloth. Use only a dry or slightly damp cloth, or an approved cleaner in spray form.

——◆ Never use strong soaps or detergents, furniture polishes, window cleaners, and so forth; such substances can cause irreparable damage to a system.

——◆ Never use strong commercial cleaners, such as alcohol, acetone, or ammonia.

——◆ Never spray anything on a dusty surface such as a keyboard. The tiny particles can cake and form a sticky layer in hard-to-reach areas that will be both damaging and difficult to remove.

——◆ Never use a strong vacuum cleaner on delicate mechanical parts such as keyboards and printers, and use an extension tube when vacuuming around your equipment. This keeps the vacuum motor and its electric fields away from your diskettes and hard drives.

The best way to "clean" your system is to do whatever you can to prevent it from needing to be cleaned. But when it does, *use only cleaners designed for use on computer component surfaces.* If a special cleaner is not available, you can use a cloth *slightly* dampened with either clear water or a *very mild* soapy solution.

### ◆ Inventory Your System

Maintain an up-to-date, itemized list that reflects all components (including software), specific models (versions or releases for software, if available), all serial numbers where available, the value, and the date and purchase place. You may wish to keep this on your system, using a data base manager or other program, but you should always keep a printed (or "hand") copy of the current system in a safe place. This could be valuable for insurance or other purposes in case of theft, damage, or destruction of part or all of the system.

If you make a practice of specially marking your possessions, you should take care when doing so with delicate electronic equipment. Avoid directly using electric engraving tools on any component that contains boards; such equipment can damage the fragile chips on these boards. If you wish to use an electric engraving tool, physically separate the part on which you will be engraving from the sensitive internal circuits before you begin. Preferable alternatives include mechanical engravers and stick-on labels.

### ◆ Insurance

Do not assume that your homeowner's or other insurance covers your computer system. Some policies either do not include computer equipment or limit the coverage without additional riders. Check with your agent to verify your company's policy. If your system is not covered, it can usually be protected at a small cost.

# ▶ Computer Viruses

One relatively new but very serious hazard to computers is the **computer virus.** This refers to a small computer program designed to "infect" computers by attaching itself to a program or part of the operating system, then duplicating itself to spread to other disks and computers. Viruses manifest themselves in a variety of ways, ranging from simple annoyances like messages or images being flashed on the screen to destructive operations that may lead to the loss of vital data files.

Whereas a virus may destroy data files, it cannot use these files as a means of transportation. Virus programs may enter a system by means of either an executable (program) file or as part of the operating system itself; once there, nothing is safe from its ravages. Viruses are roughly classified as boot or file, depending on how they manage system entry; hence, the virus infects the boot sector or an executable file, respectively. (Viruses are one example of a larger class of programs collectively referred to as **Trojan Horse** programs because they enter a computer system secretly via another program. This should not be confused with a computer virus program called Trojan.)

Despite the method used to infect a system, the one thing all viruses have in common is that they must come from an outside source—usually a contaminated floppy disk or file imported by using a modem. Most viruses are found on disks or files that have an unknown history. That is, these files come from an unknown source or have been duplicated and transferred several times. The likelihood of your computer being infected depends on how frequently you employ such sources; if you are very careful about the origin of any disk or files you use, you will greatly reduce the danger of your computer being infected. However, no disk is assumed to be virus-free. Although extremely rare, major computer manufacturers have been the victims of viruses, unknowingly passing them on to their customers.

The best way to protect against a virus is to be extremely cautious about the sources of any files you acquire. Use an antivirus program to check your computer and diskettes for infection. Make it a habit to check all new diskettes and files before using them. Unfortunately, there are now well over 3,000 known computer viruses, with still more being discovered almost daily. Because of this, any antivirus program will become obsolete very quickly, so you should keep an updated version at all times. This will normally not require purchasing an entirely new program; most major antivirus programs provide a separate file that lists the characteristics (signatures) of known viruses, and, for a nominal fee, can be periodically updated.

When running an antivirus program, there are basically three options available to you. The first is to check only for the presence of a virus. The second is to remove any known viruses that you find. The third option is to have ongoing virus protection, which is accomplished through a variety of techniques, including constant system monitoring. The better programs will provide all options; however, more economical packages may not permit continued monitoring. Although no method is infallible, persistent and diligent checking with the appropriate safeguards will provide maximum protection.

Not every user will require constant virus monitoring. Such ongoing checks can be costly in terms of system performance, often causing a computer to run noticeably slower. The test as to whether you need constant monitoring is fairly simple. If you frequently either use a modem to download files from a bulletin board (or other online sources) or make a practice of using floppy disks of unknown or questionable origin (such as passed from friend to friend), then you would be wise to implement a constant protection procedure. On the other hand, if you do not (or rarely) download files with a modem and are careful about the origin of any diskettes you use, then checking each disk you acquire before you use it should be sufficient. (Note: You can help protect against infected downloaded files by sending them directly to a diskette and checking for a virus before using any of them.)

If all else fails and you find a virus, don't panic. Do not use your computer until you can remove the virus. Many viruses are benign and may never do anything but annoy you, but others are triggered by system use and may cause irreversible damage to your data. As soon as you see any symptoms of infection (which may be indicated by unusual system performance), immediately take steps to remove the infection. Turn the computer off and reboot from a write-protected floppy disk containing the operating system. This will permit you to avoid viruses that affect the boot tracks of your hard or regular boot disk. Next, use a current antivirus program to find and remove the offending virus. A copy of an antivirus program should be kept on a write-protected floppy disk. If you do not have an antivirus program, it is worth buying. Do not run any software (other than an antivirus program) until you have purged the system of the virus.

# ▸ Computer Supplies

Most supplies, such as paper, diskettes, tapes, and printer ribbons, are available at discount prices if you purchase them in quantity. With the possible exception of ribbons, which will dry out if exposed to the air for an extended period of time, most items will keep indefinitely when properly stored.

Look for quality products. If you see a dealer selling something such as disks or paper at an unbelievably low price, inspect the quality carefully. Be sure to verify the specifications to ensure that you are getting what you want and need. All DS/HD (double-sided/high-density) floppy disks or 20-pound (20#) paper stocks are not created equally. Often, items that carry a certain rating or specification only minimally meet that standard and may be disappointing to you, either aesthetically or in their performance. If tempted but still in doubt, order a limited test supply.

Many of the larger companies now offer their own in-house brands of ribbons, diskettes, and tapes. These are usually somewhat cheaper than the most popular, nationally known name brands, but you should be cautious. You may find that the nominal extra cost for a familiar brand is well justified.

## ♦ *Floppy Disks*

Most microcomputers now use essentially the same few types of disks; however, there are still many older systems that use other kinds, which can make buying disks confusing. You will find the specifications for the floppy disks your system uses in your manual. As mentioned in Chapter 5, floppy disks come in three sizes—8, 5¼, and 3½ inches—but the 8-inch type is no longer used on microcomputers. (Diagrams of 5¼- and 3½-inch diskettes are provided in the section on floppy disks in Chapter 5.)

There are three basic considerations when buying floppy disks: single- or double-sided; the **density**; and for 5¼-inch diskettes, the **sectoring**. Your drive will most likely use double-sided, high-density, and what is known as soft-sectoring. Double-sided means precisely that—both sides of the disk will have data recorded on them. (Oddly, a number of early computers made use of only one side of the diskette.)

Density refers to how much data can be recorded on the disk and is usually referred to as **single, double, quad,** or **high**. It may also be given in capacity (kilobytes or megabytes) or tracks per inch **(tpi),** such as 48 or 96 tpi. You can always use a higher density than required, but never go to a lower one. It may work, but you run a significantly higher risk of errors and data loss.

Sectoring refers to how the beginning of the sectors, or parts of the data **tracks,** on a 5¼-inch diskette are marked by the system. All systems now use a **soft-sectoring** method, in which a single small hole near the center of the diskette is used to begin sectoring on each track. A few older systems may still be around that use **hard-sectoring,** in which a series of holes (usually 10 or 16) mark the beginning of each sector. These two types of disks are not interchangeable, so take care when ordering diskettes.

Nearly all floppy disks have a **write-protection** method. This provides you with a means to protect the data on the disk from being accidentally erased or overwritten. A small switch is used on the 3½-inch diskettes. On a 5¼-inch diskette, a write-protection tab is placed over a small notch on the side of the disk. (The system works in reverse on the older 8-inch floppy disks.)

You would be wise to buy diskettes of good to high quality; these can now be found for under $1 each. However, keep in mind that the better the quality of the disk, the less likely you are to have a data loss because of a disk failure. Many diskette manufacturers now offer a lifetime guarantee, but do not rely too heavily on this; a new diskette is of little help for your lost data. Use good quality disks for operations involving important data. You can use less expensive disks safely for storing backup or archival data, which is not used very frequently. Be wary of any diskette (except 3½-inch) that does not have a hub ring to reinforce the center hole. Such disks can be easily mangled by the drive mechanism. Hub rings can be bought separately and added.

Diskettes that have been preformatted for a specific system (such as IBM or Macintosh) are also available. These provide the convenience of not having to format each floppy disk as well as eliminating the danger of needing a formatted diskette and not having one ready. However, as might be expected, such diskettes are more expensive and are not available in all machines and programs.

### ◆ *Tapes*

Don't be put off by the cost of good quality ¼-inch tape or **data cartridges.** Remember that these tapes will contain the data from your entire system. If you do have a problem and have to restore all your files and work to your disk, you will certainly want to have a reliable tape from which to do so. One tape can easily replace a hundred or more high-density diskettes; thus, the $20 premium is well worth it.

If you acquire an older computer with a tape system that uses regular audio or video cassettes, you may find that it will not function properly with economy tapes. It is wise to buy the higher-quality tapes or even the special **data cassettes** designed specifically for this purpose. Tape prices vary widely with the type and size, but you should expect to pay at least $5 to $10 for quality cassettes.

### ◆ *Paper*

Printer paper is available in virtually any size, weight, quantity, quality, and design. Most people use either single sheets or the continuous fan-fold type that is divided by pages, but roll paper can still be found if that best suits your needs. Most stores that sell computer supplies have the more popular types. Many other varieties, ranging from unique sizes to paper preprinted with a letterhead or blank forms, can be special-ordered.

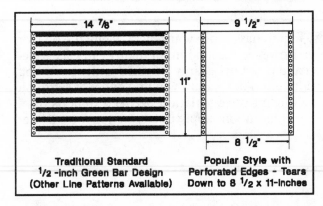

Traditional Standard
1/2 -inch Green Bar Design
(Other Line Patterns Available)

Popular Style with
Perforated Edges - Tears
Down to 8 1/2 x 11-inches

*Figure 7.7 Computer paper comes in various sizes.*

The two most popular sizes are 14⅞ x 11 inches for wide carriage work and 9½ x 11 inches for standard carriages. Many of the latter type are perforated along each side to tear down to a standard size of 8½ x 11 inches. Several other sizes are commonly available as well, and multipart (carboned) forms can be found up to four parts. You can even get paper that has been prepunched for a 3-ring binder. In many cases you will have your choice between solid white (or another color), the traditional one-half-inch green bar, or some other pattern.

Paper is available in a variety of weights, ranging from about 12 to 24 pounds. A 15-pound stock is less expensive, for example, than the 20-pound and works in most printers. However, many users prefer the added strength and reliability of the heavier forms, which are less likely to jam. When comparing the price of different papers, look at the number of forms per carton. As the pages get thicker (the heavier the stock), there are fewer pages and they have increased weight. However, heavier does not always mean higher quality. Look for key words—*bond, fiber,* or *watermark*—if that is what you want.

If you do much printing, you may want to keep more than one type of paper on hand. Aside from the obvious advantages of having more than one size, there are economic advantages to using a cheaper and/or lighter stock for printing rough drafts and development work and a better stock for printing finished products. Some people use continuous forms for the former and single sheets of high-quality bond or fiber paper for the latter.

A regular box of fanfold paper of about 2,500 to 3,500 single sheets costs from $20 to $40. The price varies with the size, weight, and quality. A box of 20-pound paper may *appear* to cost less than a similar 15-pound stock, but it contains fewer sheets, so the net price is probably higher. Multiple-part forms and odd sizes are more expensive, as are the smaller boxes that are frequently offered. With the smaller boxes of 500 to 1,500 sheets, you normally pay much more for the same amount of paper than if you bought it in larger cartons. You are paying for the convenience of the smaller size, which is much easier to carry and move about. Smaller cartons weigh only a few pounds, whereas large boxes can exceed 50 pounds.

It may take a little experimenting to find the right paper for your printer. When selecting fanfold-type paper for a particular application, take the extra time to separate the sheets. Not all fanfold papers separate easily or smoothly, sometimes tearing or leaving ragged edges. Such paper is also more likely to jam due to the sprocket holes for feeding through the printer. Also, paper with the side perforations may not tear evenly either. Paper advertised as having "fine perforations" may not be any better and can even be worse. You may have to try several brands of paper before you find one that is suitable for you. Buy small quantities initially before you find a type, or brand, of paper that works.

### ◆ Ribbons and Toner

Ribbons are relatively easy to purchase, since you generally buy the one for your particular model printer. However, the amount of inking can vary widely from one brand to another and is not necessarily reflected in the price. You might shop around and try different ribbons until you find one that suits you best. You may also find a significant price variation between ribbons from different companies. (The same precautions apply to buying toner for a laser printer.)

### ◆ CD-ROMs

Though you will not be buying blank CDs, if your system has a CD-ROM drive, you will surely acquire a collection of CD-ROM–based software. Data is not recorded on CD-ROMs in the same way it is on disks or tapes; consequently, CD-ROMs are not as sensitive to the environment as are the other media. Data is recorded on a CD-ROM by means of very tiny pits gouged into the surface; this is then covered by a transparent, protective plastic coating. Magnetic fields do not harm a CD as they do disks and tapes.

You should treat your computer CDs just as you do those for your music system. Avoid extremes in temperature and humidity. Dust and contaminants as well as direct physical damage (such as scratches) are the nemeses of CDs. Keep CDs in their protective holder and free of foreign materials. You can gently wipe the surface with a soft cloth if necessary, but *never use any kind of cleaner,* especially one that might be abrasive or leave a film.

### ◆ Storage

Inexpensive storage boxes are available for your floppy disks, tapes, CD-ROMs, and other sensitive materials. These range from small units, which store only about ten diskettes, to large files, which have the capacity to handle hundreds. You will likely find these very helpful and well worth the usually modest price. There are frugal alternatives. For example, you can make a floppy disk storage file from a sturdy shoe box and a little cardboard and tape, or you can store tapes in a box that contained a small appliance (such as a toaster). Some people even use the original packaging to store disks and tapes.

### ◆ *Cleaners*

Obtain only recommended cleaning materials for your computer. Nondamaging cleaners (which are often also antistatic) are available from most computer stores for a few dollars and are excellent for cleaning monitor screens and other external surfaces. Small microvacuum cleaners are excellent for removing tiny dust particles from keyboards, printer mechanisms, and other hard-to-reach places. Cans of compressed air and a small brush can also be effective if used frequently.

Beware of cleaners for delicate parts of your system such as disk and tape unit heads. Many effective methods are available for this, but be careful about those that are abrasive or employ messy fluids. Use only nonabrasive, dry (or semidry) methods that clean with minimal intrusion into the physical mechanism of the drive. No cleaning system should be overused. You will have to judge how often to use a cleaner depending on how heavily the unit is used, but no more than once a month should be sufficient for most systems. Overuse can be harmful with some types of cleaning methods.

### ◆ *Miscellaneous Items*

You can get extra disk or tape labels, replacement write-protection tabs, and jackets for diskettes. Printout binders are available in any size, color, quality, and style that you can imagine. There are storage and filing systems for virtually anything and in any size. If you have a printer that uses a printwheel, there are catalogs with hundreds of these in a tremendous array of fonts and pitches. Preview your needs and purchase only what is necessary.

## ▸ Updates and Upgrades

An **update** refers to the improvement of a product through a newer or corrected version. You may have an opportunity to acquire updates for many of your software packages but are not likely to change a hardware component for a newer model unless the old one is unsatisfactory. Many software vendors will notify you periodically of updates to their programs that you have purchased and registered with them. Remember that any special installation or modification that was required with the older release will likely be necessary with the newer one as well.

Occasionally a new release can introduce certain compatibility problems that you did not have previously. For example, if you are still using an old version of the operating system and have not updated it, a new release might not function properly with the older operating system. Such problems are the exception to the rule; most updates work as well if not better than the preceding editions. It is also rare that a new release does not function properly without some additional hardware component that was not previously required, such as a math coprocessor.

An **upgrade** refers to changing part or all of a system to a more powerful version. This is an expensive and complex proposition. In some respects you are starting all over with a new system. However, you probably already have a substantial investment in hardware, software, and your own data files that you need to preserve as much as possible. Also, the existence of these items can make it even harder to assemble an upgrade system that both suits your needs and preserves your files.

Some but not all, companies have a good record regarding their **upgrade path,** or the ability to change to the hardware of a newer or more powerful model and still maintain compatibility with older peripherals and software. If you purchase a system without the potential to upgrade don't despair.

The upgrade path usually involves changing the basic computer to a later version. This may, in turn, cause compatibility problems with parts from the older system—most frequently but not always the software. Some of your software programs may not be transferable, but your data files may be by simply moving them to a new disk with the new system format. You may also be able to gain new copies of much of your software without having to pay the full purchase price again. Ask your dealer to help you with this or write to the software companies and explain the problem; some may exchange disks with you for a small fee. Moving to an upgrade can also introduce problems of compatibility with the older system peripherals, but this problem is not as common as the one encountered with the software. Fortunately, few personal computer owners are ever faced with the need to do a true upgrade.

# Consumer Reports Tests

## ▸ Your Guide to Windows 95

Few consumer products in history have drawn as much fanfare as Windows 95, Microsoft's new operating system for IBM-compatible computers.

To prepare this guide to Windows 95, we drew on lengthy experience with a "preview" version that Microsoft distributed to thousands of testers and on a brief look at the official release we purchased.

Bottom line: Windows 95 does represent a big step forward for most personal computers. But when, exactly, should you upgrade?

## ▸ The Case for Waiting

If you're reasonably happy with your existing software and your current computer's capabilities, don't rush to Windows 95. It will be there if ever you change your mind.

Even if you're frustrated with the old Windows, hold off upgrading for at least a couple of months. Most software designed for the old Windows or MS-DOS will run under Windows 95, but hundreds of existing products reportedly won't run correctly or at all.

And most of the new software written to tap the full potential of Windows 95 won't be available for some time yet. So those who hold off will have more software from which to choose. Further, the first version of any piece of software, Windows 95 included, will almost surely have bugs. Whereas they will likely be fixed fairly promptly, patience can save time and aggravation.

## ▸ Software Costs

To take advantage of the increased speed and major new features in Windows 95, you must purchase new, 32-bit versions of applications software. And, for the handiest installation of a CD-ROM drive and other add-ons, you'll need some new circuitry in your computer. As the table on page 171 shows, even a few additional upgrades can make a "$90" Windows 95 upgrade cost several hundred dollars.

---

## Highlights of Windows 95

◆ A "folders on the desktop" interface, something familiar to Apple Macintosh users and those who have bought add-on "shells" for prior versions of Windows.

◆ The capability to give meaningful names to your files—up to 255 characters in a name. But older programs won't respond to the longer names.

◆ Built-in faxing and computer-linking software.

◆ Support that's supposed to make for speedier word processors, spreadsheets, and other programs.

◆ Claims of better performance when "multitasking"—running more than one program or process at a time.

◆ Plug and play—simplified installation of such peripheral equipment as a CD-ROM drive, sound card, or modem.

◆ Improved audio and video performance running games and multimedia CD-ROMs.

◆ Software for Microsoft's new on-line service.

◆ A special cursor, a larger-type display, and other aids for people who have poor eyesight or dexterity.

---

To use Microsoft Network, the company's new on-line service, you sign up and pay separate usage fees. Windows 95 is designed so that you can do that simply by clicking on an icon. That feature has drawn criticism from competing on-line services, which claim that Microsoft is using Windows 95's dominance to gain an unfair advantage.

# ▶ Hardware Costs

According to early conventional wisdom, an older computer with little memory could not handle Windows 95. But when we tried Windows 95 on a 33-megahertz 80386 DX computer with 4 megabytes of memory (an antique, as computers go), it ran multiple tasks at about the same speed as the old Windows.

Still, without more memory, a relic like the one we used won't be able to do many of the things that make Windows 95 attractive. The older machine can't run more than one major 32-bit program at a time, for example. Hence, the need for upgrades.

### ◆ Memory

On any machine, Windows 95 runs faster with 8 or more megabytes of RAM (the computer's main memory) than with 4. Upgrading RAM could be tricky. Before you invest in new memory chips, consider one of several specialty software products (about $60) that stimulate more memory. However, such software may not be as fast as "real" RAM. If you decide to buy more RAM, have someone familiar with your computer determine the type and quantity of memory you need.

### ◆ Hard Drive

You need a minimum of 50 to 55 megabytes free to install Windows 95, plus additional space for new applications. If that leaves you with less than 200 MB to spare, you may want a larger hard drive.

### ◆ Processor

Windows 95 requires at least an 80386DX processor. Upgrading to a more powerful 80346 processor will improve performance, although you still won't be able to take advantage of some new features unless you upgrade your applications, too.

---

## How Costs Can Mount

Windows 95 upgrade . . . . . . . . . . . . . . . . . . . . . . . . . . .$90
Microsoft Word upgrade  . . . . . . . . . . . . . . . . . . . . . . .$90
Microsoft Excel upgrade . . . . . . . . . . . . . . . . . . . . . . . .$90

**For an 80386 computer**
Add'l 4 MB memory . . . . . . . . . . . . . . . . . . . . . . . . . . .$160-$200
500-MB hard drive . . . . . . . . . . . . . . . . . . . . . . . . . . . .$200
New 80486 processor and board . . . . . . . . . . . . . . . .$100-$300
**Total** . . . . . . . . . . . . . . . . . . . . . . . . . . . . . . . . . . . . .$730-$970

**Minimum cost of new 80486
computer, with Windows 95,
Word, and Excel** . . . . . . . . . . . . . . . . . . . . . . . . . . . .$1,380

---

## ▶ Hands-on Advice

If you plan to upgrade:

——◆ First fix any erratic behavior in your computer or old version of Windows.
——◆ Make backup copies of important data before you install the upgrade.
——◆ Allow an hour or two to install the upgrade. Keep Microsoft's technical-support phone number handy.
——◆ Decide whether to install Windows 95 alongside the old Windows and DOS (called a dual boot) or in place of them. The former makes it easy

to work while you learn the ins and outs of Windows 95, but it uses hard-disk space. The latter makes it easier to adapt applications into Windows 95—but you can't run the previous DOS and Windows versions, a possible handicap.

# ▸Notebook Computers

Compared with a desktop computer, a notebook has clear advantages—less weight, less bulk, less clutter—not to mention the freedom to roam that battery power confers.

---

### The $2000 Portable Computer: How It's Changed

1991: A machine weighing 11 to 13 pounds, powered by a 20-MHz 386SX chip, with a 20-MB hard drive and a monochrome monitor.

1993: A machine weighing 7 to 8 pounds, powered by a 25-MHz 486 chip, with an 80- to 100-MB hard drive and a monochrome monitor.

1995: A machine weighing 7 to 8 pounds, powered by a 50-MHz 486DX2 chip, with a 340-MB hard drive and a color monitor.

---

The tradeoff: less computer for your money. Notebooks give you less computing power, a less easily read display, and less room on the keyboard for your fingers, to name some of the design compromises that make notebooks less easy to operate than a larger desk model. Nor is a notebook computer likely to have the fastest microprocessor (the electronic chip that largely determines how quickly a computer can work).

A notebook computer makes sense if its portability or size buys you something you really want—ultimate freedom and the convenience of computing almost anywhere.

---

# ▸Recent Changes

The tested models, selling for $2000 to $3500, boast many improvements over earlier models:

- ◆ *Better display*. The screens are color and larger than before—9½ to 11 inches measured diagonally, compared with 8½ inches on models of two years ago.
- ◆ *Faster processor*. Gone are the 80386 and the watered-down 80486SX used in IBM-compatibles. A 50- to 100-MHz 80486DX2 or DX4 processor is the norm, with even faster processors on the way. Processors used in *Apple PowerBooks* have also improved.
- ◆ *Larger hard drive*. Typical are drives that can store 250 or 340 megabytes

of data, plenty big enough for today's demanding software. Notebooks with smaller drives cost less.

——♦ *Longer battery life.* Nickel-metal hydride has replaced nickel cadmium as the typical battery material. Batteries using lithium, the most efficient material yet available for rechargeable batteries, are starting to show up even on moderately priced models.

——♦ *Easier-to-use keyboard and pointing device.* The makeshift clip-on trackball is gone, replaced by a number of better-designed devices. Keyboard designs have improved. Many come with built-in palm supports that prevent fatigue.

——♦ *A fax/modem.* This device, which lets you send and receive faxes and access on-line services and the Internet, is sometimes built in, but more commonly available as an add-on card.

——♦ *Multimedia capability.* Some come with built-in sound, which lets you hear the soundtrack of multimedia software played on a CD-ROM drive. Built-in CD-ROM drives are starting to appear on notebooks that cost $3000 and up.

——♦ *Pre-installed software.* Integrated "works" packages allow you to run the notebook right out of the box.

Also, look for the introduction of new, faster *Macintosh PowerBooks* (and processor upgrades for most of the current PowerBooks) based on the PowerPC processors used in *Power Macintosh* desktop models. Any time a new line is announced, prices of the old line should drop. The "500" series models for this test, because they can be upgraded, may thus turn out to be excellent buys.

What to look for in a notebook computer:

——♦ *Keyboard.* Notebooks' keyboards are no match for regular keyboards in size or design. Layouts aren't standard, so you may not find a function where you expect it. Keyboards vary in the kind of feedback they give. Some clack noisily (a drawback for library use, perhaps), some are virtually silent. Some feel stiff, some move fairly effortlessly. Keys also vary in how clearly they let you know they've worked. The Ratings note differences, but you should try before you buy.

——♦ *Display.* Nearly all notebooks have a liquid-crystal display, typically about 30 percent smaller than a desktop's monitor; words and pictures are reduced in size proportionately. If you can't adjust to such shrinkage, most word-processing programs allow you to enlarge the type. Alternatively, if you also have an external monitor, most notebooks can be hooked up to it so you can enjoy a larger screen—and, if the monitor supports it, higher resolution to boot.

Most notebooks priced under $2,500 use what's called dual-scan passive-matrix color technology (sometimes called DSTN—dual super twist nematic). Although no match for the best desktop screens, such screens generally produce images that are good enough. The screens, as found in the tests, vary little in quality from model to model. Dual-scan displays often blur the cursor arrow, or any other object on the screen, when you move it quickly. To reduce the blur, most notebooks with a dual-scan display come with software that makes the cursor more visible.

You can save a few hundred dollars by choosing a machine with a monochrome display. A monochrome display must rely on shades of gray to differentiate objects on the screen, making it less suitable for displaying complex graphics. Monochrome displays also suffer from blurring. Most manufacturers are phasing them out; Apple is one of the few that continues to offer them.

The very best notebook displays use what's known as active-matrix—sometimes called TFT (thin-film transistor)—color technology. An active-matrix screen can be viewed from a wider side angle than other types and provides a crisper, clearer image. But the improvement wasn't noteworthy enough for us to rate such a display (on the $3500 *Apple PowerBook 540c*) better than the dual-scan passive color found on most of the others. For most people, the advantages of active-matrix color are hardly worth the $800 or so it adds to a notebook's price.

You may find that some displays suit you better than others. If you can try out the notebook in the store, use this test to see how you like the display: Scroll through black text on a white background. Adjust the brightness and contrast to get the crispest image. Tilt the screen to minimize glare. If you find yourself straining to read, look for a model that's easier to work with.

◆ *Pointing device.* With Macintosh and Windows operating software, you must point to parts of the screen and click to make something happen —what's called a graphical user interface, or GUI. To move the on-screen cursor around, notebooks use a built-in device, handier than the add-on trackball of older notebooks. But a notebook's pointer, be it trackball, trackstick, or trackpad, is necessarily small and harder to manipulate than a desktop machine's trackball or mouse.

Of the three types of pointer tested, a trackstick was usually harder to control than a trackball or trackpad. To see if a notebook's pointing device suits you, try using it to drag an on-screen object across the screen. Several models' pointers had too much play for the fine movements required by some on-screen actions (see comment J in the Ratings), and the action buttons on some were hard to press.

◆ *Connections.* Most notebooks sport some built-in devices as well as an array of jacks, plugs, and slots. A built-in **diskette drive** is standard on most for installing software, transferring information to other computers, or making backups. Two PC (**PCMCIA**) **card slots** are standard on IBM-compatibles, for credit–card–sized devices such as a modem, hard drive, or CD-ROM interface. A built-in **fax/modem** leaves other PC slots free. Look for a data-transfer speed of at least 14,400 baud. A **built-in AC adapter** is more convenient than carrying a separate adapter. **Outlets** for monitor, keyboard, mouse, and audio allow you to hook up components from a desktop computer. A serial port connects with an external modem or serial printer. A parallel port connects with a parallel printer or another computer. A SCSI port adds a CD-ROM drive or other device to a Macintosh.

◆ *Battery life.* With the display and hard drive working flat out, longevity now ranges from 1½ to 3 hours, partly thanks to new battery chemistries that pack more power per pound than the older nickel-cadmium type. Nickel-metal hydride batteries are typical; lithium-ion, found on two of the notebooks tested (the *Dell Latitude XP* and *AST Ascentia 910N*), is even more efficient. But there's more to longevity than chemistry—what's being powered matters, too. The *AST Ascentia* lasted more than 3 hours, the *Dell* only 2½.

Notebooks all provide ample warning when the battery runs low, and most recharge while the computer is used plugged into an AC outlet. Various features let you extend battery life, switch batteries more easily, or save data in case the battery dies. Look for a standby mode; it lets you resume without a full restart. Some can save to the hard drive for an even longer-lived standby.

➤ *Processing speed.* How fast a computer runs is determined mainly by its processor—the electronic chip that runs its software. Processors come in families, with each family member bearing a clock speed—a number expressed in megahertz (MHz). The higher the MHz, the faster the chip.

Chip families also vary in speed. Among IBM-compatibles, the fastest processors are those of Intel's *Pentium* family. The *Pentiums* are still too expensive for moderately priced notebooks, but should soon drop in price. Notebooks such as those tested use the next fastest, processors of *Intel's 80486* family. To run Windows 95, you'll need at least a 50-MHz *80486* processor.

The new *Apple PowerBooks* will use the fast *PowerPC* family of processors. For now, *PowerBooks* use the *Motorola 68030* and faster *68LC040* processors. Models with the same processor may still perform differently because of variations in other components. Word processing, spreadsheet, and other programs were run in the tests to compare performance and measure speed. Differences between models one notch apart in the Ratings are big enough to notice. The fastest models were more than twice as fast as the slowest.

Processor type and speed are noted for each model in the Ratings.

➤ *Memory: RAM and hard drive.* When you buy a notebook, you'll have to choose how much RAM, or random-access memory, to equip it with

## Multimedia: Adding a CD-ROM to Your Notebook

Increasingly, software, games, and multimedia reference works require a CD-ROM drive. Adding one to a notebook computer and having it remain portable is something of an engineering feat. CD-ROM drives are bulky, heavy, and power hungry. To include a CD-ROM drive on the top-rated Toshiba, the manufacturer jettisoned the diskette drive, making it an external device that you must carry and plug in when needed. Because of the design difficulties, it's not clear whether notebook computers will all someday have a CD-ROM drive built in.

To run multimedia software, you also need sound circuitry and speakers. Standard on nearly all desktop computers, those features are found on only some notebooks, including all *Macs*.

Portable CD-ROM drives, from companies such as Sony, Zenith Data Systems, and MediaVision, are available. They're double-speed drives—quad-speed drives are now included with many desktop systems—priced at $300 to $500, about twice what a desktop version costs. According to tests of three such models, these portable drives work just barely adequately. If you buy one, watch out for compatibility. Some require built-in sound, and one requires a $200 adapter to work with IBM-compatibles. With headphones attached, all could be used as a portable CD player but consumed batteries voraciously.

and how large a hard drive; most models come ready to go in several configurations.

A computer's software operates in RAM. More RAM can improve performance and increase battery life in some applications. Notebooks typically come equipped with 4 or 8 MB of RAM. Windows (3.1 or 95) and Apple's System 7.5 run best with at least 8 MB.

The larger a computer's hard drive, the more software you can install and the more data you can store when the machine is turned off. The operating system alone takes 15 MB or more. Major applications, such as word processors, spreadsheet programs, and the like, typically eat up as much as 20 MB apiece. So it's fairly easy to fill a small (120 MB) hard drive. Many notebooks come with a 320-MB drive and some with a drive as large as 1 gigabyte (1000 megabytes).

You can usually upgrade RAM—figure $200 to $250 for 4 MB. Hard drives can be harder to upgrade, so buy the largest one you can afford. Software requirements are bound to keep increasing, and it's not uncommon for drives to be discontinued. IBM-compatibles can fit an add-on drive into their PC-card slots, but it takes both slots, leaving no room for other devices.

# ◗ Recommendations

If you have the room and don't need portability, get a regular desktop computer. For the cost of a notebook alone, you can buy a multimedia desktop of comparable speed and capacity, plus a printer.

If a notebook machine is right for you, any of the machines rated here

## What's Best for Special Uses?

For travelers seeking something durable and light, consider these models:

◆ *AST Ascentia 910N*
◆ *Compaq Contura 410C*
◆ *Dell Latitude XP 4100C*
◆ *Compaq LTE Elite 4/75C*
◆ *Macintosh 520c*
◆ *WinBook XP*

For students, or buyers on a tight budget, consider these models:

◆ *Compaq Contura 410C*
◆ *WinBook XP*
◆ *Epson ActionNote 660C*
◆ *Macintosh 520c*
◆ *Sharp PC-3010*
◆ *Macintosh 150*

would do the job. That includes even the lowly *Macintosh PowerBook 150*, some of whose versions are priced at less than $1,000—a pricetag that might give you a reason to put up with a design that's less than state-of-the-art.

A notebook computer is a very personal tool, and your own tastes may dictate choosing one model over another. If you're an Apple fan, for instance, your choice is reduced to a few models. Of the four tested, the *520c*, $2,600 with 8 MB of RAM, internal modem, and 240-MB hard drive, represents the best combination of value and performance. It's upgradable, too.

IBM-compatible designs vary considerably from brand to brand. To get a sense of what design you prefer, try out several models at a showroom. The *Compaq Contura 410C* and the *WinBook XP* are relatively low-priced at $2400 and $2,460 and have much to commend them. The *Toshiba T2150CDS* ($3,500) was top-rated for its speed and excellent design; it comes with a CD-ROM drive and sound for multimedia capability.

To stave off obsolescence, try to get all the capabilities you need now— 14,400 baud fax/modem, at least 8 megabytes of RAM, and at least 300 megabytes of hard-drive space—built in. A store that lets you return a model unconditionally, even if only for a limited time, has a clear advantage, given the volatile state of the computer market. Should a more capable successor come out a couple of weeks after you buy—not unlikely for many brands— you can trade up to the better model for free.

## ▶ The Tested Models

These models are considered moderate in price. Options were chosen to provide 8 MB RAM, a fax/modem, and a hard drive of about 300 MB, if available.

For the typical computer in this class , expect . . .
  ──◆ An overall package about 2 inches thick, 9 inches deep, and 10½ to 12 inches wide.
  ──◆ Backlit dual-scan color display with 640x480 (VGA) resolution.
  ──◆ One 1.44-MB 3½-inch diskette drive.
  ──◆ RAM that can be upgraded.
  ──◆ Fax/modem that's built in or is on PCMCIA card.
  ──◆ IBM-compatible models with slots for 2 Type II cards; Macs with a SCSI port for CD-ROM drives, etc.
  ──◆ Nickel-metal hydride rechargeable battery, easily replaced.
  ──◆ AC adapter/battery charger, able to charge at a lower rate while using computer, that weighs about 1 pound.
  ──◆ Ways to adjust functions to extend battery life.
  ──◆ Standby mode that saves work for quick restoration.
  ──◆ Full keyboard with keys that give adequate touch feedback and make a moderate amount of noise. On IBM-compatibles, some part doubles as a numeric keypad; on Macs, cursors are in a row, not a T, and there's no page up/down.
  ──◆ Ability to connect with external devices, including speakers if model has sound; IBM-compatibles can use expansion port to connect to many devices.
  ──◆ Installed operating system and applications, but no software manuals.
  ──◆ 1-year warranty on parts and labor.

# Computer Printers

Half the people who buy a printer now choose an ink-jet model, which prints more sharply, more quietly, and more rapidly than either a dot-matrix machine or older ink-jet models. Ink-jet printers range in price from $200, for black-and-white models, to $350 to $550 for machines that print in color.

You can now buy a laser or an LED (light-emitting diode) printer—the fastest and crispest performers of all—for as little as $400. (Prices for color laser printers remain in the stratosphere, as far as home use is concerned—$5,000 and up.) Laser and LED machines are "page printers"; they compose and print whole pages at a time, creating images with either a scanning laser or an array of LEDs. Other printer types process pages line by line.

This report includes Ratings of 22 desktop printers—color and monochrome, ink-jet and page. Also rated are three portable printers designed to be small and mobile enough to travel with a notebook computer such as those covered on page 172.

# Beyond the Ads

Specifications commonly touted in advertisements for printers can be misleading. For example, ads make much of resolution—the fineness of the machine's output, in dots per inch (dpi). While it's true that higher resolution generally yields better print quality, other factors also play a role, including the paper and ink used and how the dots are placed on the paper. Some printers with 300 dpi resolution printed better in the tests than those with 600 dpi—a resolution that's becoming the norm, even for inexpensive printers.

Be wary, too, of claims of printing speed. The pages-per-minute figures used in ads may be based on performance at the fastest possible print setting, which may produce results so poor that you'd seldom choose to print with it.

# Pressing Printer Questions

Before you hit the stores, ask yourself these basic questions:

——◆ *Mac or IBM-compatible?* A printer must be compatible with your computer type: Macintosh or IBM-compatible. Since owners of IBM-compatibles are more numerous than Mac users, they enjoy a broader selection of printers. Macintosh owners can choose among Mac-only printers marketed by Apple, which makes Macs, or Mac versions of some IBM-compatible printers. A Mac version usually costs about the same as its IBM-compatible relative, although there are exceptions—for example, the Brother HL-660, which costs $613 more in its Mac version.

——◆ *How much will you use your printer?* The cheapest printer may not be so cheap if you plan to use it a lot. Some low-priced printers are costly to use, once you add in the expense of ink or toner. Conversely, some pricey models are quite economical. Cost per page is included in the Ratings.

——◆ *Will you use the printer for graphics and photos?* Home computers handle an ever-widening array of images, including snapshots that have been transferred to floppy disk (rather than photo paper) and graphics prepared with simple kids' programs. As you prepare to buy a printer, consider how often you'll use photos and graphics on your computer and how good that art will need to look when it's printed out. A printer that excels at art may cost more than one that excels at text—and a printer that excels at both will cost still more. Pricier yet are those printers that readily handle Postscript, the file format required for professional-level graphics and desktop publishing.

——◆ *Color or black-and-white?* Ask not only how often you'll print graphics and photos, but how often they'll be in color. Although the cost of a color ink-jet printer has come down, you'll still pay a price for color capability—either in dollars or in compromises in the quality of black-and-white text, compared to a similarly priced laser printer. Unless you're sure you need color, choose a black-and-white printer.

——◆ *Do you need other home-office equipment?* If you do, and space is tight, a multifunction machine that combines a phone, ink-jet or laser printer, fax machine, photocopier, and sometimes even an image scanner might interest you. Such a unit can cost much less than buying components separately; prices start at about $700, for models with a black-and-white ink-jet printer. Expect some sacrifice in performance and features compared with separate components—and expect different models to be better at different functions.

## ▶ Toner vs. Ink: The Main Types Compared

### ◆ Page Printer

*Printing quality:* Crisp and clean. Laser and LED page printers create images electronically, using toner, much the same way a photocopier does. The tested models provided near-perfect renditions of text pages and at least good reproductions of black-and-white graphics and photos.

*Cost:* Prices have dropped dramatically in recent years. Black-and-white models now start at about $400 and run to about $800. More expensive models usually produce slightly crisper text and may have additional features or capabilities. Color laser printers start at about $5,000.

Paper and printing: about 3 to 4 cents a page.

*Advantages:*
——◆ Prints faster than ink-jets—four to six pages per minute.
——◆ Produces waterproof print that won't smudge.
——◆ Works well with plain, inexpensive copier paper.
——◆ Can print labels.
——◆ Some models have Postscript capability (for professional-level desktop publishing).

*Disadvantages:*
——◆ Costs more than the ink-jet type.
——◆ Laser models consume more energy than either LED or ink-jet printers while printing (although no printer is a heavy power consumer).

## RATINGS Notebook Computers

**As published in the September 1995 issue of *Consumer Reports***

| Brand and model | Price | Overall score<br>0    Poor—Excellent    100<br>P \| F \| G \| VG \| E | Speed | Display | Convenience | Battery life | Instructions |
|---|---|---|---|---|---|---|---|
| **IBM-COMPATIBLE MODELS** | | | | | | | |
| **Toshiba** Satellite Pro T2150CDS<br>486DX4-75, 520 MB, CD-ROM | $3500 | | ◉ | ◐ | ◉ | ◐ | ◐ |
| **Dell** Latitude XP 4100C<br>486DX4-100, 340 MB | *3500 | | ◉ | ◐ | ◐ | ◐ | ● |
| **IBM** ThinkPad 755CSE<br>486DX4-100, 340 MB | 3500 | | ◉ | ◐ | ◐ | ◐ | ◐ |
| **AST** Ascentia 910N<br>486DX4-75, 510 MB | 2900 | | ◐ | ◐ | ○ | ◉ | ○ |
| **Gateway 2000** Colorbook2<br>486DX4-100, 340 MB | 3200 | | ◐ | ◐ | ◐ | ◐ | ○ |
| **Compaq** Contura 410C<br>486DX2-50, 350 MB | 2400 | | ◐ | ◐ | ◐ | ◉ | ◐ |
| **Toshiba** Satellite T2100CS<br>486DX2-50, 330 MB | 2600 | | ◐ | ◐ | ◐ | ◐ | ◐ |
| **WinBook** XP 486DX4-100,<br>340 MB | 2460 | | ◐ | ◐ | ○ | ◐ | ● |
| **Compaq** LTE Elite 4/75C<br>486DX4-75, 340 MB | 3000 | | ◉ | ◐ | ○ | ◐ | ◐ |
| **Canon** InnovaBook 200LS<br>486DX4-100, 520 MB | 3200 | | ◐ | ◐ | ◐ | ⊖ | ○ |
| **Epson** ActionNote 660c<br>486DX2-66, 340 MB | 2300 | | ○ | ◐ | ○ | ◐ | ◐ |
| **Zenith Data Systems**<br>Z-Noteflex 486DX4-75, 340 MB | 3600 | | ◐ | ◐ | ◐ | ○ | ◐ |
| **Hewlett-Packard** OmniBook<br>4000C 486DX4-100, 340 MB | 3250 | | ◉ | ◐ | ◐ | ⊖ | ◐ |
| **Sharp** PC-3010<br>486DX2-66, 320 MB | 2200 | | ○ | ◐ | ◐ | ◐ | ○ |
| **Zeos** Meridian 800C<br>486DX4-100, 350 MB | 2995 | | ◉ | ◐ | ○ | ⊖ | ⊖ |
| **AST** Ascentia 810N<br>486DX2-66, 340 MB | 2450 | | ◐ | ◐ | ○ | ○ | ⊖ |
| **NEC** Versa M 75D<br>486DX4-75, 340 MB | 2750 | | ◉ | ◐ | ○ | ⊖ | ○ |
| **Epson** ActionNote 880C<br>486DX2-80, 340 MB | 2500 | | ○ | ◐ | ○ | ○ | ◐ |
| **APPLE MACINTOSH MODELS** | | | | | | | |
| **PowerBook** 540c 68LC040-66,<br>320 MB, Active | 3500 | | ○ | ◐ | ◐ | ⊖ | ● |
| **PowerBook** 520c 68LC040-50,<br>240 MB | 2600 | | ○ | ◐ | ◐ | ⊖ | ◐ |
| **PowerBook** 520 68LC040-50,<br>240 MB, Mono | 2300 | | ○ | ○ | ◐ | ⊖ | ● |
| **PowerBook** 150 68030-33,<br>250 MB, Mono | 1600 | | ⊖ | ⊖ | ⊖ | ○ | ● |

### Notes on the table

**Brand and model** gives the specifications for the model we tested, including the processor, its internal clock speed in megahertz, and the hard drive. IBM-compatibles use processors in the Intel 80486 family; Macintoshes the Motorola 68000 series. Unusual display types (active-matix, monochrome) and built-in devices (CD-ROM drive) are also noted. **Price** reflects recent selling prices (to within about $100); a * denotes the price CU paid. **Score** summarizes judgments of performance and features, with an emphasis on speed, convenience, display quality, and battery life. Models whose scores are within 10 points are essentially equal in quality. **Speed** shows how quickly each machine handled word processing and other typical applications, how fast it could render drawings on its screen, and how rapidly it could store and retrieve data on its hard drive. **Display** judgments are based on brightness, clarity, and color accuracy. **Convenience** includes overall design, presence of useful features, and provision of documentation. **Battery life** is based on how long computer ran under heavy, constant use; the best ran for more than 3 hrs. **Screen** size is measured on the diagonal. **Weight** includes computer, battery, and charging adapter. For models that have the charger built in, figure ¼ lb. additional for cord.

### Key to Comments
**Advantages**
A —Bundled software includes disks.

Consumer Reports Tests ◆ 18

●  ◐  ○  ◑  ●
Better ◄————————► Worse

| Screen | Total width | Weight | Pointer | Convenience notes | Comments |
|---|---|---|---|---|---|
| 10½ in. | 11¼ in. | 7½ pounds | Stick | Keys noisy, soft. External floppy drive, connects easily. 3-year warranty. **Pluses:** Built-in sound, AC adapter. | B,D,E,U |
| 9½ | 11 | 7 | Ball | Keys small. Lithium-ion battery. **Pluses:** Standby can save to disk; hard drive removable without tools. | B,C,D,E,F,O,P,Q,V |
| 10¼ | 11¼ | 7¼ | Stick | Keys noisy, firm. 3 year warranty. **Pluses:** Standby can save to disk; Built-in sound, modem. Hard drive removable without tools. **Minus:** No useful palmrest. | B,D,E,F,N,O,P |
| 10¼ | 11½ | 7 | Stick | Keys firm. Lithium-ion battery. 3-year warranty. **Pluses:** Standby can save to disk; hard drive removable without tools. Minus: No useful palmrest. | D,E,J,N,O,P,S |
| 10¼ | 11¼ | 6¼ | Stick | Keys soft. Includes padded case with strap. Pluses: Built-in sound. Hard drive removable without tools. **Minus:** No useful palmrest. | A,E,F,H,M,O,P,S |
| 9½ | 12 | 6¼ | Ball | Keys quiet. 3-year warranty. **Plus:** Standby can save to disk. | K,N,S |
| 10½ | 12 | 7 | Stick | Keys noisy, soft. Plus: Built-in AC adapter. | B,E,U |
| 10¼ | 11½ | 7 | Stick & pad or ball | Keys noisy, firm. **Pluses:** Standby can save to disk; built-in sound, modem (both optional). | A,B,J,L,P,S |
| 9½ | 11¼ | 6¼ | Ball | Keys quiet. 3-year warranty. **Pluses:** Built-in AC adaptor; standby can save to disk; hard drive removable without tools. **Minuses:** No useful palmrest; small trackball. | D,F,J,K,Q |
| 11¼ | 12 | 7¼ | Stick | Keys noisy. Includes padded case with strap. **Pluses:** Standby can save to disk; hard drive removable without tools; built-in sound. | G,L,N,O |
| 10¼ | 11 | 7¼ | Ball | Keys small, quiet. Plus: Standby can save to disk. Minus: Small trackball. | A,E,I,K,M,N,O,P,Q,R |
| 10¼ | 12 | 7¼ | Ball | Keys soft, quiet. Can take second battery. **Pluses:** Hard drive removable without tools; built-in sound. | D,E,F,I,K,R |
| 10¼ | 11¼ | 8¼ | Ball | Keys small. Can take second battery. 3-year warranty. **Pluses:** Standby can save to disk; large trackball; hard drive removable without tools; built-in sound. Minus: Can't recharge while using. | E,F,K,S |
| 10½ | 11½ | 7 | Pad | Keys small, quiet. Plus: Standby can save to disk; hard drive removable without tools. | E,I,O |
| 10½ | 11¼ | 7½ | Stick | Keys noisy. Includes padded case with strap, extra battery. **Minus:** Can't recharge while using. | A,B,H,J,M,N,O,P |
| 10½ | 10½ | 7 | Ball | Keys small. Can take second battery. 3-year warranty. **Pluses:** Standby can save to disk. **Minus:** No useful palmrest. | E,K,N,O,P |
| 9½ | 11¼ | 8¼ | Ball | Can take second battery. 3-year warranty. **Plus:** Hard drive removable without tools. **Minuses:** No useful palmrest; small trackball, requires both hands. | A,B,D,J,O,P,R |
| 10¼ | 11¼ | 6¼ | Pad | Keys small, noisy. **Pluses:** Standby can save to disk; hard drive removable without tools. **Minus:** Pointer buttons hard to press. | A,K,M,N,O,P,S |
| 9½ | 11½ | 7½ | Pad | Keys soft. Can take second battery, included. **Pluses:** Built-in sound; modem (optional). | E,i,P,R,T |
| 9½ | 11½ | 7½ | Pad | Keys soft. Can take second battery. **Pluses:** Built-in sound, modem (optional). | A,E,I,P,R |
| 9½ | 11½ | 7½ | Pad | Can take second battery. **Pluses:** Built-in sound, modem (optional). | E,I,P,R,T |
| 9½ | 11¼ | 6¼ | Ball | Mono sound, internal only. Nickel-cadmium battery. **Pluses:** Large trackball, built-in sound, modem (optional). **Minus:** Can't use external monitor. | I,M,P,S,T |

B —More printed documentation than most.
C —Battery has charge indicator.
D —"Battery-swap" mode allows quick changing without loss of work.
E —Standby mode can be activated by closing cover.
F —Diskette-drive slot on front.

**Disadvantages**
G —Small, tinny-sounding speakers.
H —PCMCIA cards protrude.
I —Can't display 1024x768 pixels with 256 colors on external monitor.
J —Play in pointing device makes fine movement somewhat difficult.
K —Pointer's buttons not easily pressed with thumb.

L —Parallel port transfers data slowly.

**Comments**
M —Comes with "works" integrated software package.
N —Comes with information-manager program.
O —Major on-line service installed.
P —Communications/fax software installed.
Q —Trackball cleaning tool.
R —Charger weighs about 1⅓ lb.
S —Charger weighs about ¾ lb.
T —Screen has wide viewing angle.
U —T2100CS also sold as T2105CS for about same price; 2150CDS also sold as T2155CDS.
V —Replaced by Latitude XP4100D.

# RATINGS Computer Printers

**As published in the September 1995 issue of *Consumer Reports***

| Brand and model | Price | Type | Color | IBM/Mac | Overall score (0 Poor—Excellent 100) | Print quality (B&W) TEXT | GRAPHICS | PHOTOS |
|---|---|---|---|---|---|---|---|---|
| **DESKTOP MODELS** | | | | | | | | |
| **Brother** HL-660 | $700 | Laser | — | ✔/$613 | | ◉ | ◐ | ◐ |
| **NEC** Silentwriter SuperScript 660I | 690 | Laser | — | ✔/— | | ◉ | ○ | ○ |
| **Okidata** OL410e | 570 | LED | — | ✔/— | | ◉ | ◉ | ○ |
| **Epson** ActionLaser 1400 | 600 | Laser | — | ✔/— | | ◉ | ○ | ◐ |
| **Hewlett Packard** LaserJet 4L | 500 | Laser | — | ✔/— | | ◉ | ○ | ◐ |
| **Texas Instr.** microLaser 600 | 829* | Laser | — | ✔/✔ | | ◉ | ○ | ○ |
| **Brother** HL-630, **A BEST BUY** | 400 | Laser | — | ✔/$80 | | ◐ | ○ | ○ |
| **Canon** LBP-430 | 565 | Laser | — | ✔/— | | ◉ | ◐ | ◐ |
| **Lexmark** WinWriter 400 | 725 | LED | — | ✔/— | | ◉ | ○ | ◐ |
| **Panasonic** KX-P4400, **A BEST BUY** | 450 | LED | — | ✔/— | | ◐ | ◉ | ○ |
| **Epson** Stylus Color ① | 520 | Inkjet | std | ✔/✔ | | ◐/◉ ② | ◐ | ◐ |
| **Apple** Personal LaserWriter 300 | 600 | Laser | — | —/✔ | | ◐ | ◐ | ○ |
| **Canon** BJC-4000, **A BEST BUY** | 350 | Inkjet | std | ✔/— | | ○/◐ ② | ◐ | ○ |
| **Hewlett Packard** DeskJet 560c ① | 425 | Inkjet | std | ✔/③ | | ○/○ ② | ◐ | ○ |
| **Hewlett Packard** DeskJet 540 ① | 270 | Inkjet | $40 | ✔/③ | | ○/○ ② | ○ | ○ |
| **Apple** StyleWriter II ① | 270 | Inkjet | — | —/✔ | | ◐ | ◐ | ● |
| **Epson** Stylus 400 ① | 200 | Inkjet | — | ✔/— | | ○ | ◐ | ○ |
| **Canon** BJ-200e ① | 220 | Inkjet | — | ✔/— | | ○ | ◉ | ◐ |
| **Apple** Color StyleWriter 2400 | 450 | Inkjet | std | —/✔ | | ○/◐ ② | ◉ | ◐ |
| **Lexmark** WinWriter 100 ① | 250* | Inkjet | — | ✔/— | | ◐ | ◐ | ● |
| **Radio Shack** JP 1000 | 399 | Inkjet | $70 | ✔/— | | ◐ | ◐ | ● |
| **Texas Instr.** microMarc Color ① | 380* | Inkjet | std | ✔/— | | ◐ | ● | ● |
| **PORTABLE MODELS (WEIGHT)** | | | | | | | | |
| **Citizen** PN60 Pocket Printer (1.7lb.) | 300 | Thermal | $7.50 | ✔/$38 | | ◐ | — | — |
| **Apple** Portable StyleWriter (4.4lb.) ① | 400 | Inkjet | — | —/✔ | | ◐ | — | — |
| **Canon** BJ-10sx (4.4lb.) ① | 250 | Inkjet | — | ✔/— | | ● | ◐ | ◐ |

① Discontinued, but remains available; see Comments for information on replacement model, which may not peform similarly.
② Score with better paper recommended by mfr.
③ Mac versions: DeskWriter 560c (for DeskJet 560c); DeskWriter 540 (for DeskJet 540).

## Notes on the table

**Price** is estimated average, based on a June 1995 national survey. An * indicates the price we paid (no average was available).

**Type.** Laser and LED printers are so-called page printers that compose and print a page at a time, using toner. **Ink-jet** and **thermal** printers print line by line, with ink.

**Color. Standard** on some ink-jet printers; **optional** on others, with the additional cost of the color cartridge and related software listed. For more, see "The Details on Color Performance," at the right.

**IBM/Mac.** Indicates whether the printer can be used with an **IBM**-compatible or **Macintosh** computer, or both. A price, if shown, is the extra cost of the Mac upgrade.

**Overall score** is based mainly on text quality and speed, with graphics and photo quality also considered.

**Print quality (black-and-white).** Reflects a staff panel's judgment of samples with identical **text, graphics** (pie and bar charts), and **photographs** produced in the best print mode. Printing was judged on plain copier paper, and additionally on any special paper recommended by the manufacturer. For graphics and photos, scores on both types of paper (if applicable) were averaged to yield a single judgment.

**Speed.** How quickly each printer turned out a page of double-spaced black text with standard margins in the best print mode. The swiftest took about 10 seconds, the slowest about 90 seconds.

**Cost per page.** For a double-spaced black-and-white document with standard margins on a single sheet of copier paper. Includes ink cartridge (for ink-jets), toner (for laser models), ribbon (for the one thermal printer), and wear to the drum or printhead.

**Resolution.** The maximum number of horizontal and vertical dots per inch, as stated by the manufacturer. While a higher resolution usually makes for higher-quality printing, that is not always the case, as the print-quality scores illustrate.

**Size.** Rounded to the nearest inch, including protrusions—cables, plugs, paper tray, and the like.

**Memory.** The **standard** and **maximum** (limit to which printer can be upgraded), in megabytes (millions of characters). The larger a printer's memory, the more rapidly a document can be downloaded to it—and the sooner the computer can do other work.

**Fonts.** The number of distinct typefaces, such as Palatino and Helvetica, built into each printer. DOS users may be restricted to these resident fonts. Windows and Macintosh users don't depend on the printer's typefaces, but a print job will be completed more rapidly if a font resides in the printer.

Better ◀———————▶ Worse

| Cost PER PG. | Speed B&W TEXT | Resolution | Size DXWXH | Memory STD. | MAX. | Fonts | Warranty | Comments |
|---|---|---|---|---|---|---|---|---|
| 3 ¢ | ● | 600x600 dpi | 27x15x16 in. | 2MB | 10MB | 18 | 1 yr. | A,E,F,H,P,W |
| 4 | ● | 600x600 | 20x15x10 | 2 | 64 | 16 | 2 | A,E,F,H,K,P,Q,W |
| 3 | ○ | 600x600 | 23x13x10 | 2 | 5 | 5 | 1 | D,J,K,M,P,S |
| 3 | ○ | 600x600 | 18x13x18 | 2 | 18 | 16 | 2 | A,E,F,H,L,P,W |
| 3 | ○ | 300x300 | 15x15x7 | 1 | 2 | 8 | 1 | E,F,K,P,T |
| 4 | ◐ | 600x600 | 22x14x14 | 2 | 10 | 4 | 1 | F,H,M,S,W |
| 4 | ● | 300X300 | 24x15x16 | 0.5 | 2 | 2 | 1 | A,E,F,P,S,W |
| 4 | ○ | 300x300 | 16x15x6 | 1 | 5 | 5 | 2 | F,K,P,T,W |
| 3 | ◐ | 300x300 | 17x15x10 | 2 | 6 | 1 | 1 | A,E,I,K,M,P,Q,T,X |
| 3 | ○ | 300x300 | 15x12x17 | 1 | 5 | 2 | 1 | D,H,L,O,P,W |
| 3 | ◑ | 720x720 | 24x19x12 | 0 | 0 | 7 | 2 | A,K,L,P,Q,S,V,Y,W |
| 3 | ○ | 300x300 | 16x16x7 | 0.5 | 0.5 | 15 | 1 | B,E,P, R,W |
| 4 | ○ | 720x360 | 22x15x11 | 0 | 0 | 8 | 2 | B,K,V,W |
| 3 | ○ | 600x300 | 19x18x9 | 0 | 0.5 | 4 | 3 | B,E,J,K,L,P,Q,V,Z |
| 3 | ○ | 600x300 | 21x17x8 | 0.5 | 0.5 | 4 | 3 | E,F,K,L,P,V, aa |
| 7 | ◑ | 360x360 | 22x14x11 | 0 | 0 | — | 1 | B,E,R,W,bb |
| 5 | ◑ | 360x360 | 16x18x7 | 0 | 0 | 6 | 2 | G,P, V,W, cc |
| 6 | ○ | 360x360 | 22x14x11 | 0 | 0 | 2 | 2 | V,W,dd |
| 3 | ○ | 360x360 | 22x15x11 | 0 | 0 | 16 | 1 | B,E,P,R,W |
| 3 | ○ | 600x300 | 28x15x14 | 0 | 0 | — | 2 | E,I,K,P,W |
| 5 | ◑ | 300x300 | 17x14x11 | 0.1 | 4 | 5 | 1 | G,J,S,V |
| 7 | ◐ | 300x300 | 23x16x8 | 0.1 | 0.1 | 5 | 1 | A,M,V,W,X |
| 31 | ● | 360x360 | 4x10x2 | 0 | 0 | 5 | 2 | C,R,S,U |
| 7 | ● | 360x360 | 9x15x7 | 0 | 0 | — | 1 | C,E,N,R,V,W,ee |
| 6 | ◑ | 360x360 | 9x15x7 | 0 | 0 | 5 | 2 | N,U,V,W, ff |

# The details on color performance

Here's how the color-capable printers we tested compare in performance and cost when printing in color. Models are listed in order of overall score, as detailed in the main Ratings table.

| Brand and model | Graphics | Photos | Color quality COPIER | OTHER | Cost INK | Type |
|---|---|---|---|---|---|---|
| **Epson** Stylus Color | ◐ | ◐ | ○ | ◐ | ● | CMYK |
| **Canon** BJC-4000 | ● | ○ | ○ | ● | ○ | CMYK |
| **Hewlett Packard** DeskJet 560c | ◐ | ◐ | ○ | ● | ◐ | CMYK |
| **Hewlett Packard** DeskJet 540 | ◐ | ◑ | ◑ | ● | ◑ | CMY |
| **Apple** Color StyleWriter 2400 | ◐ | ◐ | ○ | ◐ | ○ | CMYK |
| **Radio Shack** JP 1000 | ○ | ◑ | ◑ | — | ● | CMY |
| **Texas Instruments** microMarc Color | ○ | ◑ | ◑ | — | ● | CMY |
| **Citizen** PN60 Pocket Printer | — | — | — | — | ● | CMYK |

**Notes** Judgments reflect panelists' opinions of sharpness, resolution, and shading. Our engineers judged **color quality,** paying most attention to accuracy and richness. Where both **copier** and **other** paper recommended by the manufacturer were used, results were averaged for the graphics and photos columns. Even when special paper is used, the **cost** of printing in color goes mostly to ink. A full page of color graphics could cost several dollars to print on the costliest models; 50 cents or less on the least costly. CMYK-**type** models print a blacker black by switching back and forth automatically between black and CMY (cyan, magenta, and yellow) cartridges. On color pages, CMY printers usually print a muddy, mixed black. No printing judgments are given for the Citizen; it prints only text in color.

## Key to comments
### Printing
A —Printed test graphics faster than most.
B —Printed test graphics slower than most.
C —Cannot print graphics or photos.
D —LCD on front panel indicates printer status.
E —Printer status displayed on computer screen.
F —Has printer console program for DOS.
G —Can't print transparencies.
H —Option for Postscript capability (standard for Texas Instruments model).
I —Must use Microsoft Windows to print.
J —Optional font cartridge.
K —Has resolution enhancement, technology claimed to improve print quality.

### Paper handling
L —Winding paper path; heavy paper could bind or curl.
M —Optional paper trays.
N —Portable model has optional sheet feeder.
O —Cannot print envelopes.

### Miscellaneous
P —Has energy-saving mode.
Q —Requires more hard-disk space than other models.
R —Includes printer cable.
S —Serial interface standard or optional; allows printer hookup to computer if parallel port in use.
T —Toner cartridges can be recycled by manufacturer.
U —Battery pack costs extra.
V —Label printing not recommended by manufacturer.
W —Phone number for technical support is toll-free (phone support is available for all printers).

### Replacement models
X —No replacement; unavailable at most stores.
Y —Stylus Color II.
Z —DeskJet 660c (performed better on text, much better on color graphics & photos, and worse on B&W photos than 560C) and DeskWriter 660c (Mac version).
aa—DeskJet/DeskWriter 600.
bb—StyleWriter 1200, $270. Performed better on graphics and photos, worse on text than StyleWriter II.
cc—Stylus Color IIs.
dd—BJ-200ex, $270.
ee—Color StyleWriter 2200.
ff —BJ-30.

### ◆ Ink-jet Printer

*Printing quality:* These printers fire ink onto paper from an array of narrow nozzles that form characters or graphics. Despite improvements in that technology, text from the best ink-jet printer is still a notch below that from the best page printers. Graphics, both black-and-white and color, range from poor to excellent.

*Cost:* Prices for black-and-white ink jets range from $200 to $350. Higher-priced black-and-white models may offer color as an option. Models that come with color capability currently cost $350 to $550 or so, but prices are falling fast.

*Paper and printing:* about 3 to 7 cents per page (text); several cents to several dollars a page (color graphics).

*Advantages:*
—◆ Costs less than a page printer with comparable capabilities.
—◆ Consumes less energy than a page printer.

*Disadvantages:*
—◆ Uses water-soluble ink that smears easily (use of a highlighter can cause smudging).
—◆ Most models can't print labels.
—◆ Prints more slowly than a page printer—most ink-jets turn out three to four text pages per minute.
—◆ Will accept plain copier paper, but may require special coated paper for best results or highest resolution printing.

## ⦿ Promise vs. Performance: Test Results

### ◆ Type Quality

*Text:* The best page printers, including the NEC, set the standard with type that was crisp and dark black. Most ink-jet printers, such as the *Canon BJ-200*, produced type that was a little more jagged and a little more gray than that of the page printers, but did produce decent type. A few ink-jet printers produced far more jagged type than did the *Canon*.

*Paper:* Fancy paper made little difference to most of the printers for which it was recommended. An exception was the *Epson Stylus Color*—the highest-resolution printer tested. When it printed on the special, dime-a-sheet stock recommended by Epson, jet-black words seemed to jump off the bright white surface. On copier paper, however, the *Epson*'s print was only fair.

### ◆ Graphics

*Color:* For the most part, the color ink-jet printers did a very good job, especially with high-quality paper. Using such paper, the *Canon* excelled, turning out dense, richly colored graphics with sharp edges and fine detail. The *Hewlett-Packard 540* gave typical results.

*Black-and-white:* No type or price range of printer stood out in these tests. The *Panasonic LED* printer was among the top performers; its graphics had sharply defined black areas and gray areas that broke into many different shades. In the middle of the pack was the *Brother HL-630*. Its graphics, though quite readable, were a little dark overall.

### ◆ Photos

*Color:* Don't expect a printer to match prints from a film processor. But on special paper some, including the *Epson Stylus Color*, came close to the quality of a $50,000 commercial printer. Others, including the *Hewlett Packard 540*, produced photos that were a little muddy.

*Black-and-white:* Price and printer type were no predictor of performance, which was generally good. A few models (including the ink-jet *Apple Color StyleWriter*) stood out slightly for its sharp resolution and subtle shading. The laser *Hewlett-Packard* was a little below par.

### ◆ Other Considerations

*On-screen warnings:* Half the printers tested make you aware, on the computer screen, of any major problems after you send a print job. Others inform you via the control panel, with either a liquid-crystal display or—the least convenient option—a warning light that doesn't specify what the problem is.

*Ports for all:* Printers with both Mac and IBM-compatible ports facilitate a future change in your computer.

*A sizable difference:* Desktop printers vary dramatically in how much space they consume. Sizes of ink-jet models also ranged widely.

For a typical model, expect . . .
——◆ Much faster printing of text than of graphics and photos.
——◆ Ability to print envelopes, labels, and transparencies.
——◆ A density control to lighten printing, cut ink/toner use.
——◆ For IBM-compatible models: ability to run with either Microsoft Windows or DOS.

## The $400 Printer—How It's Changed

1991: $400 bought an early model of a black-and-white ink-jet printer—or a top dot-matrix printer, noisier than an ink-jet printer.

1993: An early model of a color ink-jet printer, with muddy black text on color pages. (Dot-matrix printers were already fading, and page-printer prices were barely below three figures.)

1995: A high-resolution color ink-jet, with crisp black text on color pages. Or a black-and-white page printer, faster than any ink-jet.

⟶◆ Quiet operation.
⟶◆ Paper tray that typically holds 100 sheets.
⟶◆ Minimal power consumption (3 to 15 watts) when idling.
⟶◆ Extra cost for printer cable.

For a typical portable, expect . . .
⟶◆ Light weight (less than 5 pounds) and very small footprint—about half the size of many desktop models.
⟶◆ Option for battery-powered operation.
⟶◆ No paper tray.

## ⧊ Recommendations

If you use a printer infrequently, for text that needn't be of the highest quality, choose a good black-and-white ink-jet printer such as the *Epson Stylus 400,* a small machine that costs just $200, the *Canon BJ-200e,* $220, or the *Apple StyleWriter II,* $270. *The Hewlett-Packard Deskjet 540,* $270, costs a bit more than most of those models, but it prints more cheaply, has a three-year warranty, and can be upgraded to color for an additional $40.

If color and graphics matter to you, choose a standout ink-jet printer such as the *Canon BJC-4000,* a Best Buy at $350. That *Canon* did a decent job printing color, and it printed text (on expensive special paper) almost as well as the priciest page printers.

---

## Portable printers

These are handy for printing on the run, but manufacturers have sacrificed quality for compactness.

*How they work:* Most are dual-powered—battery or plug in—and employ ink-jet technology, which requires little electrical energy. One model tested prints by thermal fusion: As the print cartridge moves across the page, heat transfers ink from a ribbon onto the paper.

*Print quality:* Subpar. In the tests, images and characters weren't very dark and revealed jagged or fuzzy edges. Also, printouts from these machines showed pronounced ghosting, or outline shadows.

*Cost:* Prices start at $250 or so. Paper and printing: 6 to 31 cents a page.

*Advantages:*
◆ Lightweight and portable enough to fit inside a briefcase.
◆ Battery operation enables use even when no AC outlet is handy.

*Disadvantages:*
◆ Prints very slowly—no more than two pages per minute.
◆ Limited availability of color-capable models.
◆ Some models do not print graphics or photos.
◆ High printing costs.

For printing text, a black-and-white page printer will be more economical and much faster than most ink-jet machines. The *Brother HL-630* is A Best Buy at $400 ($480 for its Mac version). Though slower than the *Brother,* the *Panasonic KX-P4400,* $450, also A Best Buy, is much better at graphics, and has a smaller footprint.

Consider the expensive printers that top the Ratings only if you demand text that's near-flawless. Portable printers are at best marginal performers and are fairly pricey, given what you get. (Some are also exorbitantly expensive to use—like the *Citizen* tested, which ran through its $7.50 black-ink cartridges in no more than 25 pages.) Buy a portable printer only if you must print pages where no desktop printer is practical.

# Manufacturers Resource Guide

The presence of a company on this list of manufacturers of computers and components should not be interpreted as a recommendation or endorsement, nor should the absence of a manufacturer be considered a disqualification. This list is not intended to be comprehensive but rather is offered here only as a convenience in helping you to contact companies and gather product information. (Companies that provide only services or supplies have not been included.)

**Acer America Technologies Corp.,**
408-432-6200

**Adaptec, Inc.,** 408-944-2541

**ADI Systems, Inc.,** 800-228-0530

**Adobe Systems Inc.,**
415-961-4400/800-833-6687

**Advanced Computer Techniques Corp.,** 212-696-3600

**Advanced Logic Research, Inc.,**
714-581-6770/800-444-4ALR

**Advanced Micro Devices,**
800-222-9323

**Aicom Corp.,** 408-453-8251

**AI Squared,** 802-362-3612

**Aldus Corp.,**
206-622-5500/800-332-5387

**Alpha Microsystems,**
714-957-8500/800-992-9779

**Alpharel, Inc.,** 805-482-9815

**Alpha Software Corp.,**
617-229-2924/800-451-1018

**Alps America,**
408-432-6000/ 800-825-ALPS

**ALR** see **Advanced Logic Research, Inc.**

**Alta Research Corp.,**
305-428-8535/800-423-8535

**Altai, Inc.,** 817-640-8911

**Amdek,** 512-343-4530/800-792-6335

**American Megatrends, Inc.,**
404-263-8181/800-U-BUY-AMI

**American Power Conversion Corp.,**
401-789-5735/800-541-8896

**AMI** see **American Megatrends, Inc.**

**Amrel Technologies, Inc.,**
800-88-AMREL

**AMS,** 818-814-8851/800-868-8108

**Antex Electronics,**
310-532-3092/800-338-4231

**AOC International (U.S.A.) Ltd.,**
408-954-0325/800-443-7516

**Apertus Technologies, Inc.,**
612-828-0300

**Apogee Software,**
214-278-5655/800-GAME-123

**Apple Computer, Inc.,**
408-996-1010/800-538-9696

**Applied Magnetics Corp.,**
805-349-1234/800-328-5640

**Archive Corp.,**
714-641-1230/800-537-2248

**ARIX Corp.,** 408-432-1200

**Artisoft, Inc.,** 602-293-4000

**ASK Computer Systems, Inc.,**
410-494-0777

**Aspen Imaging International, Inc.,**
303-666-5750/800-955-5555

**Aspen Systems, Inc.,**
303-431-4606/ 800-992-9242

**AST Research, Inc.,**
714-727-4141/800-876-4AST

**Atari Computer Corp.,**
408-745-2000/800-443-8020

**ATI Technologies, Inc.,**
905-882-2600

**Austin Direct,**
512-339-3500/800-483-9938

**Autodesk, Inc.,**
415-332-2344/800-228-3601

**Aztech Labs, Inc.,**
510-623-8999/800-886-8879

**Banner Blue Software,**
800-291-9380

Banyan Systems, Inc.,
508-898-1000/800-828-2404
Base Ten Systems, Inc.,
609-586-7010
Basis International,
505-345-5232/800-423-1394
Best Power Technology,
608-565-7200/800-356-5794
BGS Systems, Inc., 617-891-0000
Bloc Development Corp.,
305-567-9931
BMC Software, Inc.,
713-240-8800/ 800-841-2031
Boole & Babbage, Inc.,
408-735-9550
Borland International, Inc.,
408-439-1411/ 800-331-0877
Broderbund Software, Inc.,
415-382-4400/800-521-6263
Bytex Corp.,
508-366-8000/800-23-BYTEX

Cabletron Systems, Inc.,
603-332-9400
Caere Corp.,
408-395-7000/800-535-7226
Cambex Corp., 617-890-6000
Canon Computer Systems, Inc.,
800-848-4123
(800-263-1121 in Canada)
CE Software Holdings, Inc.,
515-224-1995/ 800-5CE-SOFT
Central Point Software, Inc.,
503-690-8080/800-445-4208
Cerner Corp., 816-221-1024
Cheyenne Software, Inc.,
516-484-5110/800-243-9462
Chinon America, Inc.,
310-533-0274/800-441-0222
ChipSoft, Inc.,
619-453-8722/ 800-782-1120
Cimflex Teknowledge Corp.,
412-787-3000/800-837-2685
Ciprico Inc.,
612-551-4000/800-727-4669
CMS/Data Corp., 904-878-5155
CMS Enhancements, Inc.,
714-259-5888
Cognex Corp., 617-449-6030
Cognitronics Corp., 203-327-5307
Colorado Memory Systems, Inc.,
303-669-8000/800-346-9881

Commodore International Ltd.,
215-431-9100/800-627-9595
COMNET Corp., 301-220-5400
Compaq Computer Corp.,
713-370-0670/800-231-0900
Comptek Research, Inc.,
716-842-2700
CompuSharp Integrated
Services, Inc., 214-934-9088
Computer Associates International,
Inc., 516-432-1764/800-225-5224
Computer Identics Corp.,
617-821-0830/800-343-0846
The Computer Language Co.,
215-297-5999
Computer Peripherals, Inc.,
805-499-5751/800-854-7600
Computervision Corp.,
617-275-1800
CompuTrac, Inc., 214-234-4241
Comshare, Inc.,
313-994-4800/800-922-7979
Concurrent Computer Corp.,
908-758-7000/800-631-2154
Conner Peripherals, Inc.,
408-456-4500
Consilium, Inc., 415-691-6100
Control Data Systems, Inc.,
612-482-2401
Control Vision,
316-231-6647/800-292-1160
Convergent Solutions, Inc.,
908-290-0090
CONVEX Computer Corp.,
214-497-4000
Corporate Software, Inc.,
617-821-4500
Creative Labs, Inc.,
408-428-6600/800-998-5227
CSP Inc., 617-272-6020
CTX International, Inc.,
909-595-6146
Curtis, Inc., 612-631-9512
CYBEX, 205-430-4000

Dallas Semiconductor,
214-450-0400
Data Electronics U.S.A., Inc.,
714-851-5300/800-9-LOGGER
Dataflex Corp., 908-321-1100
Data General Corp.,
508-366-8911/800-DG-HELPS

Datalux Corp., 703-662-1500
Datapoint Corp.,
210-593-7000/800-334-9968
Dataram Corp.,
609-799-0071/800-822-0071
Datasouth Computer Corp.,
704-523-8500/800-476-2120
Datastorm, 314-443-3282
Data Translation, Inc.,
508-481-3700/800-268-0427
DEC see Digital Equipment Corp.
Dell Computer Corp.,
512-338-4400/800-BUY-DELL
Delorme Mapping, 207-865-1234
Delrina Technology, Inc.,
408-363-2345/800-268-6082
DH Technology, Inc., 619-451-3485
Diamond Computer Systems, Inc.,
408-736-2000
Digital Communications
Associates, Inc.,
404-442-4000/800-348-3221
Digital Equipment Corp.,
508-467-3156/800-332-3424
Digital Research, Inc.,
408-646-6464/800-274-4374
Distributed Processing Technology,
407-830-5522/800-322-4DPT
DPT see Distributed Processing
Technology
Drexler Technology Corp.,
415-969-7277
Dynamic Graphics, Inc.,
309-688-8800/800-255-8800

Electronic Associates, Inc.,
908-229-1100
Electronic Arts, Inc.,
415-572-2787/800-245-4525
ELMA Electronics, Inc.,
510-656-3400
ELXSI Corp., 408-942-0900
EMC Corp., 508-435-1000
Emulex Corp.,
714-662-5600/800-ON-CHIP-2
Epson America, Inc.,
310-782-2698/800-289-3776
(800-GO EPSON in Canada)
Evans & Sutherland
Computer Corp., 801-582-5847
Everex Systems, Inc.,
510-498-1111/800-821-0806

Evolution Computing,
602-967-8633/800-874-4028
Exabyte Corp., 303-447-7741
Excalibur Technologies Corp.,
703-790-2110

FDP Corp., 305-858-8200
Fifth Generation Systems, Inc.,
504-291-7221/800-873-4384
Foresight Resources Corp.,
816-891-1040/800-231-8574
FormGen Corp., 416-857-4141
Frame Technology Corp.,
408-433-3311/800-843-7263
Fujitsu America, Inc.,
408-894-3980/800-626-4686
Funk Software,
617-497-6339/800-822-3865

Gateway Communications, Inc.,
714-553-1555/800-367-6555
Gateway 2000, Inc.,
605-232-2000/800-846-2058
General Automation, Inc.,
714-778-4800
General DataComm Industries,
Inc., 203-574-1118/800-777-4005
General Parametrics Corp.,
415-524-3950/800-223-0999
GENICOM Corp.,
703-949-1000/800-436-4266
Geodynamics Corp., 310-782-7277
Goal Systems International, Inc.,
614-888-1775
Group 1 Software, Inc.,
301-982-2000/800-368-5806
GTEK, Inc.,
601-467-8048/800-282-4835
Hathaway Corp., 303-426-1600
Haventree Software, Ltd.,
613-544-6035/800-267-0668
Hayes Microcomputer Products,
Inc., 404-449-8791/800-426-7704
Heath Co.,
616-925-6000/800-253-0570
Helix Software Co., Inc.,
718-392-3100/800-451-0551
Henter-Joyce, Inc.,
813-528-8900/800-336-5658
Hertz Computer Corp.,
212-684-4141/800-BE-A-USER

Hewlett-Packard Co.,
415-857-1501/800-752-0900
Hogan Systems, Inc., 214-386-0020
Honeywell,
915-585-8892/800-328-5111
Hoolean Corp.,
602-634-7515/800-937-1337
Howtek, Inc., 603-882-5200
Hutchinson Technology Inc.,
612-587-3797

IBM Corp. see International
Business Machines Corp.
ICOT Corp.,
408-433-3300/800-SNA-3270
ID Software see Apogee Software
IKOS Systems, Inc., 408-245-1900
Impulse Software, 800-6-IMPULSE
IMRS Inc., 203-321-3500
Infodata Systems Inc.,
716-381-7430
Informix Corp., 415-926-6300
Insight Direct,
602-902-1128/ 800-998-8014
Integrated Information
Technology, Inc.,
408-727-1885/800-832-0770
Integrated Systems, Inc.,
408-980-1500
Intel Corp.,
503-629-7402/800-538-3373
IntelliCorp, Inc.,
415-965-5700/800-533-0123
Intelligent Systems Corp.,
404-381-2900
Interface Systems, Inc.,
313-769-5900/800-544-4072
Intergraph Corp.,
205-730-2000/800-345-4856
Interleaf, Inc., 617-577-9800
Intermetrics, Inc., 617-661-1840
International Business
Machines Corp.,
914-765-1900/800-IBM-2468
International Power Machines
Corp., 212-953-0100
Interphase Corp., 214-919-9000
Interplay Productions,
714-545-9001/800-969-4263
Iomega Corp.,
801-778-1000/800-777-6618
IOTech, Inc., 216-439-4091

IPL Systems, Inc., 617-890-6620

Key Tronic Corp.,
509-928-8000/800-262-6006
Kingston Technology Corp.,
714-438-1850/800-435-0670
KnowledgeWare, Inc.,
404-231-8575/800-338-4130
Komag, Inc., 408-946-2300

Landmark Graphics Corp.,
713-560-1000
LaserMaster Technologies, Inc.,
612-941-8687/800-LMC-PLOT
LEGENT Corp.,
703-734-9494/800-999-5266
Logitech, Inc.,
510-792-8901/800-231-7717
Lotus Development Corp.,
617-577-8500/800-343-5414

Macola, Inc.,
614-382-5999/800-468-0834
MAI Systems Corp., 714-731-5100
Manatron, Inc., 616-375-5300
Masstor Systems Corp.,
408-988-1008
MathSoft, Inc.,
617-577-1017/800-628-4223
Maxtor Corp.,
408-432-1700/800-284-4629
McAfee Associates, Inc.,
408-988-3832/800-332-9966
MECA Software, Inc.,
203-256-5000/800-288-MECA
Media Graphics International,
Inc., 303-427-8808
Medicus Systems Corp.,
708-570-7500
Megadata Corp., 516-589-6800
Mentor Graphics Corp.,
503-685-7000
Micro Healthsystems, Inc.,
201-731-9252
Micronics Computers, Inc.,
510-651-2300/800-234-4386
Micropolis Corp.,
818-709-3300/800-395-3748
MicroProse, Inc.,
410-771-1151/800-879-PLAY
Microsoft Corp.,
206-882-8080/800-426-9400

MicroSolutions,
815-756-3411/800-890-7227
Microtek Lab, Inc.,
310-297-5000/800-654-4160
MicroTouch Systems, Inc.,
508-694-9900/800-UNMOUSE
Mindscape,
415-883-3000/800-234-3088
Mitsubishi Electronics America,
714-220-2500
Motorola Semiconductor Products,
512-873-2000, see also Universal
Data Systems/Motorola
MPC Technologies, Inc.,
714-724-9000/800-672-8088
Multitech Systems, Inc.,
612-785-3500/800-328-9717
Mylex Corp.,
510-796-6100/800-800-2MNC

Nanao USA, Corp.,
310-325-5202/800-800-5202
National Datacomputer, Inc.,
508-663-7677/800-346-1006
NEC Home Electronics (USA), Inc.,
708-860-9500/800-FONE-NEC
NEC Information Systems,508-
264-8000/800-632-4636
Network Computing Devices,
Inc., 415-694-0650
Network General Corp.,
415-688-2700/800-952-6300
Network Systems Corp.,
612-424-4888
Newbridge Networks, Inc.,
703-834-3600
Newer Technology,
316-685-4904/800-678-3726
New Image Industries Inc.,
818-702-0285
North Atlantic Industries, Inc.,
516-582-6500
Novell, Inc.,
801-429-7000/800-453-1267

Okidata,
609-235-2600/800-654-3282
On-Line Software International,
Inc., 201-592-0009/800-642-0177
Oracle Corp.,
415-506-7000/800-ORACLE-1

Osicom Technologies, Inc.,
201-586-2550/800-922-0881

Packard Bell, 818-704-3905
Panasonic Communications
& Systems,
201-392-6144/800-742-8086
Parametric Technology Corp.,
617-894-7111
PAR Technology Corp.,
315-738-0600
Passport Designs, 800-443-3210
PC Poeer and Cooling, Inc.,
619-931-5700/800-722-6555
PDA Engineering, 714-540-8900
Penril DataComm,
301-921-8600/800-4-PENRIL
Phoenix Technologies Ltd.,
617-551-4000
Philips Consumer Electronics Co.,
615-521-4316/800-242-9225
Pixel Perfect, Inc., 407-779-0310
PKware, Inc., 414-354-8699
Platinum Technology, Inc.,
708-620-5000
Plextor, 408-980-1838/800-475-3986
Poly Software International,
801-485-0466
Practical Enhanced Logic Corp.,
714-282-6188
Practical Peripherals, Inc.,
805-497-4774
Printronix, Inc.,
714-863-1900/800-826-3874
Progress Software Corp.,
617-275-4500/800-327-8445
PSI see Poly Software International
Pyramid Technology Corp.,
415-965-7200

QMS, Inc.,
205-633-4300/800-631-2692
Quadram Corp., 404-923-6666
Qualitas, Inc.,
301-907-6700/800-733-1377
Quantum Corp.,
408-894-4000/800-367-1984
Quarterdeck Office Systems, Inc.,
310-392-9851/800-387-2744
Qume Corp.,
408-952-4000/800-458-2479

Radio Shack see Tandy Corp.
Radius, Inc.,
408-434-1010/800-227-2795
Rainbow Technologies, Inc.,
714-454-2100/800-852-8569
RasterOps,
408-562-4200/800-729-2656
Read-Rite Corp., 408-262-6700
Reference Software International,
415-541-0222/800-872-9933
Retix, 310-828-3400/800-255-2333
Rexon Inc., 310-545-4441

Samsung Electronics America, Inc.,
201-229-4000/800-SAMSUNG
SBE, Inc.,
510-680-7722/800-347-2666
Scan-Optics, Inc.,
203-289-6001/800-243-3153
Scientific Software-Intercomp,
Inc., 303-292-1111
Scitor Corp.,
415-570-7700/800-533-9876
Seagate Technology, Inc.,
408-438-8111/800-468-3472
Seiko Instruments USA, Inc.,
408-922-5900/800-888-0817
Sequoia Systems, Inc.,
508-480-0800
Sharp Electronics Corp.,
201-529-8200/800-BE-SHARP
Sierra On-Line, Inc.,
209-683-4468/800-326-6654
Sigma Designs, Inc.,
510-770-0100/800-845-8060
Silicon General, Inc., 408-943-9403
Silicon Graphics, Inc.,
415-960-1980/800-338-6272
SofTech, Inc., 617-890-6900
SoftSource,
206-676-0999/800-626-0999
Software Corporation of America,
203-359-2773
Software Publishing Corp.,
415-962-8910/800-282-6003
Software Spectrum, Inc.,
214-840-6600
Software Toolworks, Inc. see
Mindscape
Sony Information Products Co.,
201-930-1000/800-222-7669
Sperry Corp., 203-729-4589

Spinnaker Software Corp.,
617-494-1200/800-826-0706
SPSS, Inc., 800-543-5833
Stac Electronics,
619-431-7474/800-522-7822
Standard Microsystems Corp.,
516-273-3100/800-762-4968
StarGate Technologies, Inc.,
216-349-1860/800-782-7428
Star Technologies, Inc.,
703-689-4400
State of the Art, Inc.,
714-753-1222/800-854-3415
StatSoft, 918-583-4149
Storage Technology Corp.,
303-673-5151
Stratus Computer, Inc.,
508-460-2000
Structural Dynamics
Research Corp., 513-576-2400
Summagraphics Corp.,
203-881-5400
Sun Microsystems, Inc.,
415-960-1300/800-821-4643
Sunward Technologies, Inc.,
619-587-9140
SWFTE International, Ltd.,
302-234-1750/800-237-9383
Sybase, Inc.,
510-596-3500/800-879-2273
Symantec Corp.,
503-334-6054/800-441-7234
Symbolics, Inc., 617-221-1000
Symix Systems, Inc., 614-523-7000
Synercom Technology, Inc.,
713-954-7000
SynOptics Communications, Inc.,
408-988-2400/800-PRO-8023
SyQuest Technology, Inc.,
510-226-4000/800-245-2278
Sysgen, Inc., 408-263-6667
System Industries, Inc.,
408-432-1212
Systems Center, Inc., 703-264-8000

System Software Associates, Inc.,
312-641-2900

Tagram System Corp., 714-258-3222
Tandem Computers Inc.,
408-725-6000
Tandy Corp., 817-390-3700
Tangent Computer, Inc.,
415-342-9388/800-223-6677
Tatung Company of America, Inc.,
213-979-7055/800-827-2850
Taxan USA Corp.,
408-946-3400/800-829-2641
Techworks,
512-794-8533/800-434-4036
Teknekron Communications
Systems, Inc., 415-649-3700
Teknike Electronics Corp.,
201-575-0380/800-962-1271
Tektronix, Inc.,
503-682-7370/800-835-6100
TeleVideo Systems, Inc.,
408-954-8333/800-624-4920
Texas Instruments,
512-250-7111/800-527-3500
3COM Corp.,
408-764-5000/800-NET-3COM
Timberline Software Corp.,
503-626-6775
Toshiba of America, Inc.,
714-583-3000/800-457-7777
TouchStone Software Corp.,
714-969-7746/800-531-0450
Traveling Software, Inc.,
206-483-8088/800-662-2652
Tripp Lite, 312-755-5400
Tri-Star Computer Corp.,
602-731-4926/800-473-6223
Tseng Labs, Inc., 215-968-0502
TSL Holdings, 805-523-0340
TVM Professional Monitor Corp.,
714-985-4788/800-822-8168
Twin Head Corp., 408-945-0808

UDS see Universal Data
Systems/Motorola

Universal Data Systems/Motorola,
205-430-8000/ 800-631-4869
US Robotics, Inc.,
708-982-5010/800-DIAL-USR

Valid Logic Systems Inc.,
408-432-9400
Vermont Research Corp.,
802-886-2256
Vertisoft Systems, Inc. see
Working Software, Inc.
Videx, 503-758-0521
View Sonic, 909-869-7976
Visual Software, Inc.,
818-883-7900/800-881-4108

Wang Laboratories, Inc.,
508-459-5000/800-835-9264
Weitek Corp., 408-738-8400
Western Digital Corp.,
714-932-5000/800-356-5787
WordPerfect Corp.,
801-225-5000/800-451-5151
WordStar International, Inc.,
415-382-8000/800-227-5609
Working Software, Inc.,
408-423-5696
WP Corp. see WordPerfect Corp.

Xerox Corp.,
716-422-3214/ 800-822-2502
Xircom, Inc.,
818-878-7600/800-874-7875
Xscribe Corp., 619-457-5091
Xtree Co.,
805-541-0604/800-634-5545

Zenith Data Systems,
708-808-4848/800-553-0331
ZEOS International, Ltd.,
612-633-6131/800-272-8993
Zitel Corp., 408-946-9600
Zylab Corp.,
708-459-8000/800-544-6339
ZYXEL, 714-693-0808

# Online Services and Bulletin Board Systems Guide

The following is a list of selected online information services and bulletin board systems (BBS). Telephone numbers and brief descriptions are included for each entry. The presence of a service on the list should not be considered a recommendation or endorsement, nor should the absence of any system be considered a disqualification. The list is a small representative sampling and is not intended to be comprehensive. It is provided mainly to assist you in gathering information about these services.

Many of the services listed are geared toward a general audience and suitable for nearly anyone; however, others are intended for and would be useful to only a narrow group of special-interest users. Check out a service very carefully before committing to a membership and any associated financial obligation. (Refer to the section on Telecommunications Software in Chapter 4 for a general discussion of what is involved in and required for connecting to an online service or BBS.)

NOTE: The type (or intended use) of phone lines are indicated as follows:

> *(V) = Voice Line*
> *(A) = Access Number (Voice)*
> *(M) = Modem Line*
> *(N) = Access Number (Modem)*

If you do not know the exact transmission protocols (when using a modem line), try either N81 or E71. Refer to your telecommunications software manual for the procedure for these settings.

**Ability Online Support Network,** (M) 416–650-5411, children/adolescent disabilities

**ABLE Inform,** (V) 800-227-0216, (FTS) 427-0280, (M) 301-589-3563, rehabilitation/disability information

**AJN Network,** (M) 800-256-4022, rural nursing forum

**ALLDATA-LINK,** (V) 800-829-8727, automotive information

**America Online,** (V) 800-827-6364, general interest

**Aquila BBS,** (V) 708-820-0480, (M) 708-820-8344, general interest

**Audiophile Network,** (M) 818-988-0452, high-end audio

**AuthorsNet,** (M) 513-848-4288, writer's interest

**AutoAdvantage,** (V) 800-843-7777, (M) 800-336-7663, automotive

**BBS Guide,** (M) 310-477-0408, bulletin boards

**Bird Info Network,** (M) 303-423-9775, exotic birds

**BIX,** (V) 800-695-4775/617-354-4137, general interest

**Book Stacks Unlimited,** (M) 216-694-5732, online books

**Boundary Waters,** (M) 218-365-6907, canoe/fishing interest

CAN/OLE, (V) 613-993-1210, technical research

Catholic Information Network, (M) 619-287-5828, religion

Channel 1, (V) 617-864-0100, (M) 617-354-3230, shareware/ public domain software library

Chemical Information System, (V) 800-CIS-USER/410-321-8440, chemical research

Chicago Syslink, (M) 708-795-4442, general interest

Christian Issues BBS, (M) 612-785-2790, religion

CICNet, (V) 800-947-4754/313-998-6103, Internet gateway

ClassiComputerFieds, (M) 317-359-5199, classified ads

Colorado SuperNet, (V) 303-273-3471, Internet gateway

Compact Audio Disk Exchange, (M) 415-824-7603, CD exchange

CompuServe, (V) 800-848-8199, (N) 800-346-3247, general interest

Corporate Data Exchange, (M) 609-683-4422, corporate newswire

CPCUG MIX, (M) 301-738-9060, computer information/support

The Cracker Barrel BBS, (M) 703-899-0020, diabetic interest

Cul-de-Sac Bar & Grill, (M) 508-429-1784, ham radio

DataLink RBBS, (M) 214-394-7438, satellite tracking

DataTimes, (V) 800-642-2525/405-751-6400, general reference

DELPHI, (V) 800-695-4005/617-491-3373, (N) 800-695-4002, general interest

Dialog, (V) 800-3-DIALOG/415-858-3785, general reference

Dow Jones News/Retrieval, (V) 800-522-3567, business/news

Dreamscape BBS, (V) 315-452-3325/800-690-9854, (M) 315-458-3482/315-452-1347, Entertainment

EarthArt, (M) 803-552-4389, Environmental Art

Environet, (M) 415-512-9108/ 415-512-9120, Environmental information

eWorld, (V) 800-775-4556, Apple/ general interest

EXEC-PC, (V) 800-EXECPC1/414-789-4200, (M) 414-789-4210, (M) 414-789-4500, general interest

FAX/Satellite, (M) 619-224-3853, NOAA weather images

FCC Public Access, (M) 301-725-1072, FCC status advisories

Games Plus, (V) 608-849-1464, (M) 608-822-2000, games

GEnie, (V) 800-638-9636, (M) 800-638-8369, general interest

GEOTeam BBS, (M) 404-246-3774, real estate

Global Gallery, (V) 715-743-2669, (M) 715-445-6000, general interest

Goldstein's Folly, (M) 310-478-3425, Jewish issues

GPO WINDO, (M) 202-512-1387, EPA/DOE/State Department data

Greenpeace Environet, (M) 415-512-9108, ecological interest

HouseNetn (M) 410-745-2037, home maintenance/improvement

IBM National Support, (M) 404-835-5300, PC users' group

ImagiNation Network, (V) 800-462-4461, entertainment

Info Globe Online, (V) 800-268-9128/416-585-5250, news/reference

Interchange Online Network, (V) 800-595-8555/617-252-5000, general interest

Investor's Online Data, (M) 206-285-5359, stock information

Islam Online, (M) 912-929-1073, Islamic issues

ITINET, (V) 305-674-1001, (M) 305-534-4440, Spanish/Latin America

Jack's Emporium, (M) 703-373-8215, genealogy research

JOBBS, (M) 404-992-8937, technical jobs listing

Macinternational, (M) 803-798-3755, Macintosh BBS

MCI Data Services see Tymnet

Microsoft Download, (M) 206-936-6735, Windows support

Minnesota Spacenet, (M) 612-920-5566, NASA topics

Monterey Gaming System, (V) 408-655-5525, (M) 408-655-5555, games

Movie BBS, (M) 718-939-5462, movie and TV reviews

NASA Spacelink, (M) 205-895-0028, NASA info/flight data

National Genealogical, (M) 703-528-2612, family history

NETCOM, (V) 800-501-8649, (A) 800-488-2558, Internet gateway

NewsNet, (V) 800-345-1301/800-952-0122/610-527-8030, comprehensive news

NIST ACTS, (M) 303-494-4775, set PC to NBS time

NOAA Space Environment Lab, (M) 303-497-5042, map data

NovaLink, (V) 800-274-2814, (M) 800-937-7644, general interest

Numisnet, (M) 301-498-8205, coin collecting

NVN, (V) 800-336-9096/713-840-9777, general interest

OCLC, (V) 800-848-5878/614-764-6000, reference/research

OERI, (M) 800-222-4922, educational information

ONLINE ACCESS BBS, (M) 404-924-3665, electronic magazine

Online Now, (M) 807-345-5522, shareware

The Opowd Crowd, (M) 708-885-8865, sports interest

Orbit, (V) 800-955-0906/703-442-0900, technology/reference

Osprey's Nest, (M) 301-989-9036, birdwatching

**PBS Online**, (V) 703-739-8464, kids/family entertainment

**PC-Ohio**, (M) 216-691-3030, general interest

**P.D.S.L.O.**, (M) 516-938-6722, national BBS list

**People Power BBS**, (M) 914-878-3112, political interest

**PHYSICS Forum**, (M) 413-545-1959, physics/astronomy topics

**Prodigy**, (V) 800-PRODIGY, general interest

**PR Online**, (M) 410-363-0834, news & journalism

**The Quality Online Forum**, (M) 913-234-6258, quality assurance

**Questel**, (V) 800-955-0906/703-442-0900, technology/news

**Reuters Money Network**, (V) 800-346-2024, financial interest

**Sahara Club**, (M) 818-893-1899, land-use/off-road interest

**Sailing IC**, (M) 301-643-1466, sailing clubs/races

**SBA Online**, (M) 800-697-4636, advice for small businesses

**SeniorNet**, (V) 415-750-5030, age 55+ interest

**Shoppers Advantage**, (V) 800-843-7777, (M) 800-336-7663, shopping

**The Sierra Club**, (M) 303-860-1242, environmental information

**SMOF-BBS**, (M) 512-467-7317, science fiction

**Star*Net**, (M) 612-681-9520, astronomy

**STN International**, (V) 800-753-4227/614-447-3600, chemical reference

**Sonshine Express**, (M) 510-651-2440, Christian family topics

**Superdemocracy Foundation**, (M) 305-370-9376, political topics

**Systematics BBS**, (M) 718-716-6198, African-American issues

**TAXACOM**, (M) 716-896-7581, botany/herbaria news

**Tiger Team**, (V) 510-540-6565, (M) 510-268-0102, Buddhism

**Traders' Connection**, (V) 800-753-4223, (M) 317-359-5199, (N) 800-386-8266, classified ads

**The Transom**, (V) 800-475-9689, young adult entertainment

**Tymnet**, (V) 800-336-0149, general interest

**UNCOVER**, (V) 800-787-7979, (M) 303-756-3600, general research

**USGS Quick Epicenter**, (M) 303-273-8672, earthquake data

**WeatherBank**, (M) 800-827-2727, city forecasts

**The WELL**, (V) 415-332-4335, modern interest

**Westlaw**, (V) 800-937-8529, legal reference

**Wilsonline**, (V) 800-367-6770/718-588-8400, indices/abstracts

**Woman's WIRE**, (V) 415-615-8989, women's interest

**Worldview**, (M) 510-676-2919, Reformed Protestant topics

If you do not see something here that fits your specific needs, check around; it's most likely available. A number of magazines, most of which periodically publish lists and reviews of services and bulletin boards, are devoted to the topic of online access. Although often more comprehensive but not quite as current, books are available with similar lists and reviews. Finally, if all else fails, check for a local computer club; there will almost always be someone there who can help you.

In addition, there are hundreds of government-sponsored bulletin boards covering topics from agriculture to transportation. These run the gamut from excellent to amazingly poor. Contact the Superintendent of Documents, U.S. Government Printing Office, Washington, DC 20401 for further information.

We would be remiss if we did not mention that numerous adult interest bulletin boards are available throughout the country. These range from uncensored discussions of daily life to explicit sex-related topics and images. If you are sensitive to this kind of material, the caution "check it out first" is especially pertinent.

# *Glossary*

This list provides definitions for the terms most commonly used in the computer industry, especially with microcomputers and their accessories, including hardware, software, and applications. If more than one term is frequently associated with the same item or concept, each is listed with a reference to the most common or preferred usage. Related terms have been carefully cross-referenced. Many of the abbreviations and acronyms used in computer terminology are also explained.

# A

**AA/AD** see **auto-answer** and **auto-dial.**

**access**
to store or retrieve data from a storage device such as a disk or tape.

**access arm**
a device that holds and moves the read/write heads to the proper position on a disk system.

**access code** see **password.**

**access technology**
a general term for hardware or software that is designed to assist persons with disabilities to gain access to using computer systems.

**access time**
the time required to locate a specific position on a storage device, such as a disk or tape, in order to store or retrieve data.

**acoustic coupler**
older terminology for a modem used to connect a computer to a telephone for telecommunications.

**acoustic enclosure** see **sound baffle.**

**active matrix display**
a high-quality, flat panel LCD display in which a separate transistor is used for each pixel. See also **passive matrix display.**

**actuator**
a device that produces action similar to an access arm of a disk unit.

**adaptive technology** see **access technology.**

**A/D** see **A to D conversion.**

**add-on**
sometimes called an add-in, refers to a component (module) that can be attached to a computer by a simple process such as plugging it into a socket.

**address**
the location of a specific value in main memory or in auxiliary storage; to send data to a specific location.

**address bus**
consists of a series of wires across which memory addresses (not data) are transmitted between the processor and memory. It is the size of the address bus that determines the amount of memory that is directly addressable by the processor. See also **data bus, local bus,** and **network bus.**

**ADP** abbreviation for **automated data processing,** same as **EDP.**

**AI**
abbreviation for Artificial Intelligence: the study of computer systems capable of simulating human thought and reasoning. See also **expert system.**

**AIM**
acronym for Apple/Intel/Motorola alliance, a cooperative effort between Apple, IBM, and Motorola (and subsequently certain other manufacturers, including Hewlett-Packard) to develop standards and new hardware and software to bridge and eventually eliminate the gap between Apple and IBM-based systems.

**AIX**
abbreviation for Advanced Interactive Executive, a version of UNIX developed by IBM for its PCs and mainframes. See also **A/UX** and **XENIX.**

**algorithm**
a specific set of instructions for accomplishing a certain task, stated in a definite number of steps.

**all-in-one case**
a case that is similar to the desktop design but is more compact, with the monitor built in. See also **desktop case, portable,** and **tower case.**

**allocation unit** see **cluster.**

**alphabetic**
containing only the letters of the alphabet.

**alphameric** same as **alphabetic.**

**alphanumeric**
containing the letters of the alphabet and/or the ten digits 0 to 9.

**alpha testing**
the test phase of a new product that takes place under controlled conditions within the company. See also **beta testing.**

**Alt key**
short for alternate key, a key found on IBM-compatible keyboards that functions in the same manner as a shift key. See also **Control key.**

**ALU**
abbreviation for Arithmetic/Logic Unit, the part of the CPU that contains the circuits to perform all arithmetic and logical operations.

**analog**
characterized by the direct representation of the measurement of continuous quantities, such as speed, length, voltage, temperature, and intensity. See also **digital.**

**analog computer**
an electronic device designed to accept and process analog data without converting it to digital format. See also **digital computer.**

**ANSI**
(an-see) acronym for American National Standards Institute, an independent organization that researches and establishes standards in many areas, including computers.

**antivirus program**
a program designed to detect, remove, and guard against computer viruses.

**Apple key** see **Command key.**

**Apple-IBM alliance** see **AIM.**

**application software**
programs written to serve a particular function for the user of a computer. Typical examples are word processors, spreadsheets, and games. See **also procedure-oriented, use-oriented,** and **system software.**

**application suite**
a package of programs designed to

work together in the Windows environment and share certain common features.

**architecture**
structure and design of a CPU or computer system.

**archival storage**
the offline storage of information that may be needed for future reference. See also **auxiliary storage.**

**archive bit**
a special bit assigned to each file by the DOS operating system that indicates whether or not a file has been changed since it was last backed up. .

**archive file**
a file that has been placed in archival storage. See also **file compression.**

**arithmetic/logic unit** see **ALU.**

**arithmetic operation**
any operation involving the addition, subtraction, multiplication, or division of numeric data.

**array**
an ordered list or arrangement. See also **table.**

**artificial intelligence** see **AI.**

**ASCII**
(ask-ee) acronym for American Standard Code for Information Interchange. This 7-bit code for data storage was originally developed by ANSI for use by terminals to establish a common format in telecommunications. It has since evolved into an 8-bit code used by most modern computers, including nearly all microcomputers. See also **EBCDIC.**

**ASCII character set**
consists of two parts, the Standard Set of 128 characters and another 128 characters of the Extended Set. The Standard Set is made up of the number digits, the letters of the alphabet, punctuation marks, and the most commonly used special symbols. The Extended Set contains pseudo-graphics symbols for drawing lines and boxes, selected foreign alphabet characters, and a few mathematical symbols.

**ASCII file**
a file that contains only characters from the ASCII character set. Such files are required for many applications and are completely portable.

**ASP**
abbreviation for Association of Shareware Professionals, a self-governing organization set up to establish policing and regulatory standards for the profession.

**assembler**
a program that translates a source program written in assembly language

into an object program in machine language that can be executed by the computer. See also **compiler** and **interpreter.**

**assembly language**
a low-level programming language that makes use of mnemonic codes to represent operations and values. Assembly language programs are rarely portable between different types of computers. See also **assembler, high-level language,** and **low-level language.**

**asynchronous**
characterized by irregularly timed operations that are usually preceded by a start signal and followed by a stop signal. See also **synchronous.**

**AT**
an IBM PC; employed the 286 processor and faster hard disks, high-density floppy drives, and a 16-bit data bus. See also **PS/2** and **XT.**

**AT keyboard**
a revision of the PC keyboard employing more traditional placement of the Shift key. See also **Enhanced keyboard.**

**A to D conversion**
the conversion of data or signals from analog to digital format. See also **D to A conversion** and **modem.**

**auto-answer**
the mode offered by many modems in which they automatically answer the phone for incoming calls. The telecommunications software must also support this feature.

**auto-dial**
the mode offered by many modems in which they automatically dial the phone for outgoing calls. The telecommunications software must also support this feature.

**A/UX**
a version of UNIX for the Macintosh. See also **AIX** and **XENIX.**

**auxiliary storage**
a method of data storage in which data is stored outside of the computer's main memory but still online and ready for use as needed. The most common type used with microcomputers is a hard disk system. See also **archival storage** and **main memory.**

**AZERTY keyboard**
a keyboard layout that is popular in Europe. It is very similar to the familiar QWERTY layout except that the A-Q and W-Z key pairs are switched, and P is on the right end of the home row. See also **Dvorak keyboard, Maltron keyboard,** and **QWERTY keyboard.**

# B

**b** abbreviation for **bit.**

**B** abbreviation for **byte.**

**backdoor**
a secret entry into a program such as an application, security system, on-line service, or BBS.

**background process**
a relatively low-priority process that is performed when the CPU is free from other processing duties. On a microcomputer, this is most often printing or data communication file transfers. See also **foreground process.**

**backup**
a copy or procedure to be used in the event of the loss of the original; or to make or set up a backup.

**backup file**
a copy of a file saved in case the original is lost or damaged.

**backup system**
a procedure used to maintain a current copy or otherwise secure against the loss of the important online data in case all or any part is damaged or destroyed. See also **grandfather system.**

**backward compatibility**
the ability of a new product to properly work with other products that use older technology. See also **upgrade path.**

**bank switching**
a technique that brings additional or alternate resources into use by simultaneously engaging and disengaging components.

**bar code**
a method for input of data that makes use of a series of usually parallel bars of varying widths and spacing. See also **UPC.**

**barrel effect**
the bowing-out on each side of the image on a monitor screen. See also **pincushion effect.**

**base memory**
conventional memory up to 640 K.

**BASIC**
acronym for Beginner's All-purpose Symbolic Instruction Code, a high-level programming language designed to be easy to learn and use, and one that is considered an excellent first language.

**Basic Input/Output System**
the part of a disk operating system that controls the input of data to and output of information from the CPU.

**batch file**
a file that causes batch processing to occur.

**batch processing**
a method whereby a series of programs are submitted to the system to be executed in a sequence. See also **interactive processing.**

**baud**
a measure of data transfer rate, practically speaking, 1 bit per second. Thus, data transferred at the rate of 9,600 bits every second is equivalent to 9,600 baud, or about 120 words per second.

**baud rate**
a common but incorrect usage for baud. Since baud is already expressed as a rate, saying "baud rate" is redundant.

**bay**
a position in a computer case to mount a drive.

**BBS**
abbreviation for Bulletin Board System, a computer system normally accessed over telephone lines that provides a source of information and often message exchange for users with common interests. Many BBSs provide a library of public domain software and shareware to be downloaded as well as "doors" into other applications, particularly games. See also **online information service.**

**BDOS**
(bee-dos) acronym for Basic Disk Operating System. See **DOS.**

**Bernoulli box**
an external, removable disk storage device commonly (but not necessarily) used in networks.

**beta testing**
the test phase of a new product that takes place under actual use conditions and is conducted by a selected group of representative users. See also **alpha testing.**

**bidirectional printer**
a character printer that prints in two, usually alternating directions to increase printing speed. One line is printed from left to right and the next from right to left.

**binary digit**
one of the two numbers (0 and 1) used in the binary number system.

**binary number system**
the number system based on the number 2. It has only two digits, 0 and 1, which makes it very useful for representing digital values in computer storage as present (1) or absent (0). Binary numbers are sometimes indicated by a subscript of 2 such as 10011102. See also **decimal number**

**system, hexadecimal number system,** and **octal number system.**

**BIOS**
(bye-ose) acronym for Basic Input/Output System, the instructions that permit a computer to communicate with the various peripheral devices.

**bi-polar**
one of the two major categories of chip design, the other being MOS.

**bit** a contraction for binary dig**it.**

**bitmapped font**
a font for which each character and point size is present in a stored pattern. See also **scalable font.**

**bit-mapping**
addressing each pixel (dot) on a CRT screen individually. This is essential for anything other than very low resolution graphics. See also **block-mapping, raster graphics,** and **vector graphics.**

**bit specification** see **word.**

**block**
a group of bytes or words treated as a unit for data storage and input/output operations to and from the storage device. See also **page** and **word.**

**block-mapping**
addressing as a single unit a group of pixels such as those required to produce a single character on a CRT screen. See also **bit-mapping.**

**BNC connector**
a coaxial design connector sometimes used with a monitor cable.

**board**
a unit on which various electronic components are mounted. See also **card, integrated circuit, motherboard,** and **printed circuit board.**

**boot**
to bring a system into operation. This normally involves loading part or all of the operating system into main memory from a disk or ROM chip. See also **bootstrap, cold boot,** and **warm boot.**

**boot disk/drive**
the disk from which the operating system is loaded.

**bootable disk**
a disk containing the bootstrap used to boot the system.

**boot sector/track**
the section of a disk that contains the bootstrap.

**bootstrap**
the part of the operating system that must be loaded into main memory in order to bring the system into operation.

**boot virus**

a computer virus that has been written into the bootstrap so that the system will be infected if it is booted from that disk.

**boss screen**

a fake, business-looking screen found on many games. It is designed to pop up at the touch of a hotkey (boss key) so your boss won't see that you are playing a game. (Use it at your own discretion.)

**bpi**

abbreviation for bits per inch, a measure of the data density of a tape or disk.

**bps**

abbreviation for bits per second, a measure of data transfer rate. See also **baud.**

**buffer**

a memory area used to hold data temporarily while it is being transferred from one location or device to another or waiting to be processed.

Buffers are essential for the efficient operation of the CPU and are often used in printers and other output devices to compensate for differences in processing speed.

**bug**

an error in a computer program.

**bulletin board** see **forum.** see **BBS.**

**bulletin board system** see **BBS.**

**burn in**

the process of running a new system or component continuously for a specific time to test for potential defaults (based on the theory that weak components are most likely to fail during their initial use); or the formation of a permanent afterimage on a monitor screen. See also **screen saver.**

**burst**

to separate continuous forms into single sheets; or a continuous stream of data on a data communications channel.

**bus**

circuits that provide an electronic interface to permit communication between two devices, usually the CPU and another unit. Common bus designs include the EISA, Micro Channel, and PC. See also **address bus, data bus, local bus,** and **network bus.**

**business graphics** see **presentation graphics.**

**bus mastering**

a bus design that permits individual boards to process data and access peripheral devices independently of the CPU.

**bus network**

a system of two or more PCs connected by a single cable and able to communicate with one another. See also **LAN, ring network,** and **star network.**

**byte**

the basic storage unit needed to store a single character, most frequently 8 bits.

# C

**C**

a high-level programming language especially useful for system software development.

**cache memory**

a block of memory that is set aside for the specific purpose of improving the performance of the computer. This is accomplished by either setting aside existing RAM using a driver or through special dedicated, high-speed memory that is part of main memory or on a controller. See also **disk cache** and **memory cache.**

**CAD**

acronym for Computer-Aided Design; programs or entire systems that teach or assist in the development of projects in design-related fields such as drafting, architecture, and engineering. See also **CAM.**

**CADAM**

sometimes used for CAD/CAM.

**CAD/CAM**

a combined CAD and CAM (Computer-Aided Manufacturing) system. Such systems can be very powerful in precision design and project planning that require great detail. See also **CAM.**

**CADD**

acronym for Computer-Aided Design and Drawing. See **CAD.**

**CAE**

abbreviation for Computer-Aided Engineering, program that provides development and analysis tools for solving a wide range of complex engineering problems.

**CAI**

abbreviation for Computer-Assisted Instruction, packages designed to provide educational training either as stand-alone units or as supplements to other materials.

**CAL**

abbreviation for Computer-Assisted Learning, same as **CAI.**

**calculator**

a device used to execute mathematical operations but usually with manual direction and operation of each step.

**CAM**

acronym for Computer-Aided Manufacturing; programs or entire systems for the development of manufacturing design projects ranging from precision machine parts to intricate electronic circuits. See also **CAD.**

**canned program**

a prepared set of computer instructions supplied by a vendor in machine-readable format that may be executed but not examined or changed in any way by the user.

**card**

a printed circuit board that is designed to serve a particular function, such as additional memory or graphics. See also **board** and **chip.**

**Carpal Tunnel Syndrome (CTS)**

a painful, potentially debilitating malady that can arise from very heavy keyboard use. Symptoms can include weakness, numbness, tingling, and burning in the hands and fingers. (The condition gets its name because it is the swelling of the tendons passing through the carpal tunnel in the wrist that puts pressure on and consequently irritates the accompanying median nerve.) See also **Maltron keyboard** and **RSI.**

**cathode ray tube** see **CRT.**

**CBT**

abbreviation for Computer-Based Training, same as **CAI.**

**CD** abbreviation for compact disc.

**CD-ROM**

a term referring to the storage of information on a CD using ROM (read-only-memory) format.

**cell**

a unit of storage as for a single character; or a position for an entry on a spreadsheet.

**central processing unit** see **CPU.**

**Centronics interface**

a common type of 36-pin, parallel connector used by most microcomputers. See also **RS-232-C interface.**

**CGA**

IBM's Color/Graphics Adapter, an older, low-resolution, color graphics standard. See also **EGA, HGC, 8514/A, MCGA, MDA, PGA, SVGA, VGA,** and **XGA.**

**channel**

a path for the transfer of data; or a track on a tape.

**character graphics**

a system of graphics display that generates images from a specified set of graphics characters; still widely used for drawing lines and boxes and certain other text enhancements in text editors and word processors.

**character printer**
a device that prints one character at a time. Also known as a *serial printer*. See also **line printer** and **page printer**.

**character set**
the letters and symbols supported by a particular system or software package. The set may consist of only the letters of the alphabet (upper- and lowercase), the ten digits (0-9), and special symbols, such as punctuation marks (the Standard ASCII Character Set), or it may include graphics characters as well.

**check bit** see **parity bit**.

**check box**
a box (usually something like [ ]) next to a selection that is checked (with an X, ✓, or other symbol) to indicate if that particular selection is to be turned on. See also **dialog box** and **radio buttons**.

**checksum**
a method of checking for errors in data transmissions.

**chip**
an integrated circuit commonly used for the microprocessor and memory of a microcomputer.

**CISC**
(sisk) acronym for Complex Instruction Set Computer, refers to processors that still make use of the complex instruction sets that have evolved over many years of system program development. Newer processors now use the faster, more efficient **RISC** design.

**client**
a single-user terminal or personal computer (workstation) used in a networking environment. See also **server**.

**client/server**
a network architecture in which the client issues processing requests to the server (microcomputer to mainframe), which returns the required information.

**clip art**
prepared graphics images that are incorporated into a document using a program such as a word processor or desktop publisher.

**clipboard**
a reserved block of memory to hold data (either text or graphics) that has been taken from an application to be placed in another, printed, or saved to a disk file.

**clock**
a circuit in the CPU that times all processes by comparing them to a set frequency such as that of a quartz crystal. See also **clock speed**.

**clock/calendar**
part of a computer system that automatically keeps track of the current date and time for reference by application programs.

**clock cycle**
the period of time it takes the internal clock to cycle ("tick") once. This is essentially the inverse of the clock speed. Thus, a 50 MHz (50,000,000 Hertz) processor would have a clock cycle of 1 divided by 50,000,000 or 0.00000002 seconds (20 nanoseconds). See also **zero wait state**.

**clock speed**
the rate at which the CPU clock operates, usually measured in megahertz (MHz). In theory, the faster the clock speed, the faster the CPU will perform its operations. Most microcomputers now work at clock speeds ranging from 25 MHz to over 100 MHz.

**clone**
used to describe systems that are copies of IBM machines.

**cluster**
also known as an allocation unit, a group of sectors on a disk treated as a single unit that forms the fundamental unit of storage.

**CMOS**
(see-moss) acronym for Complementary Metal Oxide Semiconductor; employs both NMOS and PMOS integrated circuits in a complementary arrangement; commonly used in processors' memory chips. See also **bipolar**. Also used informally to mean CMOS RAM.

**CMOS RAM**
a small memory chip with battery backup that holds the time/date and system configuration data for a personal computer; or memory made of CMOS chips.

**coaxial cable**
a type of connection used for telecommunications that can carry more data than conventional telephone lines.

**COBOL**
acronym for COmmon Business Oriented Language, a high-level language developed primarily for business applications.

**code**
a set of instructions such as a program; or to write a program; or one or more characters that perform a specific function such as a control code; or a scheme for the representation of data such as ASCII and EBCDIC.

**cold boot**
to start or restart a system from the power-off condition.

**collate**
to combine two files in a specified order into a single file in the same order.

**COMDEX**
acronym for Computer Dealers Exposition, refers to a number of annual shows displaying personal computers, components, and software.

**command**
an instruction, usually entered directly from the keyboard, to cause some action to occur.

**command file**
a program file that permits the program to be run by simply entering a single command, such as the program name.

**Command key**
a key on many Apple computer keyboards, usually designated by the symbol of an apple that functions like a control key.

**communications protocol**
the signals necessary to transmit data across a data communications channel. See also **protocol**.

**compiler**
a program that translates a source program written in a high-level language into an object program in machine language, which then must be executed (possibly after additional processing). The process usually includes an examination of the program for errors and a listing of the associated diagnostics. See also **assembler** and **interpreter**.

**composite video**
a low-resolution video input similar to regular television that was used on some early computers. See also **RGB video**.

**compressed format**
a method of data storage that eliminates all unnecessary and redundant bits. See also **condensed mode**.

**computer**
an electronic device capable of receiving instructions and data, performing the indicated logic and arithmetic operations at high speed, and issuing the result. All computers consist of the same basic components: the ALU, the control unit, main memory, and input/output devices.

**computer-aided design** see **CAD**.

**computer-aided manufacturing** see **CAM**.

**computer-assisted instruction** see **CAI**.

**computerese**
slang for the language used by those who work with computers. It is characterized by a large number of acronyms and abbreviations.

**computer literacy**
the study of computers in order to acquire the basic understanding and knowledge needed to be able to communicate and work with computers.

**computerphobia**
the fear of computers.

**computer program**
a set of instructions written in such a way that it can be entered into and executed by a computer. See also **program.**

**computer programming language**
a language designed to permit the construction of a program that can be entered into and executed by a computer. See also **low-level language** and **high-level language.**

**concatenate**
to link together into a single unit. For example, if the files that contain the chapters of a report are placed together end to end, they form a single concatenated file.

**condensed mode**
printing small or reduced characters usually in the range of 15 to 20 characters per inch (cpi).

**conference**
a simultaneous communications exchange between three or more participants. See also **forum.**

**configuration**
the design or way the various components of a computer system are connected or linked. This normally refers not only to the way the hardware is physically connected but also to how the software is set up to govern the computer and its peripherals; or the setup and operating parameters of a software program. See also **environment and platform.**

**connect time**
the duration that a terminal is actually connected to a computer. See also **CPU time.**

**context-sensitive**
responsive to a specific item or situation. For example, many software packages now come with *context-sensitive* help screens, which automatically give the correct help screen for the process or feature you are using.

**contiguous**
designates consecutive storage locations either in main memory or auxiliary storage. A contiguous file is one that is stored with all records located physically together in adjacent storage positions.

**continuous data**
analog data.

**continuous feed**
the movement of paper through a printer without a break.

**control code**
one or more characters entered into a program or command to initiate some type of action. For example, in word processing, control codes entered in the text may cause underlining, bold-

face, or the change of the font or pitch.

**controller**
a chip or board that governs the transmission of data between a peripheral device, such as a disk drive or graphics display, and the CPU and main memory.

**Control key**
a key found on IBM-compatible and other computer keyboards, usually designated by Ctl or Ctrl, used to enter control codes or issue commands.

**control unit**
the part of the CPU that directs all computer operations.

**conventional memory**
internal data storage up to 1 MB on IBM-compatible systems that can be addressed directly and sequentially by MS-DOS. Sometimes also referred to as base memory. See also **expanded memory** and **extended memory.**

**coprocessor**
a special processor designed to work with or assist the primary CPU. Coprocessors cannot stand alone, but are normally intended to enhance a particular area, such as mathematical calculations or data handling.

**copy-protected**
software that has been recorded in such a way as to protect against duplication.

**correspondence mode**
a setting available on many dot-matrix printers that produces near-letter-quality or letter-quality print. See also **draft mode.**

**courseware**
the textbook-type documentation that accompanies many educational software packages such as CAI materials.

**cpi**
abbreviation for Characters Per Inch, a measure of print pitch.

**cpl**
abbreviation for characters per line, which is sometimes used as the measure of the number of characters that can be placed on one line by a printer or on a monitor screen.

**CP/M**
a disk operating system for microcomputers that was very widely used until a few years ago. A great deal of public domain software is available for most CP/M-based systems.

**cps**
abbreviation for Characters Per Second, a measure of the speed of a character printer or abbreviation for cycles per second, or hertz, a measure of frequency.

**CPU**
abbreviation for Central Processing Unit, the part of the computer that

controls and performs all processing activities. It consists of the ALU, control unit, and main memory. See also **microprocessor.**

**CPU-intensive**
an operation that involves mostly processing within the CPU with limited disk access required. These are usually faster than disk-intensive processes but may require more memory. See also **ramdisk.**

**CPU time**
the duration required for processing by the CPU. See also **connect time.**

**crash**
an uncontrolled shutdown of the system.

**CRC**
abbreviation for Cyclical Redundancy Checking, a method of checking for errors in data transmissions. See also **checksum.**

**CRT**
abbreviation for Cathode Ray Tube, the face of which we see as the picture tube of a screen of a monitor.

**Ctl/Ctrl key** see Control key.

**CTS** abbreviation for **carpal tunnel syndrome.**

**cursor**
a symbol that marks the current position on the CRT screen and moves as the position changes. When using the keyboard, it is most often a single underline (_) or a block the size of one character (■). It may be steady or blinking. See also **mouse pointer.**

**cursor control key**
a key that can change the position of the cursor. These keys are often grouped together in a cursor control keypad.

**cursor control keypad**
a special group of keys on a keyboard that perform cursor movement functions. See also **numeric keypad.**

**cyber-**
a term relating to the rapidly growing interactive world between humans and computers.

**cyberspace**
a term first used by William Gibson in the novel *Neuromancer* to refer to a futuristic computer network into which people plugged their brains and interacted with it. It has come to refer to the increasing interaction of humans with computers. See also **Internet** and **virtual reality.**

**cylinder**
the collection on a disk of all tracks that have the same number. On a single disk unit, this is all the tracks that are in the same location on each disk surface.

# D

**D/A** see **D to A conversion.**

**daisy wheel**

an older style type of printwheel that has its characters set at the ends of a series of spokes radiating from a central hub; or a printer that makes use of a daisy wheel.

**DASD**

abbreviation for Direct Access Storage Device, which is any unit that permits direct access of data. For microcomputers this is usually a disk.

**DAT**

acronym for Digital Audio Tape, an audio cassette tape employing digital format that can be used for storing up to 2 GB of data.

**data**

an item or value to be processed.

**data bank**

basically the same as a data base except that it may also refer to a collection of data bases.

**data base**

a collection of data on a specific topic or for a designated purpose and organized for retrieval.

**data base management system** see **DBMS.**

**data bus**

the internal pathway in a computer over which data is transferred between the processor and various devices connected to the slots. See also **address bus, local bus, and network bus.**

**data cartridge**

a removable, high-quality tape designed for the storage of data on a computer. Data cartridges are most often used for backup or archival data. Typical data cartridges for home systems begin at about 120 MB. See also QIC.

**data communications** see telecommuncations.

**data communications channel**

a link used in telecommunications. The most common data communications channel for personal computers is the telephone line, but others include microwave and communication satellites.

**data density**

a measure of the amount of items or values stored in a unit length. On a tape this is usually in bits per inch (bpi), and on a disk it is in either bits per inch, tracks per inch, or both.

**data file**

a collection of related records that contains values to be processed or

information that has been processed. See also **program file.**

**data transfer rate** see DTR.

**DB-xx connectors**

a group of plugs, sockets, and pins (xx = 9, 15, 19, 25, 37, or 50) used for serial connections. The number following the "DB" indicates the number of wires available, but all are not always needed.

**DBMS**

abbreviation for Data Base Management System, a software package consisting of a set of programs that govern the organization of, access to, and the maintenance of a data base.

**D connector**

a D-shaped link used by some computers for attaching a mouse, joystick, or other device. D connectors may also be used for RGB monitor connections.

**DDP**

abbreviation for Distributed Data Processing, a loose network of computers, usually dedicated to a specific task or set of tasks. In DDP, each computer assumes responsibility for part of the processing with continuous information exchange between each member of the network as needed.

**debug**

to locate and remove the errors (bugs) from a computer program.

**debugging tool**

a utility program that may come with the operating system and with other software that assists in the debugging of programs. See also **patch.**

**decimal number system**

the base 10 number system that employs the ten digits 0-9.

**dedicated line** see **leased line.**

**default**

a value that is automatically assumed and assigned whenever no other value is entered.

**degauss**

to remove unwanted magnetic fields from a monitor screen or the read/write heads of a tape or disk drive.

**degradation**

slowing down a system under the load of processing. This is usually noticeable only on multiuser systems or microcomputers running software that permits multitasking.

**demodulation** see **modem.**

**descender**

the part of a lowercase character that prints below the line, such as in the letters *g, p,* and *y.*

**DESQview**

a multitasking user interface, incorporating many utilities and making use of resizable windows, that was popular before the dominance of Windows.

**desktop case**

a computer case design in which the drives and other components are arranged in a horizontal configuration, often with the monitor placed on top. See **also all-in-one case.**

**desktop computer**

a microcomputer using the traditional full-size case, monitor, and keyboard that are designed to be used in a stationary, "desk-centered" environment. See also **portable** and **notebook.**

**desktop publisher** see **DTP.**

**development system**

the part of a software package that is designed to permit the user to develop new programs or design new applications. See also **run-time system.**

**development tool**

a program designed to assist in the creation or modification of programs. These are normally text editors that contain certain special features to assist in program development, such as automatic indentation multiple windows, and simultaneous open files.

**device indicator**

a number, letter, or group of characters that designate a specific device for data transfer.

**diagnostic**

an error message; or a check for an error condition.

**dialog box**

a type of window for the purpose of conveying a message (such as a warning or error) or to request input (such as a choice of alternatives or a confirmation of some action). See also **check box** and **radio buttons.**

**dial-up line**

a regular connection established through the telephone system. See also **leased line.**

**digital**

characterized by the representation of data by a series of signals and the presence (on) or absence (off) of each. See also **analog.**

**digital computer**

an electronic device designed to process data in digital format. These general-purpose machines are suitable for most applications and are by far the most common type. See also **analog computer.**

**digitize**

to transfer to digital format.

**digitizer**

a device that converts an analog image (such as a picture or motion) into a series of digital values.

**DIN connector**

a German design connector. A cylindrical 5-pin DIN plug and socket is used to connect the keyboard on IBM-compatible computers. An 8-pin arrangement is used as a serial port on Macintosh computers.

**dingbats**

a typeface consisting of a group of symbols including arrows, pointing hands, stars, and many more.

**DIP switch**

acronym for Dual In-line Package switch, little switches usually in groups of eight, found on computers, printers, modems, boards, and other devices that are set to either "on" or "off" to establish certain protocols. This permits the circuit to be adjusted without the need for actual physical modifications. See also **jumper.**

**direct access**

a method of storing data that permits any record or other data items to be acquired without the need for obtaining all the preceding items. See also **sequential access.**

**direct access storage device** see DASD.

**direct file**

a method of organizing a collection of records that permits immediate access of each record. See also **ISAM** and **sequential file.**

**directory**

a listing of the files available on a disk or part of a disk. Typically, files that pertain to a specific application or job (such as word processing, project management, data base, and games) are grouped together in separate directories.

**directory track**

the section of a disk that contains the list of files on that disk.

**directory tree**

a term used to describe the organization of a disk's subdirectories into branches.

**discrete data**

digital data.

**disc**

short for *compact disc* (or CD).

**disk**

a flat, circular, metal or plastic platter coated with a thin layer of magnetic material on which data may be recorded as a series of magnetic signals arranged in circular patterns (called tracks). See also **diskette** and **hard disk.**

**disk cache**

a program designed to speed up disk operations, especially when a series of processes is involved; or a portion of main memory set aside for use by a disk cache program. See also **memory cache.**

**disk cartridge**

a removable hard storage unit of 20 MB or more that offers the speed and capacity of a hard disk and the portability of a diskette.

**diskette**

a small, portable data storage unit that consists of a single, often flexible disk used as a magnetic storage medium. Data is recorded as magnetic signals arranged in a series of circular patterns. See also **hard disk, floppy disk, minidisk,** and **microdisk.**

**disk-intensive**

a process that involves many disk transfers. These are usually slower but require less memory than CPU-intensive processes. See also **segmentation.**

**disk pack**

a removable unit made up of more than one disk, physically connected with a common center shaft. Disk packs are most often used on larger computers or those systems requiring a large amount of offline data access.

**display adapter**

an expansion device that adds the memory and software necessary to produce text and graphics displays; determines available text modes as well as the resolution and colors that can be displayed with graphics images.

**DMA**

abbreviation for Direct Memory Access, refers to the direct transfer of data from memory to memory without going through the microprocessor.

**documentation**

material that accompanies a software package or a computer system that offers explanations for such things as its setup and operation, uses, features, and capabilities.

**door**

an interface in a BBS that permits users to run and interact with certain applications stored on the system, or a drive door such as on a 5¼-inch floppy drive.

**DOS**

acronym for Disk Operating System, a set of programs that activates the computer and allows the user to perform computer functions; or used synonymously with MS-or PC-DOS.

**DOS file** see ASCII file.

**dot-addressable**

the ability to address each individual dot on a printout or video display.

**dot-matrix**

indicates characters that are formed by a series of dots, so closely spaced that the characters appear to be solid. See also **fully formed character.**

**dot pitch**

indicates the spacing (size) of dots as on a color monitor screen.

**double-density**

a data density for floppy disks at about 48 tracks per inch for 5¼-inch diskettes. Double-density 5¼- and 3½-inch diskettes have capacities of 360 K and 720 K, respectively. See also **high-density.**

**double-sided**

a term that means that data can be recorded on both sides of a diskette.

**download**

to transfer a copy of a file from a host computer to a smaller computer. See also **upload.**

**downloadable characters/fonts**

characters (or a set of characters) that can be sent to a printer or other output device to replace or supplement those normally available for use.

**downtime**

the interval a system (or any part of it) is unavailable for use.

**dpi**

abbreviation for Dots Per Inch, a common measure of the resolution of a graphics display.

**draft mode**

the normal printing mode for most dot-matrix printers. See also **correspondence mode.**

**DRAM**

(dee-ram) acronym for Dynamic Random Access Memory. See **dynamic allocation.**

**drive**

a unit that writes data to or reads it from a storage medium such as a tape or disk.

**drive door**

a panel or other device on the front of a drive that must be closed in order to secure the unit for use.

**driver**

a program that controls some component of the system such as a monitor, disk drive, or printer.

**drop-down menu** see **pull-down menu.**

**DS/DD** see **double-sided** and **double density.**

**DS/HD** see **double-sided** and **high density.**

**D to A conversion**

the change of data or signals from

digital to analog format. See also **A to D conversion** and **modem**.

**DTR**

abbreviation for Data Transfer Rate, a measure of the speed (in bits or bytes per second) at which values are transferred from one point to another, such as from a CPU to a printer or remote terminal.

**DTP**

abbreviation for Desk Top Publisher (ing), an application software package that is oriented toward output design. These programs provide for special printing features that permit the user to create and publish professional-looking layouts.

**dual scan LCD** (Liquid Crystal Display)

an improved color display technique used on passive matrix displays that employs simultaneous scanning of two halves of the display area, thereby doubling the refresh rate.

**dumb terminal**

an input/output device that has no self-contained processing capability. See also **intelligent terminal**.

**duplex**

the ability to transfer data in two directions. If the signals can go both ways at the same time, it is called full duplex; if simultaneous transmission is not permitted, it is known as half-duplex. See also **simplex**.

**Dvorak keyboard**

an alternate key arrangement that is intended to provide a more efficient use of the keys by placing the most often used keys under the most powerful fingers, thereby reducing motion and errors. See also **AZERTY keyboard**, **Maltron keyboard**, and **QWERTY keyboard**.

**dynamic allocation**

the division of main memory or other system resources so that each process is assigned whatever portion is needed as the program is being run. See also **static allocation**.

# E

**EAROM**

(ear-rom) acronym for Electrically Alterable Read-Only Memory, a nonvolatile, ROM chip that can be reprogrammed electrically and usually rather quickly without removing it from the circuit. See also **flash memory**, **PROM**, and **EPROM**.

**Easter Egg**

an undocumented feature hidden in a program.

**EBCDIC**

(ebb-see-dick) acronym for Extended Binary Coded Decimal Interchange Code, an older 8-bit coding system developed and still sometimes used by IBM. See also **ASCII**.

**edit**

to make changes in a document, data, or other file.

**edit key**

a button or combination of buttons on the keyboard that permits certain changes to be made without the need of an editor. This may be either a direct action such as with a Delete key, or it may cause a program to temporarily shift into "edit mode," in which more extensive editing is possible.

**editor**

a program that permits you to create or make changes in a document. A word processor is an advanced type of editor. Most have special features such as word wrap, headers and footers, and print enhancements (boldface, underline, italics). See also **development tool**, **line editor**, and **full-screen editor**.

**EDP**

abbreviation for Electronic Data Processing, processing data to obtain usable information by computers (or other electronic means).

**EEPROM**

(ee-prom) acronym for Electrically

Erasable Programmable Read Only Memory. See EAROM.

**EFT**

abbreviation for Electronic Funds Transfer, a system commonly used by banks and other money handlers that involves the computer-controlled money transfers between accounts.

**EGA**

IBM's Enhanced Graphics Adapter, a color graphics standard for its PCs. See also CGA, HGC, 8514/A, MCGA, MDA, PGA, SVGA, VGA, and XGA.

**EIA**

abbreviation for Electronic Industries Association, an organization of electrical equipment manufacturers that establishes standards for components used in data communications.

**80286** see **286**.

**80287**

math coprocessor for the 286 processor.

**80386** see **386**.

**80486** see **486**.

**80487**

math coprocessor for the 486 processor.

**8008**

first commercially available microprocessor.

**8080**

introduced by Intel, a successor to the 8008 and forerunner to the 8086/8088 and x86 series of chips.

**8086/8088**

early 16-bit microprocessors introduced by Intel, able to address 1 MB of RAM. These chips defined the basic architecture for the successive generations of microprocessors that followed. See also **286, 386, 486, 680x0, Pentium,** and **PowerPC**.

**8087**

the math coprocessor for the 8086 and 8088 processors.

**8514/A**

IBM's high-resolution color graphics system accompanied its Micro Channel bus. See also CGA, EGA, HGC, MCGA, MDA, PGA, SVGA, VGA, and XGA.

**EISA bus**

Extended ISA bus, introduced as a 32-bit alternative to the Micro Channel bus, it preserved compatibility with the older ISA bus systems. See also **Micro Channel bus**, and **PC bus**.

**electronic bulletin board** see BBS.

**electronic file cabinet**

a system for organizing, storing, and retrieving records using automated means, as with a data base management system.

**electronic funds transfer** see EFT.

**electronic mail** see e-mail.

**electronic shopping**

a method of shopping through catalogs and making purchases using a remote access terminal.

**electrostatic printer**

a nonimpact serial printer that produces dot-matrix characters by placing electric charges on a specially coated paper to which dry ink particles adhere.

**e-mail**

short for electronic mail, a method of sending and receiving messages through a multiuser system, BBS, on-line service, network, or other system.

**EMS**

abbreviation for Expanded Memory Specification; expands the amount of available memory and permits MS-DOS applications to make use of memory above 1 MB by swapping 64 K page frames to and from conventional memory. See also **LIM** and **XMS**.

**emulator**

a software program that permits a

computer to appear to be and/or function as a different type system.

**end user**
the final person or business to make use of a product or service. This is generally you, the consumer.

**Energy Star**
a label that designates an energy efficient rating issued to computers and electrical components by the United States Environmental Protection Agency. In order to qualify for the Energy Star standard, a device must power down after a period of inactivity to less than 30 watts of power consumption.

**Enhanced keyboard**
IBM's 101-key keyboard that replaced the PC and AT designs and is presently, with some variations, the most commonly used layout. It features the traditional dual-purpose keypad along with separate cursor-control keys plus a row of twelve function keys along the top.

**environment**
all the information necessary to describe the nature of a computer. This generally includes the type of processor and the operating system at a minimum, but may involve other factors as well. See also **configuration** and **platform**.

**EPROM**
(ee-prom) acronym for Erasable

Programmable Read-Only Memory, a ROM chip that can be reprogrammed after being exposed to high-intensity ultraviolet light for several minutes. See also **PROM** and **EAROM**.

**ergonomic**
designed with the needs and comfort of the human user in mind.

**Eurocard**
a group of European-designed expansion boards that employ a 96-pin plug rather than the more familiar edge connector pins. See also **NuBus**.

**even parity** see **parity bit**.

**executable file** see **command file**.

**expanded memory**
internal data storage beyond 640 K on IBM-compatible systems that is normally addressed by MS-DOS in 64 K blocks through the use of the EMS page frame. See also **conventional memory, EMS,** and **extended memory**.

**expanded memory specification** see **EMS**.

**expansion board**
a unit of electronic components added to the capabilities of a computer. This may be additional memory or a new feature such as a sound board.

**expansion slot**
a position for adding an expansion board.

**expert system**
an AI (Artificial Intelligence) system

that employs a data base and set of rules for solving some specific problem. Expert systems are commonly used in applications such as medical diagnostics, trip routing, financial forecasting, and behavioral analysis.

**export**
to transfer from the file format currently in use to another one. See also **import**.

**Extended ASCII Character Set** see **ASCII Character Set**.

**extended memory**
internal data storage on IBM-compatible systems beyond 1 MB. See also **conventional memory, expanded memory,** and **XMS**.

**Extended VGA** see **SVGA**.

**external bay**
a drive bay that holds a drive requiring physical access to the outside. Floppy disks, tapes, and CD-ROMs are normally housed in external bays. See also **internal bay**.

**external drive**
a drive that is physically separate from the computer. Such drives normally have their own power supply and attach to the computer through a special port on a controller that is plugged into the data bus. See also **internal drive**.

**external storage** see **auxiliary storage**.

# F

**FAT**
acronym for File Allocation Table, the part of the operating system on an MS-DOS disk that keeps track of the locations of all the files in the directory(ies) and allocates the remaining disk space to new files.

**fatal error**
the cause of premature termination of processing, often as a crash. Fatal errors can occur due to such problems as read/write errors, program bugs, system conflicts, and hardware defects.

**father file** see **grandfather system**.

**FAX board**
a board that enables a computer to send and receive FAX documents from either another computer similarly equipped or a standard FAX machine. See also **modem** and **FAX/modem**.

**FAX/modem**
a board that can act as both a standard modem as well as a FAX board.

**F connector**
a type of coaxial connector, most frequently used to connect video components such as TVs and VCRs,

but occasionally used with older computers.

**fiber optics**
cable that is made of a series of very thin, flexible glass or plastic fibers through which data is transmitted using a light beam.

**field**
an individual item of data. See also **record**.

**FIFO**
(fie-foe) acronym for First In, First Out, a process in which the first job put in line to be done is the first one to be processed. See also **LIFO** and **queue**.

**file**
a collection of related records. Data is normally stored as files. See also **data file** and **program file**.

**file allocation table** see **FAT**.

**file compression**
a procedure by which a file is reduced in size, usually for the purpose of storage or transmission. Compressed files must then be decompressed before use. Special utility programs handle file compression and can

combine one or more files into a single compressed file for later retrieval. See also **self-extracting file**.

**file extension**
an identifier of the type or purpose of a file, usually written as one to three letters following the filename and separated from it by a period. For example, the file PHONE.BAS might be a program written in BASIC while NUMBER.DAT could be a data file.

**filename**
the identification of a collection of related records in a storage system. Filenames must be unique and normally may contain up to eight characters but sometimes more.

**file server**
a high-speed computer in a network that provides a common storage and retrieval of program and data files shared by the users. See also **print server** and **server**.

**file specification**
the complete description of a collection of related records, giving the filename, extension, and device indicator, if needed. For example, the file

B:BIGDICE.COM might be a command file named BIGDICE and located on disk B. If the file is on a hard disk, a directory, such as GAMES, may also have to be given, making the complete file specification C:\GAMES\BIGDICE. COM, where C indicates the hard disk.

**file type** see **file extension.**

**firmware**
programs permanently stored on a ROM chip.

**586**
a generic term sometimes used to refer to the Pentium generation of computers; or a Pentium clone.

**fixed disk**
a nonremovable unit on which data is recorded. See also **disk.**

**flash memory**
a lower-cost, higher-density, erasable RAM memory chip, derived from the EEPROM, that is nonvolatile but requires that memory be erased in blocks of fixed size rather than individual bytes.

**flat panel display**
a thin display screen technology that may employ any number of techniques, such as LCD. Flat panel displays are commonly used on portables to reduce size and weight.

**flat-screen monitor**
refers to a monitor with a screen surface free of unnecessary curvature. Flat-screens tend to eliminate glare and image distortion near the edges.

**flexible disk** see **floppy disk.**

**floating point arithmetic**
a method of handling numbers in which the significant digits are stored as one value called the mantissa and the position of the decimal point (radix point for non-base 10 numbers) stored as an exponent.

**floating point processor**
a device designed to perform floating point arithmetic. On microcomputers, the floating point processor is normally either built into the microprocessor or achieved through a separate math coprocessor.

**floppy disk**
technically an 8- or 5¼-inch diskette,

but the term is usually used interchangeably with **diskette.**

**folder**
the Macintosh analogy of an IBM directory.

**font**
a typeface enhancement such as bold or script. Although it is not precisely correct, the term is often used to refer to a typeface style such as bookface, courier, or sans serif.

**footer**
a special message or identification placed at the bottom of a page.

**footprint**
the space on a floor or table occupied by a piece of hardware.

**foreground process**
a high-priority process that is performed while any others that are running are assigned to wait until CPU resources are available.

**format**
to initialize, such as to *format* a disk; or to shape into a specific pattern, such as a screen or report format; or a layout or pattern.

**FORTRAN**
acronym for FORmula TRANslation, a high-level programming language designed to be used primarily for mathematical, scientific, and engineering applications.

**forum**
an information exchange, usually found on online services and BBSs and confined to a single topic or area of interest.

**486**
also known as the *486DX* or *i486*, an advanced version of Intel's multitasking 386 processor. The 486 includes a built-in math coprocessor and an 8 K memory cache. See also **8086/8088, 286, 386, 680x0, Pentium,** and **PowerPC.**

**486DX** see **486.**

**486DX2**
A version of the 486DX that achieves twice the internal (not bus) speed by means of Intel's Speed Doubler chip.

**486DX4**
a version of the 486DX that has three

times the internal (not bus) speed.

**486SX**
a version of the 486 that runs at slower clock speeds and lacks the built-in math coprocessor. The 486SX can be upgraded to the 486DX by plugging Intel's OverDrive chip into the coprocessor socket.

**487**
math coprocessor for the 486SX processor.

**frame**
a block of bits transmitted as a single unit. See **page frame.**

**freeware**
software that is freely distributed without charge (other than a small service fee) to all interested users. See also **public domain software** and **shareware.**

**friction feed**
a method of moving paper continuously through a printer by using only the friction between the paper and the platen. This method is employed when single sheets are used in a dot-matrix printer. See also **pin feed, sheet feeder,** and **tractor feed.**

**full duplex** see **duplex.**

**full-screen editor**
a program that permits changes to be performed at any point on the screen by simply moving the cursor to the appropriate position and making the change. See also **line editor.**

**full-stroke key**
the type found on most keyboards, characterized by a marked give or depression when pressed, often with an associated key click. These keys are most like those on an electric typewriter and are preferred by most users. See also **limited-stroke key** and **touch-sensitive keyboard.**

**fully formed character**
a letter or symbol that is formed by a solid, unbroken image, as with a printwheel. See also **dot-matrix.**

**function key**
a key that can be programmed to perform a specific operation. This may be a permanent programming by the operating system or temporary programming by the user or the application software in use.

# G

**G** see **giga-.**

**game port**
a usually 15-pin, serial port used for attaching a joystick or other game-playing device. Game ports often come in pairs and may be found as part of the original system or possibly supplied on certain expansion boards such as **sound boards.**

**gateway**
a device, usually a specially equipped computer, which provides the connection and all necessary protocol conversions to link either a single computer or a network to another network.

**Gb** abbreviation for **gigabit.**

**GB** abbreviation for **gigabyte.**

**giga-**
a prefix meaning one billion.

**gigabit**
one billion bits.

**gigabyte**
one billion bytes.

**GIGO**
(gig-go) acronym for Garbage-In, Garbage-Out, a colorful way of saying

that the output cannot be reliable if the input is not.

**glitch**

a nonreproducible problem in a system. Glitches often result from voltage fluctuations, static discharges, and data transmission errors. See also **soft error.**

**grandfather file** see **grandfather system.**

**grandfather system**

a method of storing data for making backups that makes use of three rotating copies. The current copy is called the *son file,* the most recent copy is the *father file,* and the oldest copy is referred to as the *grandfather file.*

**graphical user interface** see **GUI.**

**graphics**

the capability to produce special characters or drawings such as graphs, charts, and picturelike representations of various objects. See also **bit-mapping, block-mapping, raster graphics,** and **vector graphics.**

**graphics accelerator**

a display adapter that has built-in software, processing capabilities, and adequate memory (usually at least 1 MB) to relieve the CPU of much of the burden of processing for graphics displays.

**graphics board** see **display adapter.**

**graphics mode**

permits graphics to be displayed.

Graphics modes vary widely with the available resolution, but may be as high as 1,280 x 1,024. See also **text mode.**

**graphics printer**

a printer that is capable of producing hard copy of graphics outputs, usually by forming images from a pattern of individual dots. See also **dot addressable.**

**graphics tablet** see **tablet.**

**GUI**

abbreviation for Graphical User Interface, a graphics-based user interface characterized by pull-down menus and icons activated by a mouse.

# H

**H**

a suffix that, when used at the end of a number (such as 384H), indicates the hexadecimal format has been used in expressing that number. See also **hexadecimal number system.**

**hacker**

a nonprofessional computer whiz; or one who tries to gain unlawful access to a computer system.

**half-duplex** see **duplex.**

**half-height drive**

a disk drive that is half the physical height of older models without sacrificing storage capacity.

**handshaking**

the communication between computers or a computer and its peripherals in which control codes are exchanged to govern the transfer of data. See also **protocol.**

**hardcard**

a hard disk mounted directly on a card. This is one method to obtain additional disk space when all bays are filled.

**hard character**

any letter or symbol entered into a text by the user. They may be moved but are normally unchanged otherwise. See also **soft character.**

**hard copy**

a reproduction that is exhibited on a permanent medium and is in user-readable format, such as a printed page. See also **soft copy.**

**hard disk**

a magnetic data storage system composed of one or more rigid platters (also called hard drive). Data is recorded as magnetic signals arranged in a pattern of concentric circles on the surfaces. Storage capacities range from about one hundred to a few thousand megabytes (gigabytes). See also **diskette.**

**hard error**

a permanent problem that is not removed by rereading the data or any other action. This usually means that there is a flaw, such as a bad memory chip or spot on a disk, that must be avoided in the future. See also **glitch** and **soft error.**

**hard-sectored**

description of a floppy disk on which holes are used to mark the positions of the individual sectors on the tracks rather than special records. See also **soft-sectored.**

**hardware**

the physical equipment of a computer system, such as the computer, monitor, and printer.

**hardware interface**

a connection between two hardware components, such as the processor and video board or modem, usually established by means of wires. See also **interface, software interface,** and **user interface.**

**hardware selectable**

a feature of some devices that permits certain of its options to be selected by switches, buttons, or dials on the unit. See also **software selectable.**

**hard-wired**

connected to the CPU with a cable; or permanently wired.

**hash total**

the sum obtained from adding the digits in one or more fields in a record. This value is then compared with a sum calculated at an earlier time to check for possible data errors.

**Hayes-compatible**

a modem (or sometimes telecommunications software) that uses and recognizes the commands and protocols of the Hayes modem systems, which have become the unofficial standard in this area.

**head**

the part of a drive that writes data to the storage medium (disk or tape) or reads data from it.

**head crash**

a condition that results when the read/write head of a hard disk drive comes in contact with the disk surface. This usually causes permanent damage to the drive head and disk surface at the point of contact, requiring replacement of the entire unit.

**head gap**

the distance between the read/write head and the surface of a tape or disk.

**header**

a special message or identification placed at the top of a page; or an identifying marker or value in a record, file, or data transfer string.

**Hercules Graphics Card** see **HGC.**

**hertz**

a measure of frequency or the number of cycles in a given time expressed in cycles per second (cps).

**heuristic**

developed by a trial-and-error approach using evaluations of prior results. See also **modular program** and **structured programming.**

**hex**

indicates that numbers are represented according to the hexadecimal number system.

**hexadecimal number system**

a number system based on the number 16 and using the sixteen characters 0-9 and A-F. Since a group of four binary digits can be expressed as one hexadecimal digit, this system is often used to express binary values in a more compact format. See also **binary number system** and **octal number system.**

**HGC**

acronym for Hercules Graphics Card,

a monochrome graphics system. It is supported by many software packages, making it an unofficial industry standard. See also **CGA, EGA, 8514/A, MCGA, MDA, PGA, SVGA, VGA,** and **XGA.**

**hierarchical design**
the arrangement of hardware, software, and processing according to some specific set of priorities. See also **top-down design.**

**high-density**
a storage system that permits 1.2 and 1.44 MB on a single 5¼- and 3½-inch diskette, respectively. See also **double-density.**

**high-level language**
a programming language such as BASIC and C that is derived primarily from the logic of the problem rather than the machine design. See also **low-level language.**

**high memory** see HMA.

**high-resolution**
showing great detail; the higher the resolution of a graphics monitor or printer, the greater the detail of a drawing or image it is able to reproduce.

**HMA**
abbreviation for High Memory Area, the first 64 K of extended memory above 1 MB on IBM-compatible machines that can be accessed by the MS-DOS operating system. See also **conventional memory, expanded memory,** and **extended memory.**

**home computer** see **personal computer.**

**hookemware**
packages, usually with limited functions, that are given away free in the hopes of "hooking" the consumer into buying the full-featured program. See also **shareware.**

**horizontal market software**
general-purpose software packages such as word processors, spreadsheets, DBMSs, PIMs, and project managers that are designed to be employed by consumers in a wide range of applications and in all industries. See also **vertical market software.**

**host computer**
a computer that serves as a source for data and information retrieval for other computers, usually networked microcomputers. See also **DDT** and **network.**

**hotkey**
a key or combination of keys that when pressed take priority in causing some action to take place. Typical uses for hotkeys include initiating menu options, activating memory-resident programs, or interrupting an ongoing process.

**hub ring**
the rigid center hole of a 5¼-inch floppy disk; it is intended to prevent the drive mechanism from damaging the disk as it closes and spins.

**hypertext**
a method of linking information in a text or other file. The linked data may be almost anything from text to graphics to programs. One common usage is to link the words in a document to permit quick cross-referencing.

# I

**i386** see **386.**

**i486** see **4686.**

**IBM-compatible**
a computer that can run software written for an IBM computer.

**IC**
abbreviation for Integrated Circuit, an assembly of electrical components deposited and connected on a silicon wafer. See also **board** and **printed circuit board.**

**iCOMP**
(eye-comp) acronym for Intel Comparative Microprocessor Performance, a comparative rating of microprocessors developed by Intel for use with its line of microprocessors.

**icon**
a graphics image, normally used to represent a specific thing or to cause a desired action to occur.

**IDE**
abbreviation for Integrated Drive Electronics, a hard disk technology. See also **SCSI.**

**IEEE**
abbreviation for Institute of Electrical and Electronics Engineers, an organization of electrical engineering professionals established to promote the advancement, propagation, and excellence of electrical, electronic, and computer technology.

**impact printer**
one that produces characters on the paper by actually striking the paper

through the ribbon, much like a typewriter. See also **nonimpact printer.**

**import**
to transfer from another file format into the one currently in use. See also **export.**

**index**
a list of the keys and associated addresses for each record in a file.

**indexed sequential file** see ISAM.

**index file**
the list of record keys and addresses that is part of an ISAM file.

**index hole**
position indicators at the beginning of a track in a diskette for soft-sectored disks and each sector for hard-sectored disks.

**information**
values that are the result of processing data.

**informational data base**
an online data base that provides an information resource, including almanacs, dictionaries, movie guides, zip and phone directories, census data, books and magazines. The data base often has hypertext links for quick cross-referencing.

**information superhighway**
a term loosely referring to the growing ease and ability to access and exchange information via electronic means over computer networks, interactive cable systems, and other methods. The Internet is presently

the "fastest" lane on this "highway."

**infoware** see **informational data base.**

**initialize**
to set up, prepare, or start from the beginning. To initialize a disk is to make it ready for use by a system. See also **format** and **boot.**

**initial program load** see IPL.

**ink-jet printer**
a serial printer that uses tiny jets of charged ink particles to form dot matrix-type characters, usually of good quality.

**input tablet** see **tablet.**

**insert mode**
an editing method offered by many software packages that permits characters to be inserted in between others. See also **overwrite mode.**

**instruction**
a command to the CPU to carry out an operation.

**integrated circuit** see IC.

**integrated software**
a programming package that offers two or more types of applications, such as a word processor, spreadsheet, and data base manager.

**intelligent terminal**
an input/output device that has independent computing power. When a micro-computer ties into another using a data communications channel, it is acting as an intelligent terminal. See also **dumb terminal.**

**interactive processing**
a method whereby immediate feedback is received from commands or messages entered into a system. This may be from the computer in response to an instruction or from another user in a network environment. See also **batch processing.**

**interface**
the boundary or connection between two components such as the CPU and a printer; or to connect two components together. See also **hardware interface, software interface,** and **user interface.**

**interlaced**
video display in which odd and even scan lines are displayed on alternate cycles. Interlaced signals require less processing and tend to be faster but can produce flicker. See also **noninterlaced.**

**interleave**
to alternate as in program instructions or the selection of data from more than one source.

**interleave factor**
the sequence in which sectors are read on a disk. A factor of 1 (1:1) means that sector 2 is immediately after sector 1.

**internal bay**
a drive bay that holds a drive not requiring physical access to the out-

side. Hard disks are normally housed in internal bays. See also **external bay.**

**internal drive**
a drive that is housed within the computer. Such drives normally derive their power from the computer's power supply and attach via the data bus using a controller or to the CPU by a local bus method. See also **external drive.**

**internal storage** see **main memory.**

**Internet**
a large, global collection of tens of thousands of government, military, commercial, and university networks. Although the Internet was originally intended as a research and communication tool for its specialized users, it is now open to anyone with a computer equipped with a modem.

**interpreter**
a program that translates a source program written in a high-level language into an object program in machine language, line by line, executing each line as it is converted. See also **assembler** and **compiler.**

**interrupt**
a temporary halt to the execution of a program during which the operating system tranfers control to another process or to cause an interrupt. See also **IRQ.**

**I/O** abbreviation for **input/output.**

**IPL**
abbreviation for Initial Program Load, essentially the same as boot but the term is more often used for larger systems.

**ips**
abbreviation for inches per second, a measurement of the speed at which a tape drive moves the tape across the read/write heads.

**IRQ**
abbreviation for Interrupt Request, one of several lines set aside to provide a means for hardware components such as disk controllers, printers, and modems to gain the attention of the CPU. See also **interrupt.**

**ISA**
(ee-za) acronym for Industry Standard Architecture.

**ISA bus** see **PC bus.**

**ISAM**
(eye-sam) acronym for Indexed Sequential Access Method, a procedure for locating files using an index that gives a key and the address of each individual record. See also **direct file** and **sequential file.**

**iterative**
repetitive.

# J

**JCL**
abbreviation for Job Control Language, a set of instructions used to control operations through the operating system. Traditionally, JCLs have not been very complex for microcomputers, but with the more powerful models now becoming available, JCLs are likely to be more important.

**job accounting system**
a program that maintains a record of all the processes run by the comput-

er. This may provide such information as what was done, who did it, from where it was done, and how long it took. Such programs are very useful when users are to be billed for their computer usage.

**job control language** see **JCL.**

**joystick**
a device for manually controlling the cursor, an object on the screen, or other screen action by the movement of a stick back and forth, right and

left, or by the push of a "fire" button. Joysticks are used with games and other programs that have graphics.

**jumper**
a short, plastic coated metal strip or clip used to close a connection (circuit) between two pins such as for configuring settings on a board.

**justification**
spacing text so that the right-hand margin is even and blocked like the left-hand margin.

# K

**k** see **kilo-.**

**K**
abbreviation for Kilobyte, which is exactly 1,024 bytes but is usually rounded off to 1,000 bytes. (Sometimes incorrectly represented by a small k, which is the prefix for kilo-.) Sometimes also used to mean 1,024 (precisely).

**kb** abbreviation for **kilobit.**

**kB** abbreviation for **kilobyte.**

**kernel**
the most rudimentary part of a program, most typically of an operating system, that remains in memory at all times. See also **interface.**

**kerning**
spacing pairs of characters such as T and A where one character overlaps into part of the space of the other.

**key**
a data item, usually a field within a record, used to identify the record uniquely; or a button on a keyboard.

**keyboard**
an arrangement of buttons in a typewriterlike layout that is used to enter, copy, move, and otherwise manipulate data manually and enter instructions to direct the computer's operations.

**keyclick**
an audible sound emitted by many keyboards whenever a key is depressed.

**keypad**
a set of keys grouped together and performing a particular function. The most common keypads are the numeric and cursor control.

**kilo-**
a prefix meaning 1,000. Because of the binary nature of computers, *kilo* is also used to refer to 1,024 (or 210).

**kilobit**
1,000 bits.

**kilobyte**
1,000 bytes.

# L

**LAN**
acronym for Local Area Network, a system of two or more PCs within a localized area (such as a building) that share some of the same facilities, such as disk, printers, and software. See also **bus network**, **ring network**, and **star network**.

**landscape**
the page orientation in which data is printed sideways or across the longer dimension of the paper. See also **portrait**.

**laptop**
a class of portable, briefcase-sized computers. Some laptops function as little more than remote terminals, while others are complete systems offering powerful and advanced features and capabilities. See also **notebook** and **portable**.

**laser printer**
a fast, versatile page printer that produces very high quality print and graphics.

**LCD**
abbreviation for Liquid Crystal Display, the dark-on-light display seen on most calculators and digital watches. See also **active matrix display**, **gas plasma display**, **LED**, and **passive matrix display**.

**leased line**
a private, permanent connection that permits continuous access, usually at a fixed rate. See also **dial-up line**.

**LED**
abbreviation for Light-Emitting Diode, a semiconductor diode that gives off light when a current is passed through it. See also **LCD**.

**letter quality** see **LQ**.

**library**
a collection of programs, routines, or subroutines available to a program or user.

**license agreement** see **software license agreement**.

**LIFO**
(lie-foe) acronym for Last In, First Out, a process in which the first job in line to be done is the last one to be processed. See also **FIFO** and **stack**.

**light pen**
an input device that consists of a stylus on the end of a cable connected to the monitor. It can sense the light from a particular position on the screen and can be used to create, delete, or move images on the screen.

**LIM**
acronym for Lotus/Intel/Microsoft, a standard in IBM-compatibles for addressing expanded memory in excess of 1 MB. See also **EMS** and **XMS**.

**limited-stroke key**
the type of key found on some keyboards and most calculators that depresses only slightly when pressed. See also **full-stroke key** and **touch-sensitive keyboard**.

**linear memory**
memory that can be addressed continuously, as opposed to being addressed using page frames.

**line editor**
a program that permits changes to be performed only on one line at a time. See also **full-screen editor**.

**line printer**
a device that prints one entire line at a time. Line printers are rarely used on microcomputers. See also **character printer** and **page printer**.

**linkage editor**
a system utility program that combines one or more object programs and any necessary library routines into a single loadable object file by establishing all required links for data transfer between the involved files.

**linking loader**
a linkage editor that performs the functions of a loader.

**LISP**
acronym for List Processing, a high-level programming language, commonly available in both interpreter and compiler versions, that is used extensively in compiler creation and artificial intelligence applications.

**list**
an ordered sequence. See also **queue** and **stack**.

**load**
to bring into memory. See also **retrieve**, **save**, and **store**.

**loader**
a system utility program that brings (loads) an object program from an aux-iliary storage unit into main memory.

**local area network** see **LAN**.

**local bus**
refers to attaching a device directly to the CPU, permitting much faster data transfer rates. Popular local bus designs include VLB and PCI. See also **address bus**, **data bus**, and **network bus**.

**logical drive**
a section of a physical drive that has been set aside and designated as an independent storage device. See also **partition**.

**logical operation**
a comparison between two items to determine a relationship, such as whether one number is larger than another or whether one name comes before another in a list.

**logic bomb**
a usually destructive program that destroys program or data files much like a computer virus. Unlike a virus, which continues its destructive activities, a logic bomb immediately does its damage, such as formatting a disk or overwriting random data elements around a disk, and is done.

**lost cluster**
records from a file that have lost the information that links them to the proper file name. Lost clusters can occur if a computer is shut down with files left open such as when power is suddenly lost or the system is turned off with applications still running.

**low-level language**
a programming language that is based on the design of the specific machine. See also **assembly language** and **high-level language**.

**lpi**
abbreviation for Lines Per Inch, one measure of the number of lines a printer prints per inch, usually either six or eight.

**lpm**
abbreviation for Lines Per Minute, a measure of the speed of a line printer. See also **pages per minute**.

**LQ**
abbreviation for Letter Quality, which indicates that the characters are of the same high quality as those from a good electric typewriter.

# M

**m** see **milli-**.

**M** see **mega-**.

**μ** see **micro-**.

**Mac**
short for Apple Macintosh computer.

**Mac clone**
a non-Apple Power Macintosh.

**machine language**
programming instructions expressed in binary format or in the basic coding of the computer.

**machine-readable format**
any format that can be read directly by the computer such as a disk or tape. See also **user-readable format**.

**machine-specific**
software that can be run on only one type or model of computer.

**Macintosh**
a general-purpose Apple computer that employs a mouse and icon-based operating system to make it user-friendly.

**Macintosh Application System** see MAS.

**macro command**
a series of instructions that can be initiated by a single short command, often a solitary keystroke or combination of keys.

**magnetic disk** see disk.

**magnetic tape** see tape.

**mainframe**
a large computer capable of handling many users and running many programs simultaneously. Such systems are extremely fast and support a wide range of peripherals. They are normally found in large businesses, universities, and government agencies.

**main memory**
the set of data storage locations found inside the computer and directly accessible by the CPU; memory can range from as little as 1 MB to as much as 4 GB. See also **auxiliary storage**.

**Maltron keyboard**
a keyboard designed to reduce stress by employing varied key heights and independent left- and right-hand modules anchored by the T-H-O-R and A-N-I-S keys, respectively. It purports to be easier to learn, enhance typing speed, and offer a reduced risk of such conditions as Carpal Tunnel Syndrome. See also **AZERTY keyboard**, **Dvorak keyboard**, and **QWERTY keyboard**.

**mark-sense reader** see OMR.

**MAS**
acronym for Macintosh Application System, emulator software that allows Macintosh applications to run on a PowerPC platform.

**matrix**
an array or an ordered arrangement. For example, 63 dots might be arranged into a rectangular matrix or array of nine rows and seven columns.

**Mb** abbreviation for **megabit**.

**MB** abbreviation for **megabyte**.

**MCGA**
IBM's Multi-Color Graphics Array, a video standard employed in its low-end PS/2 models. See also CGA, EGA, HGC, 8514/A, MDA, PGA, SVGA, VGA, and XGA.

**MDA**
IBM's Monochrome Display Adapter, an older monochrome text-only display. See also CGA, EGA, HGC, 8514/A, MCGA, PGA, SVGA, VGA, and XGA.

**meg**
short for **megabyte**.

**mega-**
a prefix meaning one million. Because of the binary nature of computers, mega is also used to refer to 1,048,576 (or $2^{20}$).

**megabit**
1 million bits.

**megabyte**
1 million bytes.

**megahertz**
1 million hertz.

**Mega VGA**
a SVGA mode with 1,024 x 768, 256 color display, requiring 1 MB of video RAM.

**memory** see main memory.

**memory cache**
a high-speed block of memory that acts between the regular memory and processor to speed the execution of instructions and processing of data. See also **disk cache**.

**memory-resident** see resident.

**menu**
a list of available options; a Menu of System Commands might show all the system utilities that can be used on that system. See also **shell**.

**menu bar**
a bar across the top of the display area that presents the first level of options for a **pull-down menu** system.

**menu-driven**
a program or system that uses a series of menus to make it more user-friendly. The user may select the desired option by clicking on an entry with the mouse, typing the corresponding letter or number, or moving the cursor to the proper selection and hitting the Return or Enter key, and the program will then automatically call up the proper routines. See also **pull-down menu**.

**merge**
to combine. A typical example would be to merge a name and address file with a form letter.

**MHz** abbreviation for **megahertz**.

**micro-**
a prefix meaning one millionth.

**micro**
a shorthand term for microcomputer, or very small.

**Micro Channel bus**
a 32-bit bus design introduced by IBM with its top-line PS/2 models. This bus offered bus mastering and eliminated the need for manual switch settings required on PC bus boards. See also **EISA bus**, and **PC bus**.

**microchip**
a very tiny chip.

**microcomputer** see personal computer.

**microdisk**
a 3½-inch diskette.

**microfloppy**
a 3½-inch diskette.

**microjustification**
the even spacing between words on each line of a text that has a blocked right margin.

**micron**
one millionth of a meter or one thousandth of a millimeter.

**microprocessor**
the CPU of a microcomputer. Microprocessors have an ALU and control unit with limited memory such as a scratchpad. The main memory is usually added separately.

**microsecond**
one millionth of a second.

**MIDI**
acronym for Musical Instrument Digital Interface, standard for the exchange of information between various musical devices, including instruments, synthesizers, and computers that are MIDI capable. See also **sound board**.

**milli-**
a prefix meaning one thousandth.

**millisecond**
one thousandth of a second.

**minicomputer**
a medium-size computer capable of handling several users and multiprogramming, and normally found in small businesses and colleges.

**minidisk**
a 5¼-inch diskette.

**minifloppy**
a 5¼-inch diskette.

**Minimal BASIC**
an ANSI-standard BASIC of only limited capability but recommended by ANSI to be included as part of all versions of that language.

**minitower case**
small version of the tower case.

**MIPS**
acronym for Million Instructions Per Second, a very rough measure of the performance of a processor in terms of the number of instructions carried out in one second. 1 MIPS = 1,000,000 instructions per second. MIPS values alone, however, are not a good indicator of relative chip performance. See also **iCOMP**.

**MM** abbreviation for **multimedia**.

**mnemonic**
a memory aid.

**mnemonic code**
a symbol or set of characters used as a mnemonic.

**mode**

a condition or set of conditions for operation, as a printer may have modes for different print qualities.

**modem**

acronym for Modulator/**Dem**odulator, used to connect digital devices to analog data communications channels. Modems perform the D to A (modulation) and A to D (demodulation) conversions necessary to translate the data from the digital format used by the computer system to the analog version required for the transfer of data over such channels as telephone lines, microwaves, and satellites. You need a modem to send a fax, to access e-mail, and to get on-line (Internet, that is).

**modular program**

a program constructed from and consisting of interacting modules. The individual modules are often developed independently and normally form self-contained units that are then combined to form the completed program. See also **structured programming**.

**modulation** see **modem**.

**module**

a section of a program that performs one or more specific functions; or a plug-in component.

**monitor**

a device having a CRT screen used for visual display with a computer. Monitors are similar to TVs but do not have a tuner and cannot receive ordinary television broadcast signals. See also **receiver**.

**monitor/receiver**

a television receiver that is also designed to act as a monitor. Such a device can display a video signal without sending it through the tuner, thus producing a sharper image.

**monochrome**

one color.

**motherboard**

a board onto which other boards are mounted, or the main board.

**Motif**

the standard graphical user interface employed with the UNIX operating system.

**MOS**

acronym for Metal Oxide Semiconductor, the newer of the two major categories of chip design, the other being bi-polar.

**mouse**

a device for manually controlling the cursor, an object on the screen, or other screen action by the movement of a palm-size device on a flat surface. A small ball on the bottom of the mouse rolls with the direction of the motion, transferring this action to the screen. Two or three buttons are also used for additional control, such as capture and release. See also **track ball**.

**mouse pointer**

a type of cursor used by a mouse or other pointing device to indicate a specific screen location. The pointer may be any number of different shapes, but the most common types are the block (■), arrow (↑) and crosshair (+ or X).

**MPC**

abbreviation for Multimedia PC; or a loose, minimal standard for multimedia PCs.

**MP/M**

a multiuser version of CP/M.

**ms** abbreviation for **millisecond**.

**µs** abbreviation for **microsecond**.

**MS-DOS**

the version of the IBM PC-DOS disk operating system used by IBM-compatible computers.

**MTBF**

abbreviation for Mean Time Between Failures, an expression of the reliability of a piece of equipment that gives the average time that the component will function before a failure occurs.

**MTTR**

abbreviation for Mean Time To Repair, an expression of a manufac-

turer's claim as to the average time to repair a certain piece of equipment.

**multifrequency** see **multiscan**.

**multimedia**

generally refers to any system or application that incorporates graphics, text, audio, and video into an integrated presentation.

**Multimedia PC**

a PC equipped for multimedia use. Common multimedia systems for home use are equipped with high-resolution graphics, CD-ROM drives and sound boards in addition to the traditional disk devices.

**multiplexor**

a device that permits more than one terminal to simultaneously share the same input/output port. Although each device has direct access to the CPU and system, the data transfer rate is reduced by the number of devices that are connected. See also **switch box**.

**multiprocessing**

the ability to perform more than one process at the same time by using more than one processor. See also **multitasking** and **time-sharing**.

**multiprogramming** see **multitasking**.

**multiscan**

designates a monitor that employs variable frequencies to achieve a higher resolution.

**multisync** see **multiscan**.

**multitasking**

the ability to run more than one program at the same time. The increasing power of 32-bit and 64-bit processors has made multitasking more efficient and popular. See also **multiprocessing** and **time-sharing**.

**multiuser**

designed to support more than one user at a time. Although most microcomputers are single-user machines, a few upper-end systems have multiuser capability. See also **time-sharing**.

# N

**n** see **nano-**.

**nano-**

a prefix meaning one billionth.

**nanosecond**

one billionth of a second.

**network**

any system of two or more computers along with all the connected peripherals organized to share resources. See also **bus network**, **LAN**, **ring network**, and **star network**.

**network bus**

a pathway through which the ele-

ments of a network communicate. See also **address bus**, **data bus**, and **local bus**.

**network server** see **file server**.

**NLQ**

abbreviation for Near Letter Quality, which indicates characters that are close to the quality of those from a good electric typewriter.

**NMOS**

(n-moss) acronym for N-channel MOS, a fast MOS design commonly used in memory chips and CMOS

designs. See also **bi-polar** and **PMOS**.

**node**

a point (terminal or computer) in a network.

**noise**

unwanted signals; or interference.

**noise filter**

an electric device designed to eliminate noise.

**nonimpact printer**

a device that produces print without physically striking the paper. See also **impact printer**.

**noninterlaced**

video display in which every scan line is displayed on each cycle. Noninterlaced signals require more processing and tend to be a bit slower but generate more stable images. See also **interlaced**.

**nonvolatile**

a main memory or auxiliary storage design in which the stored data is not lost when the power is removed from the system. See also **flash memory** and **volatile**.

**notebook**

a class of portable, notebook-size computers. Some notebook computers function as little more than remote terminals, while others are complete systems offering powerful and advanced features and capabilities. See also **portable** and **laptop**.

**ns** abbreviation for **nanosecond**.

**NuBus**

a 32-bit bus architecture defined as a 9U Eurocard.

**null modem**

connecting two nearby computers with a cable from a serial port on one to a serial port on the other.

**numeric**

containing only numbers, which may include only the ten digits 0-9, a plus or minus sign, and a decimal point.

**numeric keypad**

a group of keys set aside for the entry of numeric data and performing simple arithmetic operations. See also **cursor control keypad**.

# O

**object program**

the machine-language version of a source program that is produced by an assembler or compiler.

**OCR**

abbreviation for Optical Character Reader, an input device that can read printed material provided it is printed in a font and pitch the reader is programmed to recognize. See also **OMR** and **scanner**.

**octal**

indicates that numbers are represented according to the octal number system.

**octal number system**

a number system based on the number 8 and using the eight digits 0-7. Since a group of three binary digits can be expressed as one octal digit, this system is often used to express binary values in a more compact format. See also **binary number system** and **hexadecimal number system**.

**odd parity** see **parity bit**.

**OEM**

abbreviation for Original Equipment Manufacturer; technically, the original maker of a piece of equipment who usually markets to a reseller. However, sometimes the reseller assembles systems from a variety of vendors and incorrectly resells under their own name as the OEM. See also **VAR**.

**offline**

not connected to the CPU either physically or electronically.

**offline storage** see **archival storage**.

**OMR**

abbreviation for Optical Mark Reader, a device designed to detect the presence or absence of marks from a predetermined pattern on a page. See also **OCR** and **scanner**.

**101/102-key keyboard** see **Enhanced keyboard**.

**online**

physically connected to the CPU for ready access. This may be either through a physical connection or a telecommunications link.

**online help**

a function incorporated in many programs that provides assistance with how to operate the program. It is normally accessed by hitting a key such as F1 or selecting a menu option. Online help is often all that is needed to become proficient in using a package. See also **context-sensitive**.

**online information service**

a collection of information databases and other offerings that can be accessed over a modem. The various features range from reference material (encyclopedia and atlas) to current updates (weather and stocks) to interactive features with other users (bulletin boards and games). Popular services include America Online, CompuServe, Delphi, GEnie, and Prodigy. See also **BBS**.

**online storage** see **auxiliary storage**.

**operating system** see **OS**.

**operation**

an action taken by a computer in response to an instruction.

**optical character reader** see **OCR**.

**optical disk**

generally refers to any disk that is read or written to by means of a laser or other light-emitting/sensing device. Though the term "optical disk" is used loosely to refer to CD-ROM media, it more correctly refers to WORM or rewritable (erasable) formats.

**optical mark reader** see **OMR**.

**optical scanner** see **scanner**.

**original equipment manufacturer** see **OEM**.

**OS**

abbreviation for Operating System, the set of software programs that are necessary to control the basic operation of the computer.

**OS/2**

a single-user, multitasking operating system from IBM for IBM-compatibles. OS/2 offers a graphical interface similar to that used by Windows and the Macintosh. It can also run DOS and Windows applications and can boot as either DOS or OS/2.

**OS/2 Warp**

the latest version of the OS/2 operating system, it includes an enhanced graphical user interface, more efficient memory management, improved multimedia support, a group of Internet utilities with access through IBM's Global Network, and a large set of application software.

**OverDrive chip**

an upgrade chip from the 486SX to the 486DX.

**overlay**

a segment of a program that is loaded into main memory as needed and then overwritten by other overlays. This technique is used when the overall program is too large for it to fit in memory at one time. See also **segmentation** and **virtual memory**. The term is also used to describe a guide supplied with some software that fits over a set of keys on a keyboard to show their assigned function. Also called a **template**.

**overstrike**

the situation in which two or more characters are printed or displayed at the same position.

**overwrite mode**

an editing method offered by many software packages that causes characters to print over and replace the ones already on the screen at the cursor position. See also **insert mode**.

# P

**p** see pico-.

**P5**

Intel's codename for the Pentium processor.

**P6**

Intel's codename for the successor to the Pentium processor.

**page**

a section of a program of fixed length transferred into memory; or the amount of printed material that will fit on one printed page.

**page frame**

a 64 K block in the upper memory area used to transfer data to and from expanded memory using bank switching. See also **EMS.**

**page printer**

a high-speed nonimpact device that prints an entire page at one time. See also **character printer** and **line printer.**

**paging**

the division of main memory into page frames or the ability of an editor or word processor to automatically divide a document by pages.

**paint**

to draw directly on the CRT screen, using a tablet or other device to simulate a paintbrush.

**palette**

the selection of colors or shades available with a graphics package.

**palmtop**

a very tiny computer small enough to fit in the palm of a hand. Palmtops are often special-purpose devices and may not have a full-function keyboard or the normal input/output capabilities. See also **PDA.**

**parallel port**

a type of connection that transmits data one byte at a time. Parallel ports are most frequently used for printers on IBM-compatible systems. See also **Centronics port** and **serial port.**

**parallel processing**

a single computer design in which more than one operation can be performed at any given time. See also **pipeline processing.**

**parent-child**

a relationship in which one item springs from another. For example, in a data base, the parent file might contain name, address, phone number, and other basic data. A child file could contain sales order information, a student's grades, performance evaluations, or other related data that is dependent on the parent file.

**parity bit**

an extra bit added to a storage location and used for error checking. This is done by counting the number of bits that are "on" to determine if the sum is odd (odd parity) or even (even parity).

**partition**

the division of main memory into parts to be used in a multiprogramming system. See also **dynamic allocation** and **static allocation.** The term also describes the division of a physical drive into two or more logical drives. For example, a 400 MB hard disk might be partitioned into two 200 MB disks.

**Pascal**

a general-purpose, high-level programming language suitable for the beginner. It is considered to be a good language for learning correct programming techniques because it is designed for structured programming.

**passive matrix display**

a relatively low-quality, flat panel LCD display in which all transistors are outside the display area. Passive matrix displays are often difficult to see, may produce less than crisp color (gray-scale) images, and are frequently plagued by submarining.See also **active matrix display.**

**password**

a series of characters used as an identifying code to permit access to a system, program, or file.

**patch**

a change made in an existing machine-language program; or to make a change in a machine-language program. See also **debugging tool.**

**PC**

abbreviation for Personal Computer or sometimes used to denote any IBM personal computer; or abbreviation for printed circuit see printed circuit board.

**PC bus**

also known as an ISA bus, this is the 8- and 16-bit bus design used in IBM XT and AT machines. See also **EISA bus,** and **Micro Channel bus.**

**PC card**

see PCMCIA Card; or an expansion board for a personal computer.

**PC-compatible**

loosely used to mean IBM PC-compatible.

**PC-DOS**

the disk operating system for IBM microcomputers.

**PCI**

abbreviation for Peripheral Component Interconnect, a local bus design, popular on Pentium-based systems, that provides high-speed communications between various components and the processor. See also **VLB.**

**PCjr**

a very low end personal computer that had a compact profile for the time. The "Junior," as it was called, employed floppy disks and a cramped keyboard.

**PC keyboard**

the 84-key keyboard introduced with IBM's first PC. See also **At keyboard** and **Enhanced keyboard.**

**PCMCIA Card**

abbreviation for Personal Computer Memory Card International Association, formally known as the PC Card, a credit card–size, "plug and play" module commonly used to attach expansion devices (such as memory, modems, and drives) to portable computers.

**PDA**

abbreviation for Personal Digital Assistant, a small, usually hand-held, computer that functions as a personal organizer, calendar/reminder, notepad, electronic, address/ phone book, or other convenience feature. PDAs commonly offer special access such as wireless data transfer to a larger computer system or a cellular phone service. See also **PIM.**

**pel** see pixel.

**Pentium**

Intel's latest microprocessor, a fast, 32-bit processor (with a 64-bit internal bus) that makes extensive use of RISC technology, employs dual 8 K memory caches, and can execute two independent instructions in the same clock cycle giving it performance up to twice that of its 486 predecessor. See also **8086/8088, 286, 386, 486, 680x0,** and **PowerPC.**

**peripheral**

any hardware attachment to a computer such as a keyboard, monitor, disk, or printer.

**Peripheral Component Interconnect** see **PCI.**

**persistence**

the length of time that a monitor holds an image on the screen. If the persistence is too short, the image will tend to flicker; if it is too long, an after-image "ghost" will tend to remain very briefly on the screen.

**personal computer**

a small, single-user computer that uses a microprocessor as its CPU and designed to be both user-friendly and available at relatively low cost.

**personal digital assistant** see PDA.

**personal information manager** see PIM.

**PGA**

IBM's Professional Graphics Adapter, an early high-resolution color graphics standard, similar to VGA. See also CGA, EGA, HGC, 8514/A, MCGA, MDA, SVGA, VGA, and XGA.

**phono connector** see RCA connector.

**physical drive**

the entire disk consisting of all logical drives into which that drive has been partitioned. For example, if a 500 MB disk is partitioned into two 250 MB logical drives, then the 500 MB represents the physical drive.

**pico-**

a prefix meaning one trillionth.

**picosecond**

one trillionth of a second.

**pincushion effect**

the bowing-in on each side of the image on a monitor screen. See also barrel effect.

**PIM**

acronym for Personal Information Manager, a software program that attempts to mimic the way information is handled on a day to day basis. PIMs routinely include features such as reminder calendar, notepad, address book, phone dialer, calculator, alarm clock, and other utilities. See also PDA.

**pin feed**

a method of moving paper through a printer by fitting pins at each end of the platen into holes on the sides of the paper. See also friction feed, sheet feeder, and tractor feed.

**pipe**

the direct transfer of data from one program to another without the need of any input/output operations.

**pipeline processing**

refers to any one of several techniques that permits parallel processing within a system. Generally, pipeline processing is accomplished by moving a set of instructions (or data) into a hypothetical pipe all of which is processed simultaneously.

**pitch**

a print size, such as pica (10 characters per inch) and elite (12 characters per inch). See also point.

**pixel**

the smallest point that can be addressed on a CRT screen.

**platen**

the device (usually a cylinder) that supports the paper in a typewriter or dot-matrix printer.

**platform**

the hardware architecture on which software applications are intended to run. Also, used to denote the operating system or user interface under which the software application is intended to be used. See also configuration and environment.

**platter**

a single hard disk.

**plotter**

a device designed to produce a hard copy of graphics output by means of solid lines and curves.

**plug and play**

adding a new component without the need to perform any guesswork configuration such as setting DIP switches or jumpers. See PnP.

**plug-compatible**

units from different manufacturers that can be plugged together and will communicate and work properly.

**PMOS**

(pee-moss) acronym for Positive channel MOS, a MOS design in which the base material is positively charged. See also bi-polar and NMOS.

**PnP**

abbreviation for Plug and Play, to be used with future expansion boards and operating systems. See also Windows 95.

**POE**

acronym for PowerOpen Environment, a standard for a UNIX-based operating system running on the PowerPC platform.

**point**

a measure of the vertical height of a print character equal to $1/72$ of an inch. See also pitch; or to indicate a screen location with a pointing device such as a mouse.

**pointer**

see mouse pointer; or a marker as to a place in memory or in a file.

**port**

a position on a computer to connect a peripheral such as a printer or modem. See also serial port, parallel port, and slot.

**portable**

designates a type of computer that is easily moved from place to place and that normally contains battery power for use on the go. The most common types of portables are the laptop and notebook computers. See also desktop computer. Also refers to software that can be easily moved from one machine to another.

**portrait**

the page orientation in which data is printed lengthwise or across the shorter dimension of the paper. See also landscape.

**PostScript**

a standard for formatting output files that is device-independent. A file formatted for one PostScript device can be sent to and read by any other PostScript-compatible device.

**POWER**

acronym for Performance Optimization with Enhanced RISC, a CPU architecture used by IBM in its RS/6000 series. The PowerPC processor is a single chip version of the POWER CPU.

**power conditioner**

an electrical device designed to eliminate both voltage spikes and noise from input power sources.

**power director**

similar to a power strip except that each outlet is provided with an individual on/off switch.

**PowerMac**

the newest version of the Apple Macintosh that employs the new PowerPC microprocessor that can run IBM-compatible software (DOS and Windows) as well as traditional Macintosh applications. See also AIM.

**PowerOpen** see POE.

**PowerPC**

a product of the AIM alliance, a fast, 32-bit chip that employs advanced RISC technology. See also 8086/8088, 286, 386, 486, 680x0, and Pentium.

**power strip**

an electrical device, usually having an on/off switch and a circuit breaker, that provides multiple outlets.

**ppm**

abbreviation for Pages Per Minute, a measure of the speed of a page printer.

**preloaded system**

a system that has operating software and usually a small selection of application software loaded onto the disk at the time of purchase. See also turnkey system.

**presentation graphics**

a software program designed to create a wide variety of charts and graphs, providing output suitable for presentations such as for business or educational applications.

**primary memory** see main memory.

**printed circuit board**

a thin, laminated board with the circuit connections imprinted and the circuit elements fitted into sockets. See also board and integrated circuit.

**printer**

a device designed to produce hard copy output, usually of text materials but possibly other items such as graphics images.

**printer cable**

a cable that connects the printer to the computer.

**printhead**

the part of a serial, dot-matrix printer that produces the pattern for each character.

**print server**

a computer in a network that controls one or more printers and processes the print jobs issued by the user. See also **file server** and **server.**

**print spooler**

a software program that produces a list of files to be printed and sends these to the printer as soon as it is available, thus freeing the system for other uses.

**printwheel**

a device used on an impact, letter-quality printer to produce a given print font. See also **daisy wheel** and **thimble.**

**procedure-oriented**

describes a program or system that is designed to expedite the processes or procedures needed to complete a job or application. See also **application software, system software,** and **use-oriented.**

**processor** see CPU and **microprocessor.**

**productivity software** see **horizontal market software.**

**program**

a logical sequence of instructions designed to accomplish a specific task; or to construct a program. See also **computer program.**

**program file**

a collection of records that contains one or more instructions. Program files may also be data files if they serve as the input or output for other programs.

**programmable key** see **function key.**

**programmer**

one who writes programs.

**PROM**

acronym for Programmable Read-Only Memory, a type of ROM chip that is programmed by the manufacturer to suit the customer's individual needs. See also **EAROM** and **EPROM.**

**prompt**

a character, symbol, sound, or message sent to the screen to signal the user that the computer is ready for input; or to issue a prompt.

**proportional spacing**

the characteristic of some print fonts in which narrow characters such as I and l use less space than wider ones such as H and M.

**proprietary**

patented or copyrighted; exclusively owned by a company or individual.

**protocol**

a set of signals that must be transmitted and properly received before any data is sent in order to ensure that all parts of the system can communicate properly. See also **handshaking.**

**ps** abbreviation for **picosecond.**

**PS** abbreviation for **proportional spacing.**

**PS/1**

an economical line of IBM home computers introduced in 1990. The PS/1 used the PC bus and featured a compact, integrated case and monitor design. Both 286 and 386SX processors were used.

**PS/2**

an IBM PC that made use of the smaller 3½-inch diskette and VGA graphics. The PS/2 also introduced the Micro Channel bus architecture on certain models. Depending on the time and model, a computer with nearly any processor from the 8088 up has been available. See also **AT** and **XT.**

**public domain software**

programs that are not owned or copyrighted by anyone and are available to all who want them without restriction. These programs can usually be obtained for a small service fee. See also **freeware** and **shareware.**

**pull-down menu**

a menu system in which the options are brought down from a menu bar at the top of the screen. The menu bar may be initially hidden or dormant until brought to life using either the mouse or keyboard. See also **menu-driven.**

# Q

**QIC**

(kick) acronym for quarter inch cartridge, a ¼-inch tape cartridge system that is most frequently used as a tape backup method on personal computers.

**quad-density** see **high-density.**

**query language**

a high-level language that provides access to the information in a data base by requesting responses to specific questions (queries).

**queue**

an ordered list in which values are inserted at one end and removed from the other. Data in a queue are usually handled as a **FIFO** process, in which the first to be added to the list is the first to be processed. See also **stack.**

**QuickTime**

a multimedia extension to the Macintosh System 7 operating system. A version is also available for Windows-based multimedia applications.

**QWERTY keyboard**

the traditional keyboard layout familiar to most typist and keyboard users. The name comes from the first six letters from the left on the top alphabet row. See also **AZERTY keyboard, Dvorak keyboard,** and **Maltron keyboard.**

# R

**radio buttons**

a set of choices between several options, only one of which is available at any one time. Once a selection is made (usually indicated by a dot (●) or similar symbol), any previous choice is turned off (the dot is removed ( ).) See also **check box** and **dialog box.**

**RAM**

acronym for Random Access Memory, a read/write type of memory that permits the user to both read the information that is there and write data to it. This is the type of memory

available to the user in most systems. See also **ROM.**

**ramdisk**

the storage of files in main memory on a simulated disk drive to take advantage of the much higher processing speed of RAM. Such files can be recalled from or saved to the ramdisk area the same as with a regular disk but much faster. Ramdisk files must be saved to the disk for permanent storage. See also **CPU-intensive** and **disk-intensive.**

**random access** see **direct access.**

**random file** see **direct file.**

**raster graphics**

a method of graphics processing and display in which each scan line is composed of a series of dots (pixels), the more of which, the finer the resolution of the image. Most computers use this method of graphics imaging. See also **bit-mapping** and **vector graphics.**

**RCA connector**

a type of two-wire coaxial link, also known as a phono connector, normally used to connect audio components, which is used for composite video input to the monitor on some computer systems.

**receiver**

refers to an ordinary television when used as a visual display device. See also **monitor.**

**record**

a collection of related fields or data items. See also **file.**

**refresh**

to continuously renew or update as the image on a monitor screen or the contents of RAM or to redraw an image on the screen, such as a graphics display.

**register**

a memory location within the ALU or control unit that is used for the temporary storage of instructions or data as they are processed.

**relative file** see **direct file.**

**release number** see **version number.**

**remote access**

access to a computer through a data communications channel.

**resident**

permanently present as a program that is resident in memory remains in memory at all times.

**resolution**

indicates the degree of detail that can be perceived. The higher the resolution, the finer the detail.

**response time**

the interval between the input of a request or a command and the return of the required reply.

**retrieve**

to obtain data from main memory or auxiliary storage. See also **load, save,** and **store.**

**reverse video**

refers to switching the normal background and foreground colors on part or all of a display. This usually means displaying dark characters on a light background.

**RF modulator**

short for Radio Frequency modulator, a short-range transmitter, usually in the UHF television band, that permits an ordinary TV to be used as a monitor.

**RGB video**

short for red/green/blue video, a video input method with separate inputs that provides improved color mixing and sharpness by individually controlling the intensity of the three primary colors (red, green, and blue). See also **composite video.**

**ribbon cable**

a flat, multiwire cable design that is commonly used to connect devices to the computer internally.

**ring network**

a design in which several computers are connected together in a circular pattern. Each computer may support its own set of peripherals and share the resources of some or all of the rest of the computers in the network. See also **bus network, LAN,** and **star network.**

**RISC**

(risk) acronym for Reduced Instruction Set Computer, a chip architecture that reduces much of the complexity of the design and operation of the chip by making use of simplified instruction sets. RISC-based processors execute faster than their older, traditional CISC counterparts.

**R/O**

abbreviation for **read-only,** indicates the status of a file, disk, or device to be *read-only,* which means that data may be only read from it but not written to it. CD-ROMs and most ROM chips are examples of R/O devices. See also **R/W** and **write-protected.**

**ROM**

acronym for read-only memory, storage that permits its reading and use but not any changes. ROMs are preprogrammed at the factory for a specific purpose and are found on many boards such as graphics and in many systems that automatically boot when turned on. See also **RAM** and **PROM.**

**ROM BIOS**

a BIOS routine contained in a ROM chip. The system BIOS is one example; however, many components will have their own dedicated ROM BIOS chips.

**rotational delay**

the time required for the desired record on a disk to spin into position under the read/ write head. See also **access time** and **seek time.**

**routine**

a set of instructions to solve a specific problem.

**RS-232-C interface**

a standard 9- or 25-pin serial connector used by most microcomputers. It is most frequently used for a mouse, modem, speech synthesizer, or similar device. See also **Centronics interface.**

**RS/6000**

short for RISC System/6000, an IBM computer series introduced in 1990 employing the RISC-based POWER CPU and Micro Channel architecture.

**RSI**

abbreviation for Repetitive Stress Injury, a disorder of the hands, arms, back, neck, and even eyes that can arise from very heavy computer use. See also **Carpal Tunnel Syndrome** and **Maltron keyboard.**

**RTFM**

acronym for "Read The Flaming Manual", the "G" rated version of a somewhat more colorful expression that states the all-too-true tendency of computer users to read the manual as a last resort in resolving problems.

**run**

to execute a program; or the execution of a program.

**run-time**

the amount of time required for a program to run.

**run-time system**

the part of a software development package that permits programs to be run. The run-time system is often distributed as part of an application program. See also **development system.**

**R/W**

abbreviation for Read/Write, indicates the status of a file, disk, or device to be read/write; data may be both read from it as well as written to it. Though individual files may be set to R/O status, hard disks, diskettes, tapes, and main memory are examples of components that are normally R/W. See also **R/O** and **write-protect.**

**R/W head** see **head.**

# S

**save**

to make a copy of data in main memory and store it as a file on an auxiliary storage device. See also **load, retrieve,** and **store.**

**scalable**

capable of being sized.

**scalable font**

a font for which each character can be set to the desired size from a stored pattern. The most common varieties of scalable fonts are the TrueType fonts. See also **bitmapped font.**

**scanner**

an input device that is designed to recognize patterns of printed or drawn markings ranging from simple, fine, detailed lines to pages from a book to complex graphics symbols. Scanners are used to convert printed images into files for processing by various application programs. See also **OCR** and **OMR.**

**scratchpad memory**

a small high-speed memory used by the CPU for the temporary storage of instructions or data.

**screen blanker**

a type of screen saver that causes the screen to go blank rather than generate a moving image.

**screen reader**

specialized software, normally used in conjunction with a speech synthesizer to produce simulated voice output from a computer by phonetically reading the contents on the display screen.

**screen saver**

a software program that produces a moving image on the monitor screen to prevent permanent afterimages from being burned into the phosphors from lingering, unattended displays. See also **screen blanker**.

**scroll**

to move a graphics image or the text on a video display up, down, right, or left in a smooth, usually continuous and reversible action.

**scroll bar**

a horizontal or vertical bar containing a box that moves within the bar to both control scrolling of the display and to indicate relative position.

**SCSI**

(scuzzy) acronym for Small Computer System Interface, a parallel interface that can handle up to seven drives such as disk, tape, and CD-ROM with high data transfer rates. See also **IDE**.

**secondary storage** see **auxiliary storage**.

**sector**

the smallest unit of data that can be read or written on a disk. Each track is divided into the same number of sequentially numbered sectors.

**seek time**

the time required for the access arm of a disk drive to move the read/write heads to the proper track or cylinder. See also **access time** and **rotational delay**.

**segmentation**

the division of large programs into portions that are loaded into main memory as needed, overwriting those that are no longer required. This permits programs to be run that are larger than the available memory. See also **overlay** and **virtual memory**.

**self-extracting file**

a compressed file that is executable. When run, the self-extracting file will release and decompress all the files that have been stored within it. See also **file compression**.

**sequential access**

a method of storing data in which all records and other data items are read in order. See also **direct access**.

**sequential file**

a method of organizing a collection of records in which it is necessary to process each record in the same order that it was stored. See also **direct file** and **ISAM**.

**serial access** see **sequential access**.

**serial port**

a type of connection that transmits data one bit at a time. Serial ports are commonly used by most input/output devices. See also **RS-232-C port** and **parallel port**.

**serial printer** see **character printer**.

**serpentine pattern**

a recording method used on some tape systems in which data "snakes" back and forth from track to track.

**server**

a computer in a network, the resources of which are shared by part or all of the other users. See also **file server** and **print server**.

**shareware**

user-supported software that is copyrighted for which the author(s) usually request a ($10 to $50) fee from those who use the program. See also **public domain software**.

**sheet feeder**

a device that attaches to some printers that automatically and continuously moves single sheets through the printer, thus eliminating the need to use fan-fold or hand-feed the pages. See also **friction feed**, **pin feed**, and **tractor feed**.

**shelfware**

products that remain unused (on the shelf) either as unsold at the retailer or unused by the consumer.

**shell**

an on-screen menu found with some types of operating systems that permits system control through selecting various menu options. Shells tend to be interactive with their system, even initiating the transfer of data from one program to another. See also **pipe** and **UNIX**.

**Shift key**

a key that changes the function of a character printed by another key when pressed along with that key. See also **Alt key** and **Control key**.

**short card**

an expansion board that is half the length of a full-size slot.

**shunt** see **jumper**.

**SIG**

acronym for Special Interest Group; people who share a common interest within a specific area. SIGs are usually found in clubs, users' groups, or even on forums within a BBS or online services.

**SIMM**

acronym for single in-line memory module, a circuit board that can hold from 1 to 64 MB of RAM and plugs into a SIMM socket on the motherboard. IBM-compatibles employ an 8-bit memory with a ninth, parity bit used with some systems. Macintosh

computers use 8-bit memory and do not employ the parity bit.

**simplex**

the ability to transfer data in only one direction. See also **duplex**.

**single-density**

a low data density for floppy disks used only with 8-inch diskettes on early computers.

**single-sided**

an early diskette that could record data on only one side.

**single-user**

designed to support only one user at any one time. See also **multiprogramming**, **multitasking**, **multiuser**, and **time-sharing**.

**6502**

an 8-bit microprocessor from Rockwell International that was the heart of early Apple, Atari, and Commodore computers.

**680x0**

a series of microprocessors from Motorola that have been the heart of the Apple Macintosh personal computers. The chips (68000, 68020, 68030, and 68040) are 32-bit chips, most with 32-bit bus speeds. See also **8086/8088, 286, 386, 486, Pentium, and PowerPC**.

**slot**

similar to a port but usually used for internal expansions such as memory, graphics, and so forth, by the addition of boards.

**soft character**

a letter or symbol entered into a text by the software to perform some special function, such as in the formatting of paragraphs by a word processor. These include spaces, returns, and hyphens that are then automatically deleted if no longer required. See also **hard character**.

**soft copy**

a reproduction that is in user-readable format but is not on a permanent medium, such as a display on a CRT screen. See also **hard copy**.

**soft error**

a temporary problem that can be removed by rereading the data or some other action. See also **glitch** and **hard error**.

**soft-sectored**

a description of a floppy disk on which the sectors on each track are marked by records. See also **hard-sectored**.

**software**

the programs that are run on a computer. See also **application software** and **system software**.

**software interface**

programs, such as system utilities, compilers, and programming languages, which provide a communications link between other software. See also **interface**, **hardware interface**, and **user interface**.

**software license agreement**
a legal instrument accompanying most software packages that states the terms under which the company is providing its material to the consumer.

**software selectable**
the ability to select certain features of a component of the system directly from the software. For example, a word processor may permit you to use various print enhancements such as underline or boldface by entering control codes directly into the text. See also **hardware selectable**.

**son file** see **grandfather system**.

**sort**
to arrange information in a specified order, such as alphabetical, numerical, or chronological.

**sound baffle**
an enclosure that fits over a printer or other device to help reduce the operating noise.

**sound board**
an increasingly popular part of multimedia systems that can realistically reproduce almost any sound from music to speech to sound effects. Sound boards also interface with various devices such as stereo speakers or headphones, joysticks, MIDI devices, CD-ROM drives, and input/output from other sound equipment.

**source program**
a set of instructions written in assembly or a high-level language that is translated and processed by an assembler, compiler, or interpreter. See also **object program**.

**speech synthesizer**
an output device that simulates human speech using phonetic rules. When used with the appropriate software, a speech synthesizer can "speak" the words that are displayed on the monitor screen.

**spindle**
the central shaft of a hard disk.

**split screen**
a method of dividing the CRT screen to show two or more operations at once, but it may be that more than one is not in action at the same time. See also **window**.

**spreadsheet**
a software package designed for the development and representation of a variety of financial applications.

**sprite graphics**
a type of animation with special characters or drawings involving independent motion, usually of a figure or object against a background that is either fixed or has a different motion.

**SPSS**
abbreviation for Statistical Package for the Social Sciences, a comprehensive program that contains most of the mathematical routines necessary to perform statistical calculations.

**SRAM**
(es-ram) acronym for Static Random Access Memory. See **static allocation**.

**SS/DD** see **single-sided** and **double-density**.

**SS/SD** see **single-sided** and **single-density**.

**stack**
a list that permits items to be inserted or removed only from one end. Data in a stack is usually handled as a LIFO process so that the last item added is the first to be removed. See also **queue**.

**Standard ASCII Character Set** see **ASCII Character Set**.

**star network**
a design in which all peripherals (including microcomputers) are connected to one central computer. See also **bus network**, **LAN**, and **ring network**.

**statement** see **instruction**.

**static allocation**
the division of main memory or other system resources in which each process is preassigned a portion before the program is run and the portion does not change during the execution of the program. See also **dynamic allocation**.

**status line**
an area usually at the top or bottom of the CRT screen that provides information on the current operation of the software in use.

**STN display**
abbreviation for supertwisted nematic display, an improved implementation of the TN LCD display that employs additional twisting of the molecules. STN displays are widely used on portable computers. See also **dual scan LCD** and **TFT LCD**.

**storage** see **auxiliary storage** and **archival storage**.

**store**
to place in main memory or auxiliary storage. See also **load**, **retrieve**, and **save**.

**streamer tape**
a moderate-speed tape system most commonly used as backup for a hard disk. These tapes offer a storage capacity equivalent to a small hard disk.

**string**
a set of characters treated as a unit.

**structured programming**
a method of writing instructions that emphasizes orderly development of a program as a series of modules that

will accept, process, and output data to and from other modules. See also **heuristic** and **modular program**.

**subdirectory**
a directory that is listed as part of another directory. A subdirectory would appear as a branch under the first directory on the directory tree.

**submarining**
the temporary disappearance of the cursor commonly encountered with some LCD screens used on portable computers.

**subroutine**
a set of instructions that is repeated several times within a program or needed by several different programs.

**supercomputer**
a very large, extremely fast, powerful, and costly computer that is capable of handling very complex problems and vast amounts of data.

**supertwisted nematic display** see **STN display**.

**SuperVGA** see **SVGA**.

**surge suppressor**
an electrical device designed to eliminate voltage spikes from the input power source. See also **power conditioner**.

**SVGA**
generically known as SuperVGA; the highest-resolution graphics system commonly available to personal computer users. See also **CGA**, **EGA**, **HGC**, **8514/A**, **MCGA**, **MDA**, **PGA**, **VGA**, and **XGA**.

**switch box**
a unit that permits more than one device to share a single connection but not simultaneously. This means that while only one device can be used at any time, there is no loss in transmission speed. See also **multiplexor**.

**switched line** see **dial-up line**.

**synchronous**
characterized by operations guided by regularly timed signals. See also **asynchronous**.

**system BIOS**
a part of the operating system of a personal computer, commonly found in the form of a ROM chip on the motherboard, that contains a start-up routine for the computer, which checks and prepares the various components for operation and then loads the rest of the operating system.

**system boot** see **boot**.

**system clock** see **clock**.

**system memory** see **main memory** and **UMA**.

**system prompt** see **prompt**.

**System 7**
an upgrade to the Macintosh operating system. It includes enlarged

memory addressing, virtual memory, multitasking, TrueType fonts, and a number of enhancements to the graphical interface.

**system software**

programs required for the basic oper-

ation of the computer and its components. For microcomputers, this normally consists of the operating system and any associated utilities. See also **application software, procedure-oriented,** and **use-oriented.**

**system utilities**

programs usually supplied as part of the system software that permit and assist in basic control and maintenance of the computer and its components.

# T

**t** see **tera-.**

**table**

an ordered arrangement of data, often presented in rows and columns. See also **array.**

**tablet**

an input device used for graphics applications. Tablets consist of a touch-sensitive membrane, pressure on which (using a stylus or even a finger) is transferred to the corresponding position on the screen.

**tape**

a system of data storage using a series of parallel tracks or channels on which files are stored in a predetermined and rigid sequence. Updating or changing tapes requires making a new copy of the entire tape. The 1/4-inch data cartridge (QIC) is most common on home systems.

**tape cartridge** see **data cartridge.**

**Tb** abbreviation for **terabit.**

**TB** abbreviation for **terabyte.**

**telecommunications**

the communications between devices that are not located near each other and must make use of a data communications channel. This occurs when terminals (including other computers) link to a host computer for an exchange of data. See also **network.**

**teleconferencing**

the simultaneous communication between three or more persons. This may be via the telephone, computer telecommunications link, video image exchange, or a special network.

**template**

a device used as a guide. Two common examples of templates are a *keyboard template*, which acts as a label for certain keys to identify their function, and a *file template*, which is somewhat similar to a form letter, permitting the user to simply fill in the blanks.

**tera-**

a prefix meaning one trillion.

**terabit**

1 trillion bits.

**terabyte**

1 trillion bytes.

**terminal**

any device that acts as an input/output unit for a computer. Terminals most often have a keyboard and a

CRT screen or printer but may be in many designs. See also **monitor.**

**text editor** see **editor.**

**text mode**

permits only text to be displayed with no graphics. The standard is 25 lines of 80 characters, but most video displays will now permit more than one text mode, possibly up to 60 lines of 132 characters. See also **graphics mode.**

**TFT LCD**

abbreviation for Thin Film Transistor LCD, an active matrix LCD display that is commonly used on top-line, color portables.

**thermal printer**

a printer that produces images by using heat interaction with the paper.

**thimble**

a type of printwheel similar to a daisy wheel but with curved spokes so that it looks like a thimble.

**thin film transistor LCD** see **TFT LCD.**

**386**

also known as the 386DX or i386, an advanced Intel multitasking processor, originally called the 80386, was capable of handling both 16-bit and 32-bit data bus operations. See also **8086/8088, 286, 486, 680x0, Pentium,** and **PowerPC.**

**386DX** see **386.**

**386SL**

a chip similar to the 386SX that is designed to be used in laptops.

**386SX**

a version of the 386 that runs at somewhat slower speed and lacks the 32-bit bus handling capacity.

**387**

math coprocessor for the 386 processor.

**throughput**

the amount of work done in a given amount of time by a computer or a component of a system such as a printer.

**tickler**

a usually automated system for reminding users of pre-scheduled events. Ticklers are commonly used as reminder notices in a number of applications, including calendars, PIMS, contact managers, and utilities.

**time-sharing**

a method of processing used in multiprogramming that shares the CPU

time between two or more processes. With rapid processing speeds, the CPU can alternate between the processes without any significant loss in speed. See also **multiprocessing** and **multitasking.**

**TN display**

abbreviation for Twisted Nematic display, the low-cost, characteristic black-on-gray, passive matrix, LCD display commonly used for calculators and watches. See also **TFT LCD.**

**toggle**

a switch or control code that turns an event on and off by repeated action or use; or to turn something on and off by repeating the same action.

**toner**

a very fine, black, powdery ink used in copy machines and laser printers. The toner particles become electrically charged and adhere to the pattern of an image defined by charges on a plate or drum, which is then transferred to paper.

**top-down design**

a hierarchical structure in which the progression of ideas is arranged from the most important to the least important.

**touch-sensitive keyboard**

a type of button arrangement rarely found on computers but seen on some calculators. It is basically a touch-sensitive membrane that is very sensitive to contact and requires very little pressure to "press" a key. See also **full-stroke key** and **limited-stroke key.**

**touch-sensitive membrane**

consists of a smooth imprinted surface covering a series of sensitive switches or other sensing devices on which a small pressure in the proper place will activate the desired action.

**tower case**

a computer case design that employs an upright (stacked) arrangement of drives. Tower cases can sit on a table top, but more frequently, they are placed on the floor or a low stand adjacent to the work area.

**tpi**

abbreviation for Tracks Per Inch, a measure of data density on disks.

**track**

a circular path used for recording data on a floppy or hard disk; or a parallel data channel on a magnetic tape; or a spiral path on a CD for recording data.

**track ball**

a device similar to a mouse, which uses a ball mounted on a fixed base to control cursor movement, action on the screen, and object placement. The ball is rolled with the fingers or palm, and the movement on the screen corresponds to the direction of the ball's motion.

**tractor feed**

a method of moving paper through a printer that uses a series of pins on either side of an adjustable-width mechanism. See also **friction feed**, **pin feed**, and **sheet feeder**.

**transient**

temporary; a transient program, for example, is one that is not in memory or storage permanently.

**translator**

a program that changes another program from one form to another, such as converting a program written by humans into a form that the computer can understand (usually a neces-

sary step). See also **assembler, compiler**, and **interpreter**.

**transparent**

indicates that a program in memory does not affect (is transparent to) all other operations, even though it may have an effect on them. Also used to indicate a change in hardware or software that causes no apparent change in system performance.

**trapdoor** see **backdoor**.

**trashware**

very poorly designed software that is good for nothing but the trash can.

**Trojan Horse**

a general class of computer programs that gain system entry by attaching themselves to legitimate programs. The best-known example is the computer virus; however, not all Trojan Horses are necessarily destructive of system resources.

**TrueType**

a type of scalable font.

**TSR**

abbreviation for Terminate and Stay Resident, a program that remains in

main memory after it has run. Such programs may continue to be active or remain in the background until awakened by a hotkey or other action.

**TTL**

abbreviation for Transistor to Transistor Logic, a generic designation for digital as a TTL monitor is a digital monitor.

**turnkey system**

a ready-to-use system, usually supplied by a single vendor, that includes hardware, software, and training. See also **preloaded system**.

**twisted nematic display** see **TN display**.

**286**

an Intel multitasking processor, originally called the 80286, was introduced with the IBM AT class personal computer. The 286 could address up to 16 MB of RAM. See also **8086/8088, 386, 486, 680x0, Pentium**, and **PowerPC**.

**typeface**

the design or style of a set of print characters such as Helvetica, Orator, or Times-Roman. See also **font**.

# U

**ultra-density**

a term no longer frequently encountered for describing floppy disk capacity, but it is generally the same as high-density.

**UMA**

abbreviation for Upper Memory Area, the memory on IBM-compatibles between 640 K and 1 MB. This memory is normally used by the operating system for loading device drivers and TSRs.

**UMB**

abbreviation for upper memory block, a unit in the upper memory area available for use.

**uninterruptible power supply** see **UPS**.

**UNIX**

a popular but not user-friendly mainframe operating system that employs cryptic but powerful commands, shells, and pipes. See also **A/UX, AIX**, and **XENIX**.

**UPC**

abbreviation for Universal Product Code, a familiar bar code found on many products in food, drug, and other stores.

**update**

the process of changing software or

hardware to a newer or possibly corrected version. See also **upgrade**.

**upgrade**

the process of changing software or hardware to a more powerful version. See also **update**.

**upgradable**

a system that is designed to be easily upgraded to a more powerful processor, usually by simply unplugging the old one and inserting the new one; or any computer, component, or application that has a good upgrade path.

**upgrade path**

refers to the ability of a computer, hardware component, or software application to be changed to a more powerful or newer version without adversely affecting the remainder of the system or any pertinent data files. See also **backward compatibility**.

**upload**

to transfer a copy of a file from a small computer, usually a microcomputer, to a host computer. See also **download**.

**upper memory** see **UMA**.

**UPS**

abbreviation for Uninterruptible Power Supply, an electrical device that

contains a battery pack and will supply adequate power to a system in the event of a power failure, permitting it to be shut down in an orderly manner.

**use-oriented**

describes a program or system that is designed to expedite its use for its intended purpose. See also **application software, procedure-oriented**, and **system software**.

**user-friendly**

easy to understand and use.

**user interface**

any device, either hardware or software, that provides a bridge between the computer and the user. Examples include the keyboard, mouse, and menu programs. See also **GUI, interface, hardware interface**, and **software interface**.

**user memory** see **base memory**.

**user-programmable key** see **function key**.

**user-readable format**

any display that you can read, such as on a screen or printed page. See also **machine-readable format**.

**user-supported software** see **share-ware**.

# V

**vaporware**

hardware or software products that are announced by a company but do not appear on the market for a very long time, if ever.

**VAR**

acronym for Valued Added Reseller, a company that assembles systems, usually for a specific purpose or application, using components from various vendors. See also **OEM.**

**variable fonts**

the ability of a device such as a printer to offer more than one print typeface or style.

**variable pitch**

the ability of a device such as a printer to offer more than one print size.

**VDT**

abbreviation for Video Display Terminal, any device used to give a visual display of computer output, such as on a screen. For personal computers this is most commonly a single CRT unit called a monitor.

**vector graphics**

a method of graphics processing and display in which images are produced by a series of points, lines, and various geometric patterns. See also **raster graphics.**

**vendor**

a supplier of computer hardware or software.

**version number**

a number, usually something like 3.2, that indicates the history of the development of a software application. In general, the larger the version number, the longer the program has been around and under development, and the more revisions it has undergone. Also, the larger the difference between two version numbers, the greater the change in the program.

**vertical market software**

special-purpose packages that are designed to be used in a specific industry or for a very narrow application. See also **horizontal market software.**

**VESA**

(vee-sa) acronym for Video Electronics Standards Association, a group of manufactures of video products working toward the establishment of better industry-wide video standards.

**VESA local bus** see **VLB.**

**VGA**

IBM's Video Graphics Array, a high-resolution color graphics system. VGA was originally designed for professional applications on top-of-the-line PCs; however, it is now considered to be standard equipment. See also **CGA, EGA, HGC, 8514/A, MCGA, MDA, PGA, SVGA,** and **XGA.**

**VGA Plus** see **SVGA.**

**videoconferencing**

teleconferencing in which video images are exchanged. Though this presently involves using video cameras and monitors, routine video conferencing via computer is on the horizon.

**video display adapter** see **display adapter.**

**video display terminal** see **VDT.**

**video RAM** see **VRAM.**

**virtual disk** see **ramdisk.**

**virtual memory**

using segmentation or disk file overlays to make the total amount of available memory appear to be larger and hold more than its actual capacity would permit.

**virtual reality**

a computerized simulation of three-dimensional space in which the user can interact with and manipulate objects in the virtual world. This may be as simple as the movement through three-dimensional environments that is simulated by many games, or it may be complex, involving special devices such as a glove and helmet through which the user interacts with the projected world. See also **cyberspace.**

**virus**

a usually small computer program designed to attach to a "legitimate" pro-

gram and replicate itself, attaching to files, causing annoyance or damage to the infected system. See also **logic bomb, Trojan Horse,** and **worm.**

**virus signature**

the unique machine code (binary) pattern of a computer virus program. Most antivirus programs include a search for known virus signatures as a means for quick detection of these viruses.

**VLB**

abbreviation for VESA Local Bus, a local bus design for attaching VESA display adapters that has become very popular with 486-based machines. VLB operates at up to 66 MHz, handles 32-bit data transfers, and supports bus mastering. See also **PCI.**

**VL-bus** abbreviation for **VESA local bus,** same as **VLB.**

**voice recognition**

the ability of a computer to accept input commands or data using the spoken word.

**voice synthesizer** see **speech synthesizer.**

**volatile**

a main memory or auxiliary storage design in which the stored data is lost when the power is removed from the system. See also **nonvolatile.**

**voltage spike**

a sudden jump in electrical power. These can be very dangerous to data and, if large enough, to computer hardware as well. See also **power conditioner** and **surge suppressor.**

**volume**

a physical drive; or a logical drive if the physical drive has been partitioned.

**VRAM**

(vee-ram) acronym for Video RAM, memory dedicated to handling video processing and output.

**VSAM**

(vee-sam) acronym for Virtual Storage Access Method, a method of organizing a file that permits random and sequential access of each record.

# W

**wait state**

a halt in CPU processing for one or more clock cycles during which the processor waits for slower memory to catch up with requests; or a pause in program execution for one or more clock cycles until memory can catch up with CPU processing. See also **zero wait state.**

**warm boot**

to bring a system into operation from the keyboard or by using a reset button. This method does not always completely clear and re-initialize the system, and a cold boot may be required.

**wildcard**

a generic symbol (such as * or ?) that can stand for either a single character

or for several characters. Wildcards are frequently used in system commands.

**Winchester disk system**

a high-speed, high-density hard disk storage system that employs an airtight fixed disk on which the read/write heads lightly glide. Such systems are very reliable and do not experience head crashes.

**window**

a portion of the screen set aside for a specific display or purpose. See also **split screen.**

**Windows**

a multitasking, graphical user interface developed by Microsoft for IBM-compatible systems. The program gets its name from using movable and sizable windows in which applications are displayed. Windows supports multimedia, common printer management, TrueType fonts, and copy and paste between Windows applications. The final release of traditional windows was Windows 3.11, which is superseded by Windows 95.

**Windows NT**

abbreviation for Windows New Technology; this multitasking network-oriented operating system was designed for top-line PCs, PowerPCs and others. It is a self-contained operating system that does not require DOS; however, it can run DOS applications.

**Windows 95**

an upgrade of Windows that supersedes all previous versions except Windows NT; however, like Windows NT, it is a self-contained operating system that can run either Windows or DOS applications. Windows 95 has a graphical interface that is more like that of the Macintosh; it also provides the ability to resize icons and buttons. It supports improved memo-ry management, access to Microsoft's online service, networking, and Plug and Play capability.

**word**

a group of bits treated as a unit of storage. The larger the word size, the faster the computer can process data. Most microcomputers use 16-, 32-, or 64-bit words.

**word processor**

a software package consisting of programs designed to accept and process normal text (words) as data. Such programs may range from simple systems that are little more than a limited text editor to those with complex screen handling, editing, enhancements, and assistance features.

**word wrap**

a feature of most word processors in which the text is automatically continued from one line to the next.

**workstation**

a single-user microcomputer in a LAN; or a single-user personal computer, especially a high-performance system designed for a special function such as CAD or CAM or a terminal.

**worm**

a kind of computer program that is designed to repeatedly and rapidly reproduce itself. The effect of this is that an affected system will soon have all the available disk, memory, and other resources gobbled up leading to a system crash.

**WORM**

acronym for Write-Once-Read-Many, an optical disk system in which data may be written to the disk only once but read an unlimited number of times. Updating data on the disk involves physically destroying the old data, rendering that part of the disk unusable, and then writing the new data to an unused part of the disk.

**write-protected**

cannot be written to or changed. See also **R/O** and **R/W.**

**write-protect notch**

a notch on the side of a floppy disk that prevents the data from being altered. The 5¼-inch diskettes are write-protected by covering the notch with a write-protect tab. The reverse system is used for 8-inch diskettes.

**write-protect tab**

a small strip of opaque tape used on the write-protect notch on some diskettes to provide write-protection.

**write-protect window**

3½-inch diskettes use a small switch and window to indicate write-protect status. The disk is protected when the window is open.

**WYSIWYG**

(wiz-ee-wig) acronym for "What You See Is What You Get," indicating that the screen display is essentially the same as how the printed output will appear.

# X

**x86**

refers to Intel's series of microprocessor chips beginning with the 8086/8088 and progressing through the 80286, 386, 486, and Pentium ("586").

**XENIX**

a version of UNIX for microcomputers.

**XGA**

IBM's EXtended Graphics Array, a super high-resolution color graphics system that is very similar to SVGA, including the highest resolution modes up to 1,024 x 768. See also **CGA, EGA, HGC, 8514/A, MCGA, MDA, PGA, SVGA,** and **VGA.**

**XMS**

abbreviation for eXtended Memory Specification, permits programs on MS-DOS–based machines using a 286 or later processor to make use of memory above 1 MB as extended. See also **EMS.**

**XT**

the first IBM PC to have a hard drive; the XT made use of the 8086/8088 processors. See also **AT** and **PS/2.**

# Z

**Z80**

an early 8-bit processor from Zilog that was used extensively in CP/M-based machines.

**ZENIX** see **XENIX.**

**zero wait state**

a condition in which wait states do not occur. This is normally accom-plished by having memory with sufficiently high access speed to keep up with the processor execution speed.

# *Index*